HELL HAS TORMENTS OF *Cold*

Rebels on Johnson's Island

PAUL MCREE

Kendall Hunt
publishing company

Cover images © Shutterstock, Inc.

Kendall Hunt
publishing company

www.kendallhunt.com
Send all inquiries to:
4050 Westmark Drive
Dubuque, IA 52004-1840

Printed in the United States of America
10 9 8 7 6 5 4 3 2 1

CONTENTS

PLATE 7

Johnson's Island Civil War Prison

Fort Hill Redoubt Historical Photograph

1865

PLATE 8

Johnson's Island Civil War Prison

Officer's Quarters and Parade Grounds

no date

Courtesy National Park Service

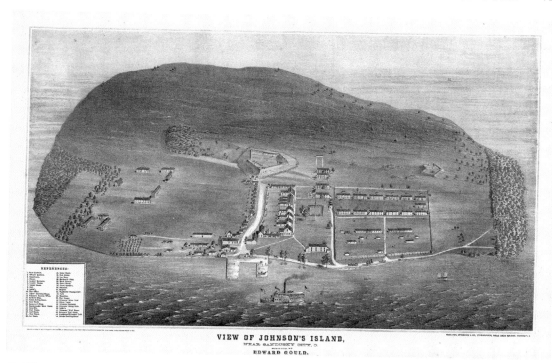

VIEW OF JOHNSON'S ISLAND,
NEAR SANDUSKY CITY, O.
EDWARD GOULD.

Chapter 1

A PRISON COMES TO SANDUSKY

"We are surrounded by beautiful scenery. Sandusky City is in sight which looks beautiful across the wide waters of Lake Erie"

—Lt. Colonel S. T. Rives, 14th Tennessee

ESTABLISHMENT OF THE CAMP

In 1861, an island owned by Mr. Johnson was sitting snugly in Sandusky Bay off the tranquil waters of Lake Erie, unaware of its destiny. The island was uninhabited; its 300 acres were of little use to the residents of Sandusky, Ohio, almost three miles away. It was an insignificant plot of earth worthy of little mention. Events elsewhere would soon change the placid nature of the island. War clouds were brewing in the South. The nation was being torn asunder. Americans would be pitted against Americans in places like Antietam, Chancellorsville, and Gettysburg. Mr. Johnson's Island would become a depot for the gentlemen of the South whose destiny in battle would place them in the hands of their enemy. These men would make the name of Johnson's Island unforgettable to people of both the North and the South. Between ten and twelve thousand Rebels would walk in and back out of the gates of the prison and would tell their countless stories to future generations, establishing this tiny island in the annals of Civil War history.

In the fall of 1861, the Civil War showed no signs that it was going to end. The "sixty-day war" had turned into six months of struggle. The South had shown its determination to the cause for which it was fighting. It became apparent to the federal government that more depots for prisoners of war were needed for a long struggle with the Confederacy. More prisons were needed to handle the captives originating from the western campaigns. A decision was made to build a prison on an island off the shores of Lake Erie.

The Quartermaster-General sent a communique to the Secretary of War on July 12, 1861, informing them that "it is to be expected that the United States will have to take care of large numbers of prisoners of war." The Quartermaster-General implemented the policy that prisoners of war "are entitled to proper accommodation, to courteous and respectful treatment, to one ration a day and to consideration according to rank." The recommendation was brought forward that an island off Sandusky in Lake Eire be rented as a depot.[1] On October 7, 1861, Lieutenant Colonel William Hoffman, Commissary-General of Prisoners for the United States, was assigned to locate an appropriate site for a new federal prison. Hoffman was a veteran of the Mexican War and of Indian frontier wars. He was stationed in Texas on frontier defense duties when the hostilities began. In January 1861, the federal forces in Texas were surrendered to the Confederate authorities. Hoffman became a prisoner. He was quickly released on parole, on the grounds that he could never serve in the field. He remained in federal service in the war prisoner department and was made Commissary-General of Prisoners, a noncombat duty, in accordance with his parole, on October 23, 1861. He held that post until November 3, 1865.[2]

Colonel Hoffman was to survey the Put-in-Bay and Kelly Islands in Lake Erie and report which one was more suitable for a prison. The order also gave him permission to review other sites in the same vicinity.[3] Hoffman reviewed several sites in and around Lake Erie. He visited the islands requested and did not like their location. These islands were vulnerable to an attack from Confederate raiders from Canada (a nation sympathetic to the South) and were difficult to supply. Both problems were compounded because during the winter the lake would freeze solid. The land was not well suited for a large compound, the soil was thin, and gusts off the lake were strong. Families had divided up all the land and had working farms and their private homes scattered over the islands. The islands also contained a wine and brandy establishment, too much of a temptation to the guards.[4] Hoffman had to take into account the price of the land, security, building materials, supply logistics, and local populations. He continued looking for a more suitable location.

---

[1] *War of the Rebellion: A Compilation of the Official Records of the Union and Confederate Armies*, Series II, Vol. 3, 8.

[2] Frohman, Charles E., *Rebels on Lake Erie* (Columbus, OH: The Ohio Historical Society, 1965), 1.

[3] *War of the Rebellion: A Compilation of the Official Records of the Union and Confederate Armies*, Series II, Vol. 3, 49.

[4] Ibid., Series II, Vol. 3, 54–55.

The businessmen of Sandusky made a bid to have the prison located in Sandusky or on Johnson's Island. When W. T. West, owner of the West Hotel and a prominent merchant, discovered the intention of Hoffman's visit, he took him over to Johnson's Island for inspection. He quickly arranged for estimates on construction.[5] The merchants thought that the prison would greatly benefit the town in trade. The building and maintaining of the prison would put federal dollars into the local economy and the stationing of a garrison of troops would help the merchants. The merchants also saw the possibility of selling goods to the prisoners of the island. The businessmen promised financial aid to the government if the island was selected.[6] Hoffman had also visited Detroit, Toledo, and Cleveland for possible sites. Hoffman was inclined to favor a site elsewhere, but after the efforts of the local merchants, especially West, he recommended Johnson's Island as the best location for the prison.[7]

Johnson's Island comprised 300 acres, forty acres of which was already cleared of timber when Hoffman inspected the island. Even though only half of the island was leased for $500 a year, the government was granted full control of the island and could use the lumber on the other side of the island for fuel. The cleared area faced the city of Sandusky, the close proximity of which made the transporting of supplies and prisoners easier.[8]

Colonel Hoffman estimated that the total cost of construction of the prison would be $26,266. Each block would roughly cost $1,400. Originally, four blocks were to be built for enlisted prisoners, an additional four blocks for officer prisoners, and one hospital block. For the guards: one building for officers, one block for enlisted men (about 100–150 men) and miscellaneous other buildings. Contracts were awarded to the Gregg & West Company of Sandusky, with assurances from many people of Sandusky that they were men of energy and integrity. The lateness of the season induced Hoffman to award the contract without delay and competing bids were not accepted.[9] Construction of the prison began with a target completion date of February 1, 1862. Hoffman stated in a November 15th report that the cost was more than expected because of the expansion of the number of buildings for the camp and lumber was more expensive than planned. The new total was estimated between $28,000 and $30,000. He also

---

[5] Mitchell, E. O., "Johnson's Island: Military Prison for Confederate Prisoners," *Sketches of War History 1861–1865*, vol. 5 (1903), 118.

[6] Knauss, William H., *The Story of Camp Chase* (Nashville, TN: Publishing House of the Methodist Episcopal Church, 1906), 186–188.

[7] Frohman, Charles E., *Rebels on Lake Erie*, 2; *War of the Rebellion: A Compilation of the Official Records of the Union and Confederate Armies*, Series II, Vol. III, 56; Knauss, *Camp Chase*, 186–188.

[8] *War of the Rebellion: A Compilation of the Official Records of the Union and Confederate Armies*, Series II, Vol. III, 55–56.

[9] Ibid., Series II, Vol. III, 436–437.

reported that four more blocks could be built and an additional row of blocks could be added to the bay side to greatly expand the number of prisoners accommodated.[10] John Carr, a Sandusky contractor, complained to Secretary of War Stanton of fraud in the awarding of the contracts, but Hoffman stated that Carr did not have the means to handle the contract and assured the Secretary that favoritism was not the case.[11] The Secretary did not act upon Carr's complaint.

Colonel Hoffman made arrangements to locate a doctor for the prison compound. On January 17, 1862, he sent a request to track down a competent physician to employ on Johnson's Island. He knew the difficulty in hiring a camp doctor with the army's standard compensation of $80 a month. To prevent any interruption in the opening of the prison he ordered the Surgeon R. S. Satterlee of New York to send to Sandusky medical provisions for six months' supply for 1,000 men.[12] The Surgeon General in Washington authorized Hoffman to offer $100 per month, owing to the fact the physician would have to live on the island away from the city.[13] Dr. Woodbridge was hired mid-February at the same time as mumps had broken out with the newly raised guard unit.[14]

By late February 1862, several complications had forced Hoffman to delay the opening of the prison. The problems included: Ice was still in the bay, lanterns had not yet arrived to illuminate the security fence, and the guards were without their revolvers. The delay, Hoffman argued, was beneficial because the guards needed additional training. The colonel also decided to construct an additional barrack, for he found the one already established too crowded for the guards.[15]

The prison continued to expand and change its character before the grand opening. On March 10, 1862, the Quartermaster-General approved the construction of four more prisoner barracks to expand the capacity of the prison to around 3,000 to 5,000 men. These barracks were to be the "cheapest shed huts."[16] Six days later Colonel Hoffman declared the prison ready to receive 250 officers and 700 or 800 enlisted men even though construction was ongoing.[17] To prevent officers from encouraging the

---

[10] *War of the Rebellion: A Compilation of the Official Records of the Union and Confederate Armies*, Series II, Vol. III, 136.

[11] Frohman, Charles E., *Rebels on Lake Erie*, 4.

[12] *War of the Rebellion: A Compilation of the Official Records of the Union and Confederate Armies*, Series II, Vol. III, 196.

[13] *War of the Rebellion: A Compilation of the Official Records of the Union and Confederate Armies*, Series II, Vol. III, 204.

[14] *War of the Rebellion: A Compilation of the Official Records of the Union and Confederate Armies*, Series II, Vol. III, 284.

[15] Ibid, 326–327.

[16] Ibid, 366.

[17] Ibid, 382.

enlisted men to rally against the guards, the Quartermaster-General recommended that Johnson's Island be used solely as an officer's prison. The Secretary of War agreed and ordered on April 13, 1862, three days after the first prisoners arrived, Johnson's Island would be an officer's prison only.[18]

DESCRIPTION OF PRISON

Johnson's Island is an island about a mile and a half long and a third of a mile wide. The city of Sandusky was almost three miles across the bay. To the north of the island is a peninsula running west, where it meets the mainland. The island has a slow incline up to a ridge, called the "Hog's Back," that ran the length of the island. The soil is a mixture of clay and loam, from two to eight feet deep covered by very fine grass. When the island was originally contracted by the military, it was covered with about 260 acres of timber, but by the time the government released the island at the end of the war, it was nearly bare.[19]

The island was a very beautiful location with many commenting on the lay of the land. One guard commented on putting rebels on such beautiful land: "Secessia, as we have christened the Rebel's retreat on JI, is looking lovely in its summer robe—much too comfortable and picturesque to be the abode of traitors even in confinement."[20] Depending on which block a prisoner was quartered, he would either have a good view of the lake or of the back side of the island. Barber, a prisoner, noted: "To a person facing the rising sun the scene was beautiful. Before him lay the smooth waters of Sandusky Bay, beyond which a long narrow thickly wooded promontory ran out from the mainland, terminating in Cedar Point. On this point were two lighthouses, one at a little distance out in the lake. On the right two and a half miles away on the main shore, the city of Sandusky was visible, lying along the water's edge for more than a mile."[21] Captain Bingham's room faced the interior of the island and still had beautiful scenery. "The sunset was lovely. The light rested in a soft, rich glow on the little line of Woods to the North on the lake border—& stretching across the lake lighted it lovely. There are woods behind our block—to the west, & thro[ugh] the trees yet dripping from the [rain] shower the light crept, glimmering among the trees & peering thro[ugh] the drooping leaves making them glisten like diamonds"[22] All of the prisoners would enjoy the beauty of the lake.

---

[18] Ibid, 439, 448.

[19] *War of the Rebellion: A Compilation of the Official Records of the Union and Confederate Armies,* Series II, Vol. VII, 330.

[20] Stem (USA), June 30, 1862.

[21] Barber, Flavel C., *Holding the Line: The Third Tennessee Infantry, 1861–1864,* 51.

[22] Bingham, Robert, *Diary,* 29–30.

Captain Bingham continued: "The lake is beautiful and its face is as various as the hues of a mountainside. It is very beautiful. The sun and moon rise across it—and the setting sun steals over it. I have watched it at all times of the day—& hardly ever seen it the same. I have listened at night to its low plaintive wail. If I had lived this long free near it, this lake would be part of my life—my inner life."[23] A rebel prisoner elegantly stated: "We are surrounded by beautiful scenery. Sandusky City is in sight which looks beautiful across the wide waters of Lake Erie, none less are the boats and ships as they sail in every direction as if guided by some supernatural power. There is a pleasant breeze all the time, it is very pleasant."[24]

The prison at Johnson's Island was located on the southeast side of the island facing the town of Sandusky, Ohio. The prison compound comprised fifteen acres surrounded by a plank fence about fifteen feet high. Outside of the bull pen were the guards' barracks and administration buildings. The pine planks formed a solid wall on three sides of the prison. On the side facing the bay, the planks were positioned with gaps in between them. The prisoners could see the bay glistening through these gaps. The prisoners nicknamed the enclosure the "Bull Pen." There was a walkway about three feet from the top of the fence where the sentinels maintained a commanding view of the inmates.[25] Stairs led from the outside of the bull pen up to the walk at regular intervals so the guards could quickly mass soldiers at any part of the fence. The block house, or main gate, was very secure. It was two stories with firing slots all around. One prisoner described the blockhouse: "On either side of the main entrance was a sliding panel through which, on occasions, a little Leon gun loaded with grape and canister could be projected."[26] If the prisoners tried to storm the gate, the Napoleon guns, or "Leon" cannons could disrupt the charge with a devastating blast of grape shot, in effect they would act like huge shotguns; a common way to break up an infantry charge during the Civil War. At each corner of the wall were smaller block houses with smaller secondary gates. They also could use cannons at these corner blockhouses.[27] In addition to the corner blockhouses, guard shacks were installed at intervals to protect guards from the cold.

In July 1864, the federals moved the west wall, the wall opposite of the lake, back about ninety-five feet to increase security.[28] The Yankees knew this might encourage

[23] Bingham, Robert, *Diary*, 52.

[24] Rives Letter, June 15, 1863.

[25] Hundley, D. R., *Prison Echoes of the Great Rebellion* (New York: R. W. Green, Printer, 1874), 77.

[26] Todd, Westwood, *Reminiscences of Westwood Todd*, 317.

[27] Mills, Luther Rice, Papers, Webb, 666.

[28] *War of the Rebellion: A Compilation of the Official Records of the Union and Confederate Armies*, Series II, Vol. VII, 681; John Washington Inzer, *The Diary of a Confederate Soldier*, ed. Mattie Lou Teague Crow (privately published, 1977), 87.

a rush at the partial wall so they heightened security. W. A. Wash stated, "Nearly the whole garrison was under arms and watching our manoeuvers, so the wise and prudent ones among us said it was best to be right easy. Some monstrous brave fellows with more courage than discretion ranted around and called for volunteers to charge the loyal troops."[29] No charge took place.

Lanterns were employed at regular intervals along the fence to keep a watch over the prisoners.[30] Thirty feet from the inside of the fence was the "dead line"; beyond which no prisoner was allowed. This area was marked with wooden stakes driven into the ground, about twenty-five to thirty feet apart. On the lake side of the pen, the stakes were forty to fifty yards from the wall that encompassed the condemned men's cells and the pest house, which were forbidden to visit.[31] No line or rope connected these stakes, so the prisoner had to estimate this unmarked boundary. A miscalculation could result in the prisoner being shot.[32]

The prisoners were housed in thirteen two-story wood buildings called "blocks." Each block was roughly 130 feet long by 25 feet wide. They were arranged in two parallel rows of six blocks each. Each block was numbered, with even numbers running near the western wall of the prison and odd numbers in a second row about one hundred feet to the east of the first row. Between these two rows of blocks was a large promenade where the prisoners would exercise. Block 13 was placed at the east end of this promenade between Blocks 11 and 12. Block 6 was used as the prisoners' hospital. Access to the upper stories was through outside staircases, with very small balconies, pointed toward the inside of the avenue. To make sure the prisoners understood the rules of the prison and could not plead ignorance of said rules, "Pierson's Ten Commandments" were posted in every room.[33]

If the commandant or other prisoners wanted to communicate with postings, a bulletin board was erected in front of Block 3. One prisoner noted his admiration of the bulletin board: "Our want of medium for communication was well supplied by a large bulletin board. It was about eight feet long by four feet wide, and I have spent many pleasant hours reading the racy, well-worded advertisements with which its two sides were always filled. Advertise for anything you might want and you would be almost sure to hear from it in an hour or two."[34] Colonel

---

[29] Wash, W. A. *Camp, Field and Prison Life*, 241.

[30] Horace Carpenter, "Plain Living at Johnson's Island," *Century Magazine* (March 1891), 710.

[31] Barziza, Decimus et Ultimus, *The Adventures of a Prisoner of War, 1863–1864*, 76–77.

[32] Horace Carpenter, "Plain Living at Johnson's Island," *Century Magazine* (March 1891), 711.

[33] Norman, 202–203.

[34] Mills, Luther Rice, Papers, 7.

Hundley said it "is visited during the day by almost every man in the bull-pen who is not sick."[35]

The blocks were made cheaply of white pine boards, butted against each other. The outside weatherboarding, the horizontal boards were nailed to upright beams with no plastering or interior boarding. Over time, humidity and varying temperatures caused the boards to warp, causing huge gaps to develop between the boards. These gaps were welcomed in the summertime because they improved the ventilation in the rooms, somewhat relieving their stuffiness. However, when the frigid winter winds blew through the blocks, these gap-filled walls offered little protection against the cold. Major Henry Kyd Douglas noted that "there were many knotholes, through which one lying in bed could look out upon the moon or the water; but when the weather got below zero, the scenery was scarcely compensation for the suffering." Douglas noted that there was a stove in the middle of every room, which kept men comfortable "within a certain range, except in very cold weather. It was like living in a canvas tent.[36] To compound this problem, the prisoners themselves cut holes in the boards to allow even more ventilation during the warm summers, thinking that they would be exchanged before winter. With the arrival of winter, the prisoners would stuff newspapers, rags, or whatever they could find into the openings. This odd assortment of stuffing pushed through every gap and hole gave the prison blocks an ungainly patchwork appearance.[37]

Not all of the blocks were built to consistent measurements or quality levels. Blocks 1 through 4 were built to accommodate officers, while the other blocks were originally built for enlisted soldiers.[38] These first four blocks were built to a higher quality standard. Initially, officers were considered gentlemen and deserving of better quarters. As the war dragged on and more prisoners were taken, necessity closed the gap between the quality of quarters of officers and their subordinates.

The first four blocks were divided into twenty-two sleeping rooms each fourteen by sixteen feet, with eleven rooms on each side of a long hall. The ceiling was nine feet high. Twelve men usually shared each room. Two rows of bunks three high were located on either side of the room with a rough pine table sitting in the center. The rest of the furniture consisted of two benches, a chair, a spittoon, footlockers, and an

[35] Hundley, D. R., *Prison Echoes of the Great Rebellion*, 82.

[36] Douglas, Henry Kyd., *I Rode with Stonewall* (Chapel Hill: The University of North Carolina Press, 1940), 261. All quotes from letters and diaries use the prisoner's original grammar, spelling, and punctuation.

[37] Wash, W. A., *Camp, Field and Prison Life* (Saint Louis: Southwestern Book and Publishing Co., 1870), 354.

[38] Hundley, D. R., *Prison Echoes of the Great Rebellion*, 77.

oil lamp.[39] For ventilation, each of these rooms had two windows. Each room was equipped with a wood-burning stove. On the ground floor, there were cook rooms, dining rooms, and wash rooms, in addition to the sleeping quarters.[40] They had ceilings of plaster and, consequently, they were the warmest blocks in the winter. The small rooms in the officers' quarters housed fewer soldiers, which gave these lucky prisoners a greater degree of privacy. Not all of the rooms were consistent in minor details or occupancy. W. A. Wash stated in his diary, "I got [Block 4] room No. 19, having four beds in it, hoping to avoid taking in another man, as myself and three Lieutenants filled the beds. We did not have to increase our number, and our room proved one of the best in the block."[41] One prisoner was said to have had one room completely to himself. Because of the enhanced conditions, the first four blocks were the most desirable of the thirteen blocks.

Blocks 5 through 12 were originally erected for enlisted prisoners. Each upper story had three rooms measuring thirty feet by twenty-five feet, each containing twenty-seven bunks. Each bunk slept two men, giving a total of fifty-four prisoners per room.[42] In every room, there were three rows of bunks three tiers high and three bunks deep against one wall. On the opposite wall, there were five tables, with benches, that accommodated eight to ten prisoners each. Three windows lighted these five tables. A wood-burning stove stood in the center of each room.[43] In these cramped rooms, the prisoners sometimes cooked, washed, and stored their supplies. Just like the upper blocks, there were minor differences with the lower blocks in arrangement and numbers. Captain Bingham moved from Block 11 to Block 8, and noticed that Block 8 was better: "In the other room, the spaces we occupied by bunks where only the windows & a little light could come in from way down such a narrow lane between two bunks but here one side of the room is left vacant, leaving two windows clear—& on the other side there is 2 or 3 feet vacant on each side of the window, so we can sit by the stove & read comfortable."[44] Major Caldwell commented about the improvement when his entire mess moved from Block 11 to Block 8 as well: "The room is much quitter [sic] . . . There are, I believe, only 32 in the room. I have an excellent bunk, with a place for a window of its own. I shall improve it still more, though it is nearly papered etc. now.

---

[39] Ibid., 76.

[40] Ibid.

[41] Wash, W. A., *Camp, Field and Prison Life*, 88.

[42] Dooley, John., *John Dooley, Confederate Soldier: His War Journal*, ed. Joseph T. Durkin (South Bend, IN: University of Notre Dame Press, 1963), 138.

[43] Felix Hays Blackman to Maggie, October 18, 1863, Author's Collection, hereafter referred as Blackman.

[44] Bingham, Robert, *Diary 2*, 21.

I hung up a blanket curtain before my bunk. Am enabled to enjoy quite a degree of privacy."[45] Colonel Murphey explained an ingenious method to increase the space in the rooms: "Necessity is the mother of invention and in order to afford space necessary for locomotion, we suspend our bunks upon leather hinges from the sides of the walls with legs fixed by the same means and have the entire room free and unencumbered."[46]

The bunks had a tick of straw as bedding, with a wooden frame and support boards. The prisoner initially could have one or two men assigned to each bunk. At any time, you could be ordered to take on additional personnel in your room or a second occupant in your bunk. Major Caldwell was ordered on December 28, 1864, to make room for an additional bunkmate. He commented that he would rather have an old inmate bunk with him instead of a new one because they have a better quality blanket than new arrivals.[47] Double bunking actually gave the prisoners an advantage because they could share two blankets and could stay warmer together than separate.[48] Colonel Inzer was caught by the whims of command about what room you occupied. He somehow procured an extra plank to widen his bunk that he shared with another inmate, only to be moved into a different room two days later.[49]

Officially, all cooking and washing was to be done in the lower part of the block, but this was not strictly followed. The lower story consisted of two little rooms on each end used for cooking and washing, with a dining hall in the middle; a heating stove was at each end of the dining hall.[50] Bunks were installed on one side only.[51] Captain Barziza described in his memoir the system of dining: "Each block was, for convenience, divided into two messes—No. 1 and 2; each mess usually numbered about one hundred and forty men, who did their cooking in one stove, about two feet and a half or three feet square. Each mess was again sub-divided at pleasure, into smaller ones. There was a 'head' of each main mess—one of our own men—appointed by a Yankee corporal, whose duty it was to call the roll or assist in it, and to receive the rations, and who otherwise acted as a 'go-between' for the corporal and ourselves."[52] With regards

[45] Caldwell, James Parks, *A Northern Confederate at Johnson's Island Prison: The Civil War Diary of James Parks Caldwell*, 155.

[46] Murphey, V. S., *Diary*, 119.

[47] Caldwell, James Parks, *A Northern Confederate at Johnson's Island Prison: The Civil War Diary of James Parks Caldwell*, 171–172.

[48] Knauss, William H., *The Story of Camp Chase*, 241

[49] Inzer, John Washington, *The Diary of a Confederate Soldier: John Washington Inzer*, 96–97.

[50] Barziza, Decimus et Ultimus, *The Adventures of a Prisoner of War, 1863–1864*, 76.

[51] Horace Carpenter, "Plain Living at Johnson's Island," *Century Magazine* (March 1891), 709

[52] Barziza, Decimus et Ultimus, *The Adventures of a Prisoner of War, 1863–1864*, 76.

to cooking, all "rank disappeared, and the man who could command the most money was the big man. Sometimes a mess composed of lieutenants would hire a colonel to cook for them."[53]

Blocks 5 through 13 were not originally ceiled. Because of the lack of ceiling and the warped perforated walls, these blocks were very, very cold during the winter months. Somehow prisoners started to ceil their individual rooms themselves in preparation for the winters. The storms that struck in the summer of 1864 and did so much damage to the pen gave the prisoners a quantity of pre-cut scrap lumber to use to double plank the outside walls. Other prisoners papered their walls with old newspapers or whatever ingenious methods available. An inspection report dated October 23, 1864, by Lt. Colonel Scovill (USA) contained the following about ceiling: "There are four blocks in the prison that are not ceiled, Nos. 5, 11, 12, and 13. The prisoners in some of them have applied for permission to purchase lumber and put ceiling on themselves. I would respectfully recommend that, in view of their exposed condition to all winds and their open condition, the above-named blocks be ceiled by the prisoners, the Government furnishing the material. I think the saving in fuel would nearly compensate the expenditure."[54] Colonel Hoffman declined because he felt the request for the tools and lumber could be a ruse to escape. He then said that they could be ceiled with plaster of clay, but then gave no further instructions about if the purchase of the plaster clay should be from the prisoners' or the prison's funds. He then apathetically stated the barracks "have been used one winter and it is not deemed advisable to ceil them now unless it is absolutely necessary."[55]

Block 13 was the last and crudest block built. Construction began once Block 11 and 12 were nearing completion, in the summer of 1862, while prisoners occupied the other blocks. Colonel Hoffman specified that guards were to make sure no contact happened between the prisoners and the civilian workman. He also ordered that no furniture was to be installed until prisoners occupied it, as theft might occur.[56] This add-on block consisted of four large rooms, two rooms on each floor, measuring about fifty feet long and twenty feet wide. The inmates christened this block the "boar's nest" for it was a "living sweltering, stifling lot of humanity."[57] When a new prisoner arrived at Johnson's Island, he was usually sent first to the "boar's nest." From there, the prisoner

---

[53] Mills, Luther Rice, Papers, 4.

[54] *War of the Rebellion: A Compilation of the Official Records of the Union and Confederate Armies*, Series II, Vol. VII, 120.

[55] *War of the Rebellion: A Compilation of the Official Records of the Union and Confederate Armies*, Series II, Vol. VII, 1050.

[56] *War of the Rebellion: A Compilation of the Official Records of the Union and Confederate Armies*, Series II, Vol. III, 591.

[57] B. W. Johnson, "Record of Privation in Prison," *Confederate Veteran*, Vol. IX (1901), 165.

worked to get transferred, through the help of friends and comrades, to one of the more comfortable blocks.[58] Block 13 was indeed the worst block at Johnson's Island.

Situated behind each Block were twelve latrines called "sinks." These pits measured eighteen feet long by five feet wide and five feet deep. Sheds of the same construction as the blocks covered these open pits.[59] At night, the Confederates could have only two or three prisoners visit the sinks at one time. Visits to the sinks at night were a dangerous proposition because the guards had permission to fire upon any prisoner outside the blocks. To gain safe access to the sinks, a prisoner had to get permission from one of the guards atop the wall. He would then be watched as he went to and from the sinks. If he deviated from the path, he was liable to be shot.[60] Since dysentery was a constant problem for the prisoners, this process caused great distress.

The sinks were excavated to a depth of five feet and reached the limestone substructure of the island, which prevented drainage. The poor drainage of these sinks, compounded by the speed at which they were filled, caused the sinks to become great pools of human waste. The foul smell from the sinks permeated the air of the prison camp. In an inspection report, dated October 10, 1863, the examiner noted that the sinks were in filthy condition and almost full, with no new ones under construction.[61] Hoffman was furious about the mismanagement of the prison and ordered new sinks to be built immediately. He added that this matter should not have had to be resolved by an inspection report or an order from Washington.[62] The next summer, 1864, an inspection report stated the sinks were a nuisance and "the commanding officer [said] that as many vaults had been constructed as the ground would permit." The inspector commented that something "will have to be done soon to meet the emergency; probably boxes upon wheels, that could be emptied every night in the lake and washed out, would be the proper thing."[63] In the hot summer of 1864, the unsanitary conditions stemming from the poorly draining sinks were temporarily alleviated when the order was given to blast through the limestone to make new, deeper sinks. In addition, more lime was issued, upon occasion, to cover the waste.[64] This problem could not

---

[58] Hundley, D. R., *Prison Echoes of the Great Rebellion*, 76.

[59] *War of the Rebellion: A Compilation of the Official Records of the Union and Confederate Armies*, Series II, Vol. VI, 365.

[60] Horace Carpenter, "Plain Living at Johnson's Island," *Century Magazine* (March 1891), 710.

[61] *War of the Rebellion: A Compilation of the Official Records of the Union and Confederate Armies*, Series II, Vol. VI, 365.

[62] *War of the Rebellion: A Compilation of the Official Records of the Union and Confederate Armies*, Series II, Vol. VI, 396.

[63] *War of the Rebellion: A Compilation of the Official Records of the Union and Confederate Armies*, Series II, Vol. VII, 485.

[64] Wash, W. A., *Camp, Field and Prison Life*, 237.

or would not be remedied. An inspection report, dated March 2, 1865, a late date in the course of the war, noted: "Owing to the geological formation sinks cannot be dug more than eight feet deep, and blasting to a greater depth is extremely difficult, owing to the character of the rock and the position of its strata. It follows that in a few weeks' time the sinks become full and new pits have to be opened. This has been so often repeated that the ground north and south of the prison barracks for a distance of fifty feet on either side may now be considered as one continuous sink, very superficially covered, and saturating the whole ground down to the rock. At my inspection these sinks were in the filthiest condition imaginable, the excrementitious [sic] matter in some of them rising high above the seat and covering the floor." The report then recommended a water pipe and water-closet system to remedy the problem with "water-tight boxes, lined with zinc, or with cast-iron troughs connected with water pipes, to be kept flushed with water and drained into the bay on the south side of the island by 6-inch iron pipes."[65] This system was never introduced. Johnson's Island always had problems with the sinks.

In the southwest corner of the bull pen was a building that housed the four condemned men. The men were John Mars, George Sims, William Burges, and Thomas Campbell, all of whom had been convicted of spying, bushwacking, and recruiting for the Confederacy. They were sentenced to death but were given an indefinite stay of execution from Abraham Lincoln. The building was constructed in the same style as the main buildings but had higher security measures. A regular prisoner, Decimus et Ultimus Barziza, described their lot: "The house in which they have been confined since May of 1863, is divided into eight small compartments or cells, each about seven feet high, two and a half feet wide, and long enough to lie down in; a little window, about six inches in length, and one inch and a half in width, admits light and air. At sunset each is locked up separately. Each had a ball, weighing sixty-four pounds, with a chain attached, six feet long, on one leg: shackles riveted upon their ankles with about fourteen inches play, and handcuffs on the wrists. During the day they were allowed to sling their balls on their shoulders, and walk within the stakes, a space about fifteen feet square."[66] These condemned men lived this way until the end of the war.

The other buildings inside the prison pen were the sutler's stand and a pest house. The sutler's stand was a general store for the prisoners and was located just inside the main gate and to the south. The pest house was a temporary structure located on the far southeast corner of the pen, constructed to isolate smallpox victims and prisoners with other contagious diseases.

---

[65] *War of the Rebellion: A Compilation of the Official Records of the Union and Confederate Armies*, Series II, Vol. VII, 330–331.

[66] Barziza, Decimus et Ultimus., *The Adventures of a Prisoner of War, 1863–1864*, ed. R. Henderson Shuffler (Austin: University of Texas Press, 1965), 96–97.

By the summer of 1864, improvements had been made to the prison compound. The soil of Johnson's Island did not drain well; consequently the bull pen became very muddy. [67] In March of that year, a gravel walkway was laid through the center of the yard and behind the blocks. The gravel walkways helped alleviate some of the messy conditions in which the prisoners walked. An inspection report in October 1864 noted that not all of the sinks had gravel walks completed and so there were still mud problems in those locations.[68]

In May 1864, the federals excavated a deep ditch that surrounded the inside of the prison wall. This ditch had two purposes. First, it was excavated down to the bedrock so any escape tunnel would terminate before it reached outside of the wall. Second, the ditch would help drain the compound.[69] One prisoner noted that the ditch "seriously interfer[ed] with the programme [sic] of those having a finger in the tunnel pie."[70] The ditch was four to five feet away from the wall, except where the main gate was located. The main gate and blockhouse angled away from the pen. The ditch, running straight, was subsequently ten or twelve feet away from the blockhouse. A bridge was built over the ditch at this juncture for traffic.[71] Both improvements made escape a greater challenge.

In July 1864, a federal inspector submitted a report on the cleanliness of the prison camp. He stated: "No general mess rooms exists. Besides the large messes there are sub-messes of eight to ten, having small private cooking-stoves purchased by the prisoners, consequently I saw but few rooms which are not used as kitchen and mess-room, as well as sleeping apartment." The Inspector recommended that two large mess halls with kitchens be built along with a wash house in order to improve prison health and cleanliness.[72] In August 1864, the federals began construction of the new buildings. The original specification for the mess halls was one building thirty feet wide and eight hundred feet long, 80 windows and 6 lanterns.[73] It appears from artists' drawings that two halls were built of the same width but each about four hundred feet long. The mess halls were built one hundred and five

---

[67] *War of the Rebellion: A Compilation of the Official Records of the Union and Confederate Armies,* Series II, Vol. VII, 484.

[68] *War of the Rebellion: A Compilation of the Official Records of the Union and Confederate Armies,* Series II, Vol. VII, 1025–1026.

[69] Ibid., 681.

[70] Wash, W. A., *Camp, Field and Prison Life,* 226.

[71] Hundley, D. R., *Prison Echoes of the Great Rebellion,* 201.

[72] *War of the Rebellion: A Compilation of the Official Records of the Union and Confederate Armies,* Series II, Vol. VII, 484.

[73] Ibid., 484–487.

feet to the east and parallel to the eastern most row of blocks.[74] The halls were the same type of construction as the blocks except that gravel was used as flooring for the halls. The federals tried to recruit prisoners to help construct the dining halls. Colonel Hundley noted: "The Yankees are engaged building a dining hall for the prisoners, and have had the generosity to offer five cents a day to any rebel who will work on it. I am glad that no Southren [sic] has proven himself so base as to accept of the offer."[75]

In September 1864, the mess halls were completed. The Rebels moved all of their cooking and eating utensils into the new enclosures.[76] Not all the prisoners were happy with the new cooking arrangements. W. A. Wash reported that the "cooking facilities of at least 1,200 men were now crowded into a place about forty feet square. Imagine twelve large cook stoves in that space, with about fifty cooks, and rations, wood and water to cook for a thousand men interspersed, and you have a very slight idea of the disadvantages."[77]

The removal of the cooking requirements from the blocks freed up space for more prisoners. The rooms previously used for kitchens were very desirable. Wash described what occurred. "And now came the exciting question of who should occupy the cook and mess rooms just vacated. The rooms being small, were desirable, as winter was coming on, and it was almost impossible to keep warm in the large rooms during cold days. No one could change his quarters without leave from the prison superintendent, to whom at least two hundred applications were made."[78] It is assumed that the lower rooms had bunks installed for more prisoners. The prisoners knew that with these dining halls more prisoners were going to be brought in.

The wash house was a multifunction building. It was located to the southeast of the compound, between the sutler's shop and the condemned men's cells. Prisoners could bathe inside it or wash their clothes. It was constructed to stop the prisoners from washing their clothes and other items in their blocks and to give warm baths in the winter. A federal report stated that "the prisoners are allowed to wash their clothes in every part of the camp, even in the hall of the barracks, consequently dirty soap-suds meet you on every turn." In order to tidy up the compound, a wash house was constructed thirty feet by forty feet and contained two large boilers of thirty to sixty

[74] Ibid., 876–877.

[75] Hundley, D. R., *Prison Echoes of the Great Rebellion*, 108.

[76] Patterson, Edmund Dewitt., *Yankee Rebel, the Civil War Journal of Edmund DeWitt Patterson*, ed. John G. Barrett (Chapel Hill: North Carolina Press, 1966), 192.

[77] Wash, W. A., *Camp, Field and Prison Life*, 261.

[78] Ibid., 262.

gallons, for heating water. The wash house allowed the prisoners to bathe in hot water and wash their clothes protected from the weather.[79]

Most prisoners who were incarcerated at Johnson's Island felt that this prison was better than the other northern prisons. Prisoner Wharton Green stated, "On the whole it was a decided improvement over the last two prisons [in which he was incarcerated] as it was more commodious and roomy."[80] Captain Drummond was impressed with the blocks: "We have much more room in our sleeping quarters than we had at Governor's Island [Prison]".[81] Edmund Dewitt Patterson liked Johnson's Island more than any other Union prison. What impressed him most of all was the fact that the guards were not generally seen inside the prison but remained on the pulpit. The Confederates enjoyed the limited contact the despised Yankees.[82] Captain Bingham noted, "We get a beautiful view of the lake. It adds very much to the landscape. This place is a great improvement upon Ft. Delaware—as pleasant a place, indeed as we can expect & we have as many liberties as we could wish almost. [The guards] are very reasonable. The enclosure is about 16 acres & one can go all about during the day."[83]

When the federal government built Johnson's Island, they were looking for a secure, cheap, and temporary facility for the confinement of Confederate prisoners of war. Johnson's Island was the only Union prison that was built solely for the purpose of housing prisoners of war. Since the design of the facility was to be a prison, the comfort and security of the prisoners were well planned.

GUARDING THE REBELS

An 1864 engraving by Edward Gould showed a multitude of federal buildings on the outside of the prison walls. These included guards' barracks, officers' barracks, head-quarters, horse stables, a bakery, laundry houses, and barbershops. The buildings were of similar construction to the prisoners' blocks except they were built to a higher quality standard. No prisoners were allowed outside the fence to utilize any of these Union facilities. To the north of the prison, in the center of the island, were two forts, manned by federals to help quell any prisoner uprising against the guards and to repulse any external attack. These forts were an intimidating presence.

---

[79] *War of the Rebellion: A Compilation of the Official Records of the Union and Confederate Armies*, Series II, Vol. VII, 484-487; Vol. VI, 702.

[80] Green, Wharton Jackson., *Recollections and Reflections: An Auto of Half a Century and More* (no place: Edwards and Broughton Printing Company, 1906), 182.

[81] Drummond, Edward W., *Confederate Yankee: The Journal of Edward William Drummond: A Confederate Soldier from Maine*, 76.

[82] Patterson, Edmund Dewitt, *Yankee Rebel: The Civil War Journal of Edmund DeWitt Patterson*, 124.

[83] Bingham, Robert, *Diary*, 22–23.

A garrison was needed to guard the prisoners. Governor William Dennison of Ohio was ordered to organize a company of volunteers for Johnson's Island. The governor requested that the garrison be called the Hoffman Battalion in honor of the Commissary-General.[84] An advertisement was placed in the *Sandusky Register* calling for volunteers. They were given a $100 reward for enlisting and told that they would be garrison troops on Johnson's Island. They would receive the same pay and same instruction as regular troops.[85] Many enlisted for the money or the good rations, but most knew that they would not be sent to the front and would be close to home.

Even though the guards were garrison troops, they were kept in full readiness for combat. Colonel Hoffman gave specific orders that they not be allowed to grow soft or neglect their duties as soldiers just because they were guarding prisoners. Hoffman ordered: "Each man of the guard will fire one shot with his revolver besides discharge of his musket. Have a target three feet by six, with a vertical and horizontal line, and let them fire fifty yards with muskets and fifteen with revolvers. It is very important that your command should be well drilled and you must order two drills a day, one in the morning of one hour for squads and a company drill in the afternoon." New recruits are to "drill three times a day."[86] Private Mortimer Thompson of the Hoffman's Battalion complained they had "to get up every morning at four o'clock and drill one hour before breakfast and then we haf [sic] to thrash flies the balance of the day."[87] In addition to typical military duties that would be seen at any encampment, about fifty-four men manned the fence daily. In January 1864, the guard at night was increased to eighty-four.[88] Lieutenant Mitchell explained extra duties of the men: "When an exchange of prisoners was ordered, a company was detailed to guard them to the place of destination, and at other times, when the draft was going on in Ohio detachments were located at Mansfield, Toledo, Lima, and other places, doing provost duty."[89] In the spring of 1864, the Hoffman's Battalion was expanded into a regiment called the 128th Ohio Infantry; however, the moniker of Hoffman's Battalion remained.

The prisoners' opinions of the guards recorded in diaries, letters, and memoirs, varied from kind to very bitter. Henry Kyd Douglas said, "The officers and guards,

---

[84] *War of the Rebellion: A Compilation of the Official Records of the Union and Confederate Armies,* Series II, Vol. III, 123–124; Frohman, *Rebels on Lake Erie,* 6.

[85] Frohman, Charles E., *Rebels on Lake Erie,* 6.

[86] *War of the Rebellion: A Compilation of the Official Records of the Union and Confederate Armies,* Series II Vol., 591.

[87] Morimer Thompson letter.

[88] Wash, W. A., *Camp, Field and Prison Life,* 194.

[89] Mitchell, E. O., "Johnson's Island: Military Prison for Confederate Prisoners." *Sketches of War History, 1861–1865,* 127.

with rare exceptions, were civil and considerate."[90] Captain Barziza had the opposite opinion: "This battalion comprised as graceless, impudent and insulting a set of ruffians as was ever gotten together. The petty lieutenants too would sometimes promenade the yard, and assume the most ridiculous airs and attitudes, much to the disgust of the prisoners."[91] This anger was most likely a combination of personality conflicts and anger from being completely subservient to these guards. Colonel Barbiere illustrates the combining of the two by stating, "our rolls are called by a sergeant of eighteen years of age, who, with an impudent air, orders, 'Fall in boys, I'm in a hurry,' and this to his seniors in age, rank, position, and everything that constitutes a man, soldier, and gentleman."[92]

William Steward Pierson, a former mayor of Sandusky, was commissioned a major and made commandant of the prison and placed in command of the Hoffman Battalion on December 17, 1861. Pierson was highly regarded by people of Sandusky. Hoffman stated he was "an intelligent and experienced man of business, particular in administrative affairs."[93] He was thirty-six years old and from a distinguished Connecticut family. He was a Yale graduate but had no previous military experience.[94] Hoffman wanted a man with greater military experience and age. He thought that a man with military experience would be better able to handle the position. An alternative was sought, but a suitable candidate could not be found. Hoffman felt Pierson had many of the qualities he was looking for—Pierson was gentlemanly, courteous, and industrious—but was lacking confidence in himself and might not have the ability to make prompt decisions.[95] Colonel Hoffman made an agreement with Pierson to allow him to resign when another commandant was selected.[96] All in all, Pierson was not well liked by the prisoners and many negative connotations can be sifted out of numerous diaries and memoirs about him. Colonel Joseph Barbiere had a low opinion of him and stated: Major Pierson "is an arrant [sic] hypocrite and would make an elegant lobby-member, if he had any brains. Pierson is a harmless individual, ostensibly, but is a dangerous man in the dark."[97]

---

[90] Douglas, Henry Kyd, *I Rode with Stonewall*, 263.

[91] Barziza, Decimus et Ultimus, *The Adventures of a Prisoner of War, 1863–1864*, 78.

[92] Barbiere, Joe, *Scraps from the Prison Table, At Camp Chase and Johnson's Island*, 80.

[93] *War of the Rebellion: A Compilation of the Official Records of the Union and Confederate Armies*, Series II, Vol. III, 163.

[94] Frohman, Charles E., *Rebels on Lake Erie*, 6.

[95] *War of the Rebellion: A Compilation of the Official Records of the Union and Confederate Armies*, Series II, Vol. III, 163.

[96] Ibid., 479–480

[97] Barbiere, Joe, *Scraps from the Prison Table, At Camp Chase and Johnson's Island*, 77–78.

Colonel Pierson submitted his resignation when Colonel Hoffman found a temporary replacement to take over as commandant of the prison. On January 18, 1864, Brigadier General Harry D. Terry of the VI Army Corps assumed command, but was commandant for just a short time. General Terry was not a satisfactory commander: An inspection report noted that "General Terry is an intelligent, clever gentleman, but quite fond of a social glass of whiskey as of attending to the duties of command."[98]

Although Colonel Charles Hill was put in charge of the prisoners on May 11, 1864, he was still under the command of General Terry until he became full commandant of Johnson's Island on December 19, 1864.[99] The comments made in prisoners' diaries were generally kinder toward Colonel Hill than they were towards Colonel Pierson. Major Caldwell, a prisoner, noted Colonel Hill had been in command for several days and then he penned in his diary: "we hail his return as a deliverance from some few of our evils."[100] Not all of the comments, of course, were positive about Colonel Hill. Westwood Todd wrote in his diary: "The Col., though a very respectable looking man, had by no means a marked air, but rather the appearance of 'a sly man of business.' His profession, which was that of a lawyer in Toledo, Ohio was abundantly indicated by his fondness for speech making, and glibness of tongue. He frequently made the numerous communications received by him from prisoners an excuse for making a 'few remarks to them by way of a general reply to their requests and complaints.' He was very plausible, as smooth as oil, in fact 'too sweet to be wholesome.' He was believed by the prisoners to be hypocritical, or to use a hateful word, he was considered a fraud."[101]

E. A. Scovill, who went from the rank of Captain to Lt. Colonel while stationed at Johnson's Island, was probably the most written about Union officer at the prison. He had the most contact with the prisoners and had direct command of the prisoners for most of the war. W. A. Wash, a prisoner, commented, "Captain Scoville [sic], who was in charge of the internal affairs of the prison, visits all parts of the institution frequently and is very kind in listening to the various questions and supplying the wants of the prisoners."[102] Wharton Green, another prisoner, stated he was one "of the most popular of our jailers . . . who for the life of him couldn't say 'No.' He had charge of approving all papers emanating from the inside on the powers that be."[103] Even Colonel

---

[98] Hesseltine, William., *Civil War Prisons* (Kent, OH: The Kent State University Press, 1972), 110.

[99] Schultz, Charles R., "The Conditions at Johnson's Island Prison during the Civil War" (Master's Thesis, Bowling Green State University, 1960), 22.

[100] Caldwell, James Parks, *A Northern Confederate at Johnson's Island Prison: The Civil War Diary of James Parks Caldwell*, 164.

[101] Todd, Westwood, *Reminiscences of Westwood Todd*, 318.

[102] Wash, W. A., *Camp, Field and Prison Life*, 155.

[103] Green, Wharton Jackson, *Recollections and Reflections: An Auto of Half a Century and More*, 190–191

Barbiere, who was very negative in his writings, praised Scovill as "an officer that has the bearing and appearance of a soldier, and would pass for a gentleman."[104] Captain Wash recorded a typical act of kindness by Scovill: "I learned that Major Scoville [sic] had a library at his office, and seeing that he was inclined to accommodating, I asked him if he would bring me in something to read. To my pleasant surprise, he asked me to go out with him to his office and make a choice from his library, which I did."[105]

Of course not all prisoners had a positive opinion of Scovill. Colonel Inzer, of Alabama wrote: "went to the express, found the goods. Could not get them without the permission of the infernal Maj. Scoville [sic]. He was 100 yards off. Several gentleman interested with myself went to him and requested him to deliver the goods. It would have taken but a few minutes. Positively refused, treating the gentleman with great indignity."[106] Captain Bingham believed him to be a liar with promises to prisoners he cared not to keep. Scovill "is the biggest liar I ever saw, but really polite, a pleasant liar. He [would] sign anything. Some one wrote an order for a blanket, shoes, etc. & 6 pieces artillery & 600 revolvers—old Scovill signed it as usual. Some one asked if he was in the first squad that [would] be removed. Scovill said 'Yes, I saw your name myself.' What is my name? asked the rebel. 'Really' said Scovill, a good deal chagrinned, 'I do not know.'"[107]

Scovill must have battled illness in 1864 as he was missing from the camp at certain times. In an official report dated July 23, 1864, concerns were raised about his health interfering with duties. It stated: "The major is somewhat of an invalid, not however, so sick as to be confined to his quarters at all times; judging from his appearance, able to direct. A necessity exists for placing in charge of the prisoners an efficient, practical officer, who knows what good police is, and with decision sufficient to enforce his orders."[108]

The other officers of Hoffman's Battalion were occasionally mentioned in diaries and memoirs. Captain Follett "is some fifty winters, stern, taciturn, and with little of the milk of human kindness in his composition; takes a delight in irritating those, whom the fortunes of war have thrown under his charge, and is a bear generally."[109] But another prisoner called him "a nice, clever man."[110]

---

[104] Barbiere, Joe, *Scraps from the Prison Table, At Camp Chase and Johnson's Island*, 78.

[105] Wash, W. A., *Camp, Field and Prison Life*, 187.

[106] Inzer, John Washington, *The Diary of a Confederate Soldier: John Washington Inzer, 1834–1928*, 77.

[107] Bingham, Robert, *Diary* 2, 81.

[108] *War of the Rebellion: A Compilation of the Official Records of the Union and Confederate Armies*, Series II, Vol. VII, 484.

[109] Barbiere, Joe, *Scraps from the Prison Table, At Camp Chase and Johnson's Island*, 78.

[110] Gresham, *Confederate Veteran*, XVI, 518.

Lieutenant Benson, from Sandusky, as Colonel Barbiere described, had "made himself obnoxious, to the entire prison community, by his boorish disposition, and his ruffian manners and will catch many a castigation, if the chances of the field should throw him in the way of some of our gallant men, he has so often wantonly insulted."[111] The Rebels had the opposite view of Lieutenant Williams. W. A. Wash stated that Williams "had been calling our roll for some time, and whom we all liked for his kindness, came in to bid us adieu before leaving for the front. We gave him a letter of recommendation for good treatment in case he should be captured, and promised to reciprocate his kind deeds if we should ever have charge of him."[112] Colonel Barbiere gave his opinions on two more officers: "Lieutenant Wells, post adjutant, performs his duties faithfully, and is a good officer, and a gentleman. Lieutenant Lennelle is a negative character, yet is attentive to our wants, and makes himself acceptable to the prisoners."[113]

On November 10, 1863, a rumor that Confederates in Canada were planning to make a raid on Johnson's Island sent northern Ohio into turmoil. Reinforcements were needed immediately. The newly created 12th Cavalry Regiment, which was training in Cleveland, got the message to deploy to the island at once. The official history of the regiment stated: "The 12th Cavalry was not ready for service; its men were but imperfectly uniformed and not a weapon had yet been placed in their hands. The order reached the camp on that cold winter night . . . [and] muskets and infantry accoutrements were distributed to the men, a hasty ration of raw pork and hard bread issued, and before midnight . . . were on the march to the depot." Johnson's Island had no shelter prepared for this influx of men. The 12th Cavalry had to set up camp on open ground near the buildings of the Hoffman Battalion. Winter was in full rage, "the damp, muddy snow lay thick upon the ground, and the keen winds swept across the lake and howled round their rude huts." The men built a temporary camp with "the help of a few old tents that were finally secured, huts were erected and a reasonable degree of comfort attained." [114] Two regiments of Ohio militia (or 100 days men as they were called) were raised and sent to the island. The 24th Ohio Artillery Battery was sent with some of their men and cannons stationed on the island and some at Cedar Point across the bay.[115] These units were on the island when the temperature dropped to record lows that were recorded in the 12th Cavalry's unit history:

---

[111] Barbiere, Joe, *Scraps from the Prison Table, At Camp Chase and Johnson's Island*, 78.

[112] Wash, W. A., *Camp, Field and Prison Life*, 226–227.

[113] Barbiere, Joe, *Scraps from the Prison Table, At Camp Chase and Johnson's Island*, 78–79.

[114] The Twelfth Ohio Cavalry, 15–16.

[115] The Twelfth Ohio Cavalry, 16.

The first, second and third days of January were an epoch in the weather record of this country. From a warm fitful rain the wind suddenly veered to the northward and brought on a gale and storm of unexampled severity. The mercury dropped, within twelve hours from about 50 degrees Fahrenheit to 28 degrees below zero. The gale increased rather than diminished and the biting air pierced through the warmest clothing and punished the slightest indiscretion with a frozen hand or foot. During this trying period guard duty was a work of no ordinary hazard. On the parapet of the prison the guards were doubled, and, although relieved four times every hour, many a man came out of the ordeal with nose and fingers bitten or with his health seriously impaired.[116]

A few days later, on January 13, 1864, four regiments of veteran infantry, under the command of General Alexander Shaler, were immediately transferred from the Army of the Potomac to Johnson's Island. The 23rd and 82nd Pennsylvania Infantry and the 65th New York Infantry were quartered on the island in tents and the 122nd New York Infantry was stationed in Sandusky.[117] General Shaler was transferred back east a little while later and left General Terry in command of the regiments.

For the remainder of the winter, an odd mix of soldiers guarded the Rebels. The island consisted of men who joined Hoffman's Battalion to avoid the front, militia, untested cavalryman, and four regiments of combat veterans. The militia were the most troublesome as they were "unused to the privations of army life, and their constant complaints resulted in their securing the lion's share of whatever comforts and supplies could be furnished."[118] The veterans looked down on the Hoffman's Battalion. A prisoner, Wharton Green noted an altercation between the veterans and the prison guards when one of the locals said, "You fellows treat these rebels with as much politeness as if they were some of our folks;" to which Shaler's man replied: "And you fellows, who have never smelt powder, treat them as if they were dogs. If you had helped to catch them as we have, you would have more respect for them, for we know what they are."[119] Captain Bingham had a conversation with an old veteran where he commented: "There is the greatest difference between the old soldiers and these infamous Hoffman men and there is a most cordial hate between them and the battalion."[120] Most of the prisoners enjoyed the presence of the veterans as Wharton Green stated there "was no more needless shooting of prisoners after their coming, as there had been under the redoubtable 'stay-at-homes,'

---

[116] Ibid., 17.

[117] Mitchell, E. O., "Johnson's Island: Military Prison for Confederate Prisoners." *Sketches of War History,* USA, 119–120.

[118] The Twelfth Ohio Cavalry, 16.

[119] Green, Wharton Jackson, *Recollections and Reflections: An Auto of Half a Century and More*, 183.

[120] Bingham, Robert, *Diary* 2, 71.

who enjoyed, of all things, some slight excuse for making a target of some of us." Green felt "grateful to those old war veterans for their marked courtesy and civility."[121]

With the threat of a raid over, the reinforcements started leaving for the front to participate in spring campaigns. The 12th Ohio Cavalry left on February 10, 1864.[122] On April 14, 1864, three of the four veteran regiments left for the Army of the Potomac leaving just the 23rd Pennsylvania behind. They left for the front in May.[123]

Johnson's Island was used to "season" National Guard units in case they were needed at the front. By June 1864, four regiments of infantry and one artillery unit were on the island. Colonel Webb, a Rebel, stated: "Two-thirds of the Yankee force are national guards or militia. Some of them are mere children in appearance and present a strange contrast to the grim warriors whom they guard."[124]

The 171st Ohio Infantry was sent to Kentucky to stop a raid by John Hunt Morgan. They were surrounded, captured, and paroled back to Johnson's Island. John Sargent commented on this disaster: "One day a regiment of Ohio volunteers [171st] were marched out amid much elation and beating of drums. Their bright new uniforms, fluttering flags, and glistening guns made a sad contrast to the boys inside the walls." But when they returned, "Of all the dilapidated broken down sets of men ever seen, these surely were the worst. They appeared as if a 'cyclone had struck them.' From what had been the exultant departure, their dejected return made a pleasing contrast."[125] Horace Carpenter of Louisiana noted: "A regiment of hundred day's men was in camp outside the 'pen' and when Morgan was on one of his raids this regiment was sent out to meet him. As they marched by, one of their number sang out, 'Boys we're going to bring John Morgan to keep you company.' In due time they returned. They had met Morgan and had exchanged their accoutrements for a parole. As they went by, one of our numbers shouted, 'Boys, where's your guns?' and quickly came back the retort, 'Morgan's got them: where's yours?' No reply was made to this."[126]

In September 1864, the 6th U. S. Veteran Corps, under Lt. Colonel Frederick Palmer, arrived at Johnson's Island to reinforce the guard for the winter. One prisoner noted: These [guards] knew how to treat the brave, whose misfortune it was to be prisoners. Those gallant and chivalrous men did their duty as guards, but showed

[121] Green, Wharton Jackson, *Recollections and Reflections: An Auto of Half a Century and More*, 183–184.

[122] Wash, W. A., *Camp, Field and Prison Life*, 203.

[123] Knauss, William H., *The Story of Camp Chase*, 192,; Caldwell, James Parks., *A Northern Confederate at Johnson's Island Prison: The Civil War Diary of James Parks Caldwell*, 110.

[124] Webb, R. F., "Prison Life at Johnson's Island." *Histories of the Several Regiments and Battalions from North Carolina in the Great War, 1861–65*, 680.

[125] John Sargent, *Confederate Veteran*, Vol. I, 340.

[126] Horace Carpenter, "Plain Living at Johnson's Island," *Century Magazine* (March 1891), 717.

to us and . . . in broad contrast to the Hoffman Battalion, how the brave can be generous."[127] In late October, Colonel Hill left on furlough and Colonel Palmer assumed temporary command of the prison. The prisoners may have felt the guards were kind and gentlemanly but they had a different opinion about Colonel Palmer. Major Caldwell wrote in his prison diary that the first contact with Colonel Palmer was when the prisoners had a general muster. Some of the men brought chairs out and sat while the roll call was held. Caldwell reported that Colonel Palmer ordered the Corporal to take the chairs away and "knock down" those who refused to give them up.[128] Colonel Hundley had a scathing account in his diary: "Awhile back one could bribe the Yankees to bring in coffee, sugar, and such little delicacies, 'underground,' but not now. Colonel Hill being absent, this post is now commanded by a Lieutenant Colonel Palmer, at one time a cab-driver and New York pimp, and afterward police detective, whose natural instincts lead him to regard us as criminals whom he must watch as well as guard. Colonel Hill, with the education of a gentleman, could not stoop to pry into such small matters, but this upstart Palmer pries into everything, and even has his commissioned officers searched upon entering or returning from the prison yard."[129]

EXCHANGE

The first prisoners arrived at Johnson's Island on April 11, 1862, while construction of the prison was still being completed. The majority of prisoners from this first group were exchanged in September 1862. In keeping with European military tradition, prisoners were exchanged; for example, 100 Union lieutenants held in southern prisons would be exchanged with the North for 100 Confederate lieutenants. As the war intensified in the spring of 1863, the prison population at Johnson's Island swelled to the approximate size it would be for the duration of the war, with new prisoners coming in and existing prisoners departing being exchanged. The prison held an average of 2,480 for the years of 1863 and 1864.[130] Exchanges were common until early 1864 when the exchange system broke down for various reasons. One prisoner stated, "During the earlier part of our stay we constantly looked forward to exchange, and it was this hope that served in a measure to mitigate the ills of our prison life. It was toward the fall of 1864 that I began to give up all hope of exchange, and could see no prospect of release save

---

[127] Wash, W. A., *Camp, Field and Prison Life*, VIII.

[128] Caldwell, James Parks, *A Northern Confederate at Johnson's Island Prison: The Civil War Diary of James Parks Caldwell*, 156.

[129] Hundley, D. R., *Prison Echoes of the Great Rebellion*, 179–180.

[130] Knauss, William H., *The Story of Camp Chase*, 192.

the close of the war or death."[131] After that time, most prisoners who left the island were invalids, special exchanges, or transfers to other prisons. In April 1864, about 150 sick and disabled prisoners were exchanged. By the fall of 1864, two groups left Johnson's Island, one of forty and the other of fifty.[132] These invalids would drain resources of the North and fuel outcry of abuse if they perished in captivity. In addition, they were too disabled to help the southern army. The decision was made to allow their special exchange. With the hope of general exchange evaporated, these officers were "overwhelmed with messages to be delivered to dear ones in Dixie."[133] In January 1865, with victory for the Union army virtually assured, the exchange commenced once again with some prisoners leaving the confines of Johnson's Island to return to Dixie.

RULES OF THE PRISON

In April 1862, Major Pierson issued ten regulations for the inmates to follow. The prisoners quickly called them "Pierson's Ten Commandments."[134] They were posted inside the prison and read as follows:

Order No. 1—It is designed to treat prisoners of war with all kindness compatible with their condition, and to other ends, as few orders as possible will be issued respecting them, and their own comfort will be chiefly secured, by prompt and implicit obedience.

Order No. 2.—The Quarters have been erected at great expense, by the government, for the comfort of prisoners of war, the utmost caution should be used against fire, as in the case of their destruction, the prisoners will be subjected to much exposure and suffering, for want of comfortable quarters, as others will not be erected, and rude shelter only provided.

Order No. 3.—All prisoners are required to parade in their rooms, and answer to their names, half an hour after reveille and at retreat.

Order No. 4.—Meals will be taken at breakfast drum, dinner drum, and half an hour before retreat.

Order No. 5.—Quarters must be thoroughly policed by 10 o'clock in the morning.

Order No. 6.—All prisoners will be required to remain in their own quarters after retreat, except when they have the occasion to visit the sinks, lights will be extinguished at "taps," and no fires will be allowed after that time.

---

[131] Ibid., 247.

[132] Hundley, D. R., *Prison Echoes of the Great Rebellion*, 151; Patterson, 162.

[133] Hundley, D. R., *Prison Echoes of the Great Rebellion*, 132.

[134] Knauss, William H., *The Story of Camp Chase*, 243.

Order No. 7.—Quarrels and disorders of every kind are strictly prohibited.

Order No. 8.—Prisoners occupying officers' quarters in blocks 1, 2, 3 and 4 will not be permitted to visit the soldiers' quarters in blocks 5, 6, 7 and 8 nor go upon the grounds in their vicinity, nor beyond the line of stakes between the officers' and soldiers' quarters; nor will the soldiers be allowed to go upon the ground in the vicinity of the officers' quarters, or beyond the line of stakes between the officers' and soldiers' quarters.[135]

Order No. 9.—No prisoner will be allowed to loiter between the buildings, and the north and west fences, and they will be permitted north of the buildings, only when passing to and from the sinks, nor will they approach the fences anywhere else nearer than thirty feet, as the line is marked out by stakes.

Order No. 10.—Guards and sentinels will be required to fire upon all who violate the above orders. Prisoners will, therefore, bear them carefully in mind, and be governed by them, to forget under such circumstances is inexcusable, and may prove fatal.[136]

Conclusion

The living conditions at Johnson's Island were entirely dependent on the prevailing mood of the country. In the first two years of its existence, prison life was not overly uncomfortable. The quality of lodging, food, clothing, and medical attention was kept as high as one could expect. But, when the mood of the country turned to bitterness and revenge, the prisoners at Johnson's Island suffered. The flow of supplies was unnecessarily cut off in 1864 (see Chapter III). Johnson's Island could have been without a doubt the best prison during the Civil War. The majority of the physical suffering endured on Johnson's Island was a result of the reduction or restriction of rationed commodities necessary for healthy existence.

---

[135] This was no longer a valid order when the prison was designated for officers only.

[136] Knauss, William H., *The Story of Camp Chase,* 194–195.

Chapter 2

DAILY LIFE

"Very much like young fellows first going off to college, we were smartly puzzled when we first entered, not knowing where to go or what to do."

—Captain W. A. Wash, 16th Tennessee

AN AVERAGE DAY

The prisoners' daily routine started at dawn with breakfast, consisting of coffee (until that commodity was declared contraband) and bread. Sometimes breakfast would include meat, or whatever the prisoner could scrounge up from friends outside the prison or purchase from the sutler, a military store inside the prison. No one was allowed outside the blocks until a little after sun-up. The signal for the day to officially begin was the raising of the garrison flag above the parade ground of Hoffman's Battalion. Prisoners could wake up at any time and move around inside the block before they were required outside for roll call at 7:30. At which time, a drumbeat would signal for all prisoners to muster for roll call. A Union corporal, one for each of the thirteen blocks, entered the bull pen and called roll in front of the prisoners' respective blocks. No distinction was given to rank; the prisoners were called by their civilian names. The corporal would count the prisoners to see that the number who answered "here" matched the number of prisoners standing in front of the block.[137] The roll call occurred rain or shine, snow or blizzard. The procedures never fluctuated because of the weather, and put undo suffering upon the prisoners. In winter many of the prisoners complained the roll call was unnecessarily continued outside in the freezing snow

---

[137] Wash, W. A., *Camp, Field and Prison Life*, 152.

and they argued the corporal could have just as easily conducted the roll call inside the block. Upon returning to their respective blocks, prisoners had difficulty shaking off the chill created by standing outside for upwards of an hour because little heat was furnished in the blocks.

After roll call, the prisoners would collect all the articles they needed for the day. The sutler came in with newspapers, eatables, and supplies to sell to the inmates. His inventory fluctuated over time and had to adhere to the prescribed regulations from the commandant on what could be sold to the prisoners. The approved articles varied depending on the political mood of the time. The Rebels purchased northern newspapers, the only papers allowed, from the sutler to keep up with the war and the happenings at home. The contents were eagerly devoured. The prisoners purchased food to supplement their meager rations. Later in the day the prisoners might return to the sutler to peruse and purchase other goods such as writing paper and candles.[138]

The guards brought in and distributed rations to each mess. The quantity and quality of provisions varied from time to time. In 1863 to early 1864 rations were generally good; however, later in 1864, in retaliation for the stories of hunger coming from Andersonville and other Southern prisons, rations were severely reduced (see Chapter III). In addition to the rations, wood was also provided to the prisoners. Lieutenant Carpenter wrote "rations were brought in daily, and to each mess were delivered an ax and a bucksaw. These were collected and taken out each night; and should any mess fail to return them, no wood was brought in until the missing tools were given up. This happened once during my stay . . . and the ax and saw showed up."[139]

The mail and express came at about 10 o'clock A.M. provided that the weather cooperated. The arrival of the mail was eagerly anticipated. The postmaster of the mess distributed the mail to his mates. The express wagon entered the pen with packages mailed to the prisoners from friends outside. Colonel Hundley gave a testament to the value of the express, writing "after roll call, the 'Express' comes in, being usually a wagon heavily laden with boxes of clothing, eatables, etc., sent to the prisoners by relatives and sympathizing friends throughout the 'loyal states'; and of truth, if it were not for these boxes of provisions, many of the prisoners here would die of scurvy or starvation."[140]

Water was another item that had to be procured by the prisoners (see Chapter III). The drinkable water supply, deficient in both quality and quantity, was always a problem for the prisoners on Johnson's Island. They needed water for drinking, cooking, and washing themselves and their clothes. Water was available either out of the wells

---

[138] Frohman, Charles E., *Rebels on Lake Erie*, 15–16.

[139] Knauss, William H., *The Story of Camp Chase*, 241.

[140] Hundley, D. R., *Prison Echoes of the Great Rebellion*, 82.

or the pumps. During winter the pumps froze and prisoners were allowed to go to the lake and cut a hole through the ice for water. In the summertime the prisoners were given permission to go out into the lake for bathing and swimming. They could venture out about three times a week in shifts of 100 men. Many prisoners believed a bath in the lake added to their comfort and relieved in some degree the tedium of prison life.[141]

After the daily provisions were acquired, the prisoners had to find ways to pass the time. The prisoners had almost free range within the prison pen. However, no correspondence was allowed with the condemned prisoners on the south side of the pen and no prisoner could walk within thirty feet of the wall, as this was the dead line. One inmate described how prisoners "collect[ed] in groups on the various woodpiles, stairsteps or shady plot of grass and [told] of adventures in the wars, travels, incidents, manners of society and characters of the people where we have been, and [got] off good jokes on each other." He continued, "The end of Block 1 was rather a famous place, . . . it was a place of resort to witness [the Hoffman's Battalion] dress parade, look at the visitors to the island, and whatever was going on about headquarters. Full many a pleasing hour have I whiled away at that point watching the movements of the world without."[142]

The prisoners organized games and activities to defeat their boredom. The prisoners put on plays, sang songs, attended classes, and engaged in discussions about a variety of subjects. Activities were initiated by prisoners for prisoners without contact with the outside world. W. A. Wash noted in his dairy, "This evening, about one hundred of us, engaged in an exciting game of town ball, furnishing fun and exercise till the flag went down, sometimes we have foot races, and at other times the boys wrestle—in fact, anything is done that will give exercise and keep up an excitement."[143] John Dooley described how the less athletically inclined passed the time: "Another source of recreation to a much larger number is a quiet promenade during the cool of the evening. Then you may see hundreds of promenaders passing up and down the prison enclosure in quiet, pleasant but melancholy converse."[144]

The prison had all the trappings of a small town. Businesses and services sprang up throughout the pen. Some inmates were unaccustomed to daily chores and had money to pay the other inmates for their cleaning duties. Some poorer prisoners would cook and clean for a mess that had wealthy inmates. John Lewis stated that he did "washing and ironing, and by them made my tobacco [money]; for be it known that

---

[141] Patterson, Edmund Dewitt., *Yankee Rebel: The Civil War Journal of Edmund DeWitt Patterson*, 172.

[142] Wash, W. A., *Camp, Field and Prison Life*, 153, 287.

[143] Ibid., 168.

[144] Durkin, Joseph T., *John Dooley, Confederate Soldier: His War Journal*, 163.

we had millionaires in prison."[145] W. A. Wash described the business activities of the camp: "[Y]ou may find one fellow making pies to sell, while another deals in lemonade, a third sells ice cream, and a fourth has cakes and beer to exchange for sutler's checks. Two tailors are kept all the time employed, and to wind up we have a boot and shoe shop."[146] All materials to support this trade were either bought from the sutler or smuggled in via bribed guards.

Many prisoners spent the evenings writing letters home, logging entries into their journals, or just reflecting on their situation. Edmund Patterson would spend his nights writing in his diary internalizing his thoughts and reflecting on all he observed. His friend Mosely would study French with great enthusiasm, rehearsing his enunciation and diction for the day he can put his practice to the test. On another bunk, Captain Ballentine of Florida is immersing himself in a novel about some adventurous spirit engaging in battle, wondering if the protagonist will brave the slings and arrows to emerge victorious and win honor and the hand of a fair maiden. Two more roommates, Dennis and Clark, are engaged in game of chess as Lieutenant Butchell looks on. Captain Brown read the papers of the day. On the other end of the room, a table is occupied by parties playing whist, euchre, solitaire, and other card games. At the far extreme of the room two men are writing letters to loved ones far away in physical distance but not in their hearts.[147] Another prisoner noted, "the inmates are sitting out on the verandahs discussing war and home topics; others are in their quarters. Some are sitting or standing in groups, singing a familiar hymn or a favorite war song while others are writing to the dear ones at home. Some are fast asleep, while others are merrily scuffling around and over them."[148]

Gambling was a favorite pastime of the prisoners who wagered on ball games, wrestling, and marbles. Card games, the most common betting event, helped pass the time in late afternoon. When the drum was beat to return to quarters, and once prisoners were inside, these games would take center stage. Poker, euchre, and seven-up were the favorite games. The usual medium of currency for betting was sutler checks, but cash was also used. The gambling continued even when some inmates were holding prayer meetings or church in the same block.[149]

One prisoner, Ham Chamberlayne, wrote to loved ones at home a summary of his daily routine: "Let me sketch you the general outline of my life; after breakfast a certain time always devoted to study (after, if it should chance to be my day, in rotation,

---

[145] Lewis, John H., *Recollections from 1860–1865* (Washington DC: Prake & Company, Publishers, 1895), 89.

[146] Wash, W. A., *Camp, Field and Prison Life*, 129.

[147] Patterson, *Yankee Rebel*, 131; Barziza, *The Adventures of a Prisoner*, 142.

[148] Wash, W. A., *Camp, Field and Prison Life*, 168.

[149] Patterson, *Yankee Rebel*, 131; Barziza, *The Adventures of a Prisoner*, 98.

cleaning the room, bringing water etc.) then walking, visiting for some hours, then dinner, then writing letters, reading some book of entertainment and in the evening I spare my eyes and [engage in] conversation, cards, chess, etc. [to] consume my time. Some employ much time in making trinkets, rings etc., but I do not incline to that way."[150]

Just before dark the drum would signal for the prisoners to return to their blocks.[151] At the sound of a second drum, between 9:30 and 10:00, prisoners would blow out the candles and retire. All lights had to be extinguished. If a guard saw a light in a block, he had permission to shoot into the block. On many occasions shots were fired and the ricocheting bullets hit a few inmates, which caused much resentment. Many complained lighting a candle at night to check on a sick friend might result in a shot being fired into the block.

"FRESH FISH"

Prisoners would arrive in Sandusky by train from their former destinations. This could have been from mass surrenders, individual captures, or from transfers from other prisons. The prisoners would march from the train station to the docks to cross the bay to Johnson's Island. During the winter, the bay would be frozen and they would walk across the ice, under guard, to the island. For the rest of the year steamers would be contracted to ferry prisoners. Colonel Hundley explained the process: "Upon reaching Sandusky this afternoon, we were immediately marched on board the steamer *Princess*, which plies regularly between Sandusky and Johnson's Island. The sun shone brightly, the lake was scarcely ruffled by a breath of wind, and being invited by my Yankee captain to accompany him to the hurricane-deck, I had a splendid view of my present residence before reaching it. Upon landing, we were marched immediately to Colonel Hill's in two separate squads—the officers from the Virginia Army in one, and those from Johnston in another. We were divested of our money, and our names and rank and date of capture being taken down carefully in a book, we bade adieu to the outer world; the gate to the prison yard swung open; we entered, our guards still on either side of us, and beheld some thousand or fifteen hundred brother rebels formed in line on either side of the walk over which we were soon to be conducted, many of them brawling out lustily, 'Fresh fish!' It was a strange, sad sight, that crowd of badly-dressed, yellow-looking gentleman, shouting out the slang salutation of convicts and felons to their unfortunate comrades, fresh from the fields of glory."[152] So entered the southern gentleman into the confines of Johnson's Island.

---

[150] Chamberlayne, Ham., *Virginian – Letters and Papers of an Artillery Officer in the War for Southern Independence*, 12–23–63.

[151] Durkin, Joseph T., *John Dooley, Confederate Soldier: His War Journal*, 140.

[152] Hundley, D. R., *Prison Echoes of the Great Rebellion*, 75–76.

Once inside the bull pen and after the hollers of "fresh fish," the prisoners would have to find quarters. While the prison was below capacity, a group of prisoners might be sent into an empty block, being the first to occupy it. During these early days, W. A. Wash described it as "very much like young fellows first going off to college, we were smartly puzzled when we first entered, not knowing where to go or what to do."[153] Once the prison was filled, the "custom, in the pen was to place the 'fresh fish' in blocks 11, 12, & 13, and let them work their own way up to better quarters."[154] New arrivals were now seen as competition for valuable resources. The mood had soured on new arrivals as Major Caldwell discussed the indignity of fresh fish meeting the "cold shoulder." He regretted that the experienced inmates of Johnson's Island would treat their brethren with apathy and even discourtesy.[155]

LETTERS

Writing and receiving letters were the two most important pleasures at the disposal of a prisoner at Johnson's Island. The prisoners were locked away far from home with limited prospect of receiving visitors. The only means of communication with the outside world was through these coveted letters as days turned into weeks, weeks into months, and months into years. Time hung heavy on the prisoners' hands. Writing helped pass the time and relieved the monotony of the prison routine. Some prisoners kept journals, but most wrote to love ones at home as a release to the frustrations of being imprisoned.

Prisoners also wrote letters home to dispel their blues. Many times depression would strike and letter writing would lighten the spirits of the inmates. One prisoner wrote, "And while my heart is filled with sadness I can not express, I have sat down and written a happy cheerful letter to one who is dear to me, but far away in Dixie This is one of the commonest of the many expedients resorted to here to dispel the gloom which hangs like a pall over this ill-fated spot; and I find it affords one of great relief."[156] Captain Felix Blackman stressed his happiness at writing to his sweetheart: "I know of no better way to spending the day than writing to you."[157]

Upon analysis of the vast numbers of letters written from Johnson's Island, few prisoners complained of their predicament. The writings in journals and reminiscences were much more descriptive of the prisoners' hardships. This was explained in Colonel R. F. Webb's diary when he stated, "I write cheerfully to my friends, particularly

---

[153] Wash, W. A., *Camp, Field and Prison Life*, 88.

[154] Thompson, 210.

[155] Caldwell, James Parks., *A Northern Confederate at Johnson's Island Prison: The Civil War Diary of James Parks Caldwell*, 166.

[156] Hundley, D. R., *Prison Echoes of the Great Rebellion*, 79.

[157] Blackman, Felix Hays, *Letters to Maggie Sexton* (1863–1865), October 18, 1863.

to my wife. I have two reasons for this. One is I dare not complain [for fear of retaliation]; the other, I do not wish to add to her unhappiness by letting her know the truth of my situation."[158] Most of the letter recipients at home were wives, in the culture of the time; one did not get political or too worldly with sheltered females. Letters with descriptions of hardships or containing too much negativity toward the government might be destroyed. The patriotic examiners could have considered any such remarks as treason and refused to let the letters pass. The prisoners were always careful not to lose their letter privileges.

For the prisoners, a far greater happiness came from receiving letters from loved ones. A prisoner wrote home telling of the degree of adulation receiving letters have on the camp: "Could you but witness the delivery of letters here in the morning—the smile of triumph the proud flash of the eye—the excited quiver of the lips as the fortunate one is announced."[159] Captain Blackman wished his correspondent could "take a peek into my heart and see the sunshine and joy that follows your letters. I open the door to receive your letters and called upon to make room for the accustomed compassions [sic] 'joy' 'gladness' and when [I] read and reread them the sweet messengers still linger long." Letters from home were treasured possessions of the prisoners. Any time a prisoner felt lonely, he would pull out his letters and immerse himself in the familiar writing of a loved one. Captain William Norman expressed how the letters comforted him: "The letters I get from [my wife] Letitia are read many times as I love to read her letters. I look at every letter and syllable and esteem it very highly indeed."[160] Colonel Hundley exclaimed with joy over a special letter: "I have received a Dixie letter . . . from my wife! No language can express how great a weight of care and anxiety a few brief lines from those one loves, can remove from the overburdened heart of the exile."[161] The opposite effect was felt by those who did not receive any letters from home. E. J. Ellis tersely wrote, "I never look now for letters from any of you. Hope has been baffled and expectation disappointed so often that I cease to hope or expect."[162]

Most of the prisoners were young, and their confinement on the island was the first time, except for their service in the army, they were separated from family and friends. To be in a strange land, surrounded by strangers, and guarded by sometimes cruel guardians made these prisoners feel utterly alone. They longed for the familiar sounds and voices from home. Since this was impossible, letters were their best substitute.

---

[158] Webb, *Prison Life at Johnson's Island,* Howell Webb Autograph Book, 1863–1864, 675.

[159] Houston, Thomas D., *Prisoner of War Letters: 1863–1865. From Johnson's Island,* 11, October 21, 1863.

[160] Norman, William M., *A Portion of My Life,* 206.

[161] Hundley, D. R., *Prison Echoes of the Great Rebellion,* 117–118.

[162] Ellis, E. J., to "My Dear Sister." December 27, 1864.

Even though they might have received only one letter a month, the prisoners would stop by the post office on a daily basis, inquiring about a possible message from sunnier places. W. A. Wash wrote a touching entry in his journal: "I got a letter from my mother, the first one since I left her side two years before. The missive was full of interesting news which I swallowed down like a sponge imbibes water, and the kind, sympathetic words of my mother made my heart swell and flutter with ecstatic joy, and my soul felt that it was good to be once more in communion with my best friend on earth. As I read the endearing, maternal sentiments, briny tears coursed their way down my cheeks, and for a good while I was overcome with feelings that pen can not portray."[163] The letters jogged the prisoners' memories of their life outside the prison walls. They daydreamed of the time they could return to the shelter and comfort of their family and home.

The Commandant issued rules governing the writing and receiving of letters on the island. The post office was attached to the side of Block 3. The prisoners would write their letters and drop them off, unsealed, to the Rebel postmaster, Tommy Stevenson, or "Old Pap," as he was called. The federal postmaster came in at ten o'clock and picked up and dropped off any letters.[164] Federal authorities read and inspected all letters for contraband news.[165] Any letter coming in or departing the prison could be destroyed if the letter writer violated the prescribed regulations. The most common way a prisoner lost a beloved letter was for its being too long. Upon the slightest infraction, the prisoner found his whole letter destroyed. The inspectors had to read each outgoing and incoming letter. When the number of prisoners was multiplied by the number of friends and family writing multi-page letters, the final total was staggering. Letters going in and out of the prison created thousands of pages that had to be read and approved daily. As the war wore on and the bitterness toward the prisoners increased, the length and regularity of the letters were restricted.

When Felix Hays Blackman entered the compound in the fall of 1863, he wrote home stating prisoners were allowed to write as long a letter as they pleased. He could write long letters but he had to bribe the examiner ½ cent for each additional page over the first one.[166] Henry Kyd Douglas also noted in his diary that the charge was ½ cent per page.[167] Later this cost per page was raised to 2½ cents. Edmund Patterson explained that you could write letters of any length as long as you enclose the money

---

[163] Wash, W. A., *Camp, Field and Prison Life*, 96–97.

[164] Ibid., 130, 170.

[165] War news was contraband, but regulations have not been found that listed all contraband issues.

[166] Blackman, Felix Hays, *Letters to Maggie Sexton* (1863–1865), October 11, 1863.

[167] Douglas, Henry Kyd., *I Rode with Stonewall*, 264.

for the extra length. The prisoners speculated that each examining clerk would make several dollars per day, a tidy sum for the era, from the illicit arrangement.[168]

In January 1864, when a new commandant, Brigadier General Terry, took command of the prison, the prisoners were once again restricted to one page. A prisoner, unaware it was actually a bribe, had complained to the new commandant that he was taxed for writing long letters.[169] General Terry put an end to the bribery. A rumor even circulated around the prison yard that Colonel Pierson was arrested for bribery and complacency.[170] The examiners were probably nervous about the new commandant's disapproval of the old arrangement and were more cautious about taking bribes for the long letters. It seemed most of the prisoners were restricted to one-page letters for the duration, although a few prisoners stated they continued to write long letters, perhaps because of secret individual bribes to the inspectors.

Captain Blackman explained, "in compliance with the present regime I am limited to one page and one letter per day. I hope soon some arrangement may be effected similar to the former agreement—until then however I can write only one page."[171] He explained how he wrote one letter every day, each day had a routine: "We can only write once per day now and yours [his girlfriend] and Susies [home] fill up four days of the week thus leaving me three unoccupied."[172] Many letters were received from Johnson's Island to people who were not family. However, one prisoner noted an order stating only relatives could be corresponded with; henceforth, "the officers here have a large number of cousins and aunts."[173] For example, Captain Blackman began every letter to his sweetheart with "Dear Cousin Maggie" apparently to get around the restrictions.

Another indiscretion General Terry halted was the stealing of stamps by the examiners. Colonel Webb explains: "The custom was for the clerk who read the letters to appropriate the stamps on all contraband letters to his own use, and he made money by the operation, as more letters were condemned then were sent off. And in consequence the general has issued an order that on all letters condemned, the envelope and stamp shall be returned to the writer."[174] Even though some of the examiners may have stolen stamps, it is doubtful more letters were destroyed than approved.

---

[168] Patterson, Edmund Dewitt., *Yankee Rebel: The Civil War Journal of Edmund DeWitt Patterson*, 145–146.

[169] Thompson, 211.

[170] Bingham Findley Junkin, *Civil War Diary of Bingham Findley Junkin*, 65.

[171] Blackman, Felix Hays, *Letters to Maggie Sexton (1863–1865)*, January 28, 1864.

[172] Blackman, Felix Hays, *Letters to Maggie Sexton (1863–1865)*, March 24, 1864.

[173] Webb, R. F. "Prison Life at Johnson's Island." *Histories of the Several Regiments and Battalions from North Carolina in the Great War 1861–65*, 675.

[174] Webb, R. F. "Prison Life at Johnson's Island." *Histories of the Several Regiments and Battalions from North Carolina in the Great War 1861–65*, 676–677.

Incoming mails initially had no limits. One prisoner wrote home "correspondents are not limited in their length of letters." He continued, "I hope in announcing this you will write a good long one."[175] In June 1864, the rules about letter length changed for incoming mails. Incoming letters could be written on only one side of one page. It seems the authorities did not pre-warn the inmates of this limitation. Captain Blackman told of a fellow prisoner who had received "a letter or rather the envelope two or three days since. The letter [was marked] contraband on account of length. Last week an order was issued prescribing all letters coming in as well as going out of more than one page of ordinary letter paper [was forbidden]. Many lamentations or maledictions too have been called forth since the enforcement of the orders."[176] Two days later, Blackman himself would feel the effects of the order. He wrote to his future wife, "I wrote you a few days since telling you of the order . . . to day I reaped the fruits. An envelope with the simple sentence written across the back, Over length—from Maggie."[177] In December, apparently to cut down again on the task of reviewing letters, incoming mail was restricted to three letters a week.[178]

In September 1864, Colonel Hill, the third commandant, limited the prisoners to two mails per week. Letters would leave only on Mondays and Thursdays. No prisoner was allowed to write more than one letter at a time.[179] The prisoners could circumvent this order by signing the name of another prisoner, one who did not write home.[180] The family would undoubtedly recognize the handwriting regardless of the name signed. Felix Blackman somehow got around the limit because he stated in his letters how he wrote his sweetheart twice a week and still wrote home, too.[181] Letters were so important to prisoners that they found ways of evading most restrictions concerning letters.

There must have been some confusion about what was the definition of one page. In February 1865, an "Order published on the Bulletin Board, allowing but 28 lines common letter paper, or 42 lines of commercial note paper" was allowed.[182] This was for incoming and outgoing mails.[183]

---

[175] Houston, Thomas D., *Prisoner of War Letters: 1863–1865. From Johnson's Island*, 11, Oct 21, 1863.

[176] Blackman, Felix Hays, *Letters to Maggie Sexton* (1863–1865), June 6, 1864.

[177] Ibid., June 8, 1864.

[178] Inzer, John Washington., *The Diary of a Confederate Soldier: John Washington Inzer 1834–1928*, 113.

[179] Patterson, Edmund Dewitt., *Yankee Rebel: The Civil War Journal of Edmund DeWitt Patterson*, 191.

[180] Hundley, D. R., *Prison Echoes of the Great Rebellion*, 148.

[181] Blackman, Felix Hays, *Letters to Maggie Sexton* (1863–1865), September 28, 1864.

[182] Inzer, John Washington., *The Diary of a Confederate Soldier: John Washington Inzer 1834–1928*, 124.

[183] Shepherd, Henry., *Narrative of Prison Life at Baltimore and Johnson's Island,* 17.

A Captain Stagg from Louisiana had other troubles with the inspectors. His wife, living in New Orleans, could not read or write English. She wrote her husband in French. The examiners, not being able to read French, would not let them pass and destroyed the letters. Stagg wrote to an outside friend in the Union army and he resolved the matter by reading the letters for the inspectors.[184]

The prisoners wanted to express their feelings freely without the inspectors reading and possibly destroying their letters. They made several attempts to get uncensored messages home. The prisoners concocted ways to conceal messages from the eyes of the inspectors: invisible ink and lemon juice, for example.[185] O. E. Mitchell, an officer of the Hoffman Battalion, told of one trick. A letter would appear to be written on only half a page, but when it was brought near the heat of a candle, a full page of writing was revealed.[186] In attempting this, the letter writer risked losing his mailing privileges. Captain Bingham noted in his diary how an innocent act put a temporary hold on his letter writing privileges. "I wrote to my wife & put a little thing or two under the stamp—just for her that I did not care for the Yanks seeing. The Yanks found it. I wrote no harm—only told my wife how much I loved her. The worst of it is they have stopped my letters home." The examiners thought the note was a signal for a hidden message as others "had written with chemical ink - & [instructed under the stamp] to hold the page to the fire. He was put into the same category as those with malicious intent until he wrote to Colonel Pierson explaining his innocence.[187]

When a prisoner left for exchange or was released as an invalid, he was given letters from the other prisoners that he tried to smuggle by the inspectors. Many letters were concealed in boot linings, hat crowns, coat linings and other ingenious places.[188] Whether there was a regulation against hand carrying correspondence from other prisoners or if they were just trying to avoid censorship is not clear.

When Felix Hays Blackman was paroled to leave, he was told he would have to burn his letters from home. On March 16, 1865, he states, "a few days ago I learned that we would not be allowed to carry away our old letters. I took down the packet and again looked over them thinking of burning them but again put them back in their place. I could not burn them. I could not give up my treasures—Too many sad and lonely hours have been spirited away by these 'connecting links' of the chain binding me to absent friends to be rudely thrust into the flames. These I shall reserve till the drum shall sound for my appearance at the gate for departure. Then with a heart

---

[184] Douglas, Henry Kyd., *I Rode with Stonewall*, 261–262.

[185] W. Frazer, untitled, *Confederate Veteran,* Vol. IV (1896), 438.

[186] Mitchell, E. O. "Johnson's Island: Military Prison for Confederate Prisoners." *Sketches of War History*, 1861–1865. 124.

[187] Bingham, Robert, *Diary*, 64.

[188] Wash, W. A., *Camp, Field and Prison Life*, 121.

bounding with joy I can yield up treasured relics of my imprisonment. The profusion of happy emotions will drown the loss of my 'gems' of sweetness amid such bitterness." He continued in a letter on the 23ʳᵈ March: "Would I could take them with me but the authorities say we can not. To burn them is like tearing out sacred relics & dethroning divinities, which I have loved to treasure. But though these must be given up I will carry their sacred impress through life."[189] John W. Inzer's diary stated that all diaries and autograph albums were destroyed when some invalids attempted to carry them out of the prison in April 1864.[190] Yet, Inzer's own diary survived. The extent to which the prisoners were forced to destroy their letters and diaries is not known. Vast quantities of diaries, autograph books, and letters have survived.[191]

NEWSPAPERS

Newspapers were brought in to Johnson's Island for the prisoners to keep up with the outside world and obviously the war. Only northern newspapers were allowed inside as southern newspapers might rouse the sentiment of a possible victory or incite incorrigible behavior. Colonel Hundley wrote in his diary about the newspapers: "In my own mess are received the *New York Herald, Times, News*, and *World* as well as the *Cincinnati Enquirer, Chicago Times, Cleveland Herald, Sandusky Register* (which is received the same day it is published and every day except Sunday). From these papers we gather very accurate information of all that is taking place in the North, and as they usually contain copious extracts from the Southern journals we also have a pretty clear idea of that is taking place in Dixie as well."[192] In May 1864, because of the presidential campaign, anti-war fervor reached a climax. The authorities became concerned about a possible rebellion or insubordination inside the prison encouraged by the divisive news from the papers. In response to this, Colonel Hill restricted certain newspapers from entering the prison. Colonel Inzer noted, "Old Hill got mad to-day because the copper-head papers were telling too much truth. He refused to let any of said papers in."[193] Edmund DeWitt Paterson had written in his diary that the Herald or the Tribune was allowed as long as it agreed with the Lincoln administration's policy.[194] The Rebels read these pro-Union papers, but always with a hefty level of skepticism.

---

[189] Blackman, Felix Hays, *Letters to Maggie Sexton* (1863–1865), March 16, 23, 1865.

[190] Inzer, John Washington., *The Diary of a Confederate Soldier: John Washington Inzer 1834–1928*, 74.

[191] It is not known if the destruction of letters and diaries was a policy that ended at a certain date or if some prisoners were singled out.

[192] Hundley, D. R., *Prison Echoes of the Great Rebellion*, 83.

[193] Inzer, John Washington., *The Diary of a Confederate Soldier: John Washington Inzer 1834–1928*, 78.

[194] Patterson, Edmund Dewitt., *Yankee Rebel: The Civil War Journal of Edmund DeWitt Patterson,* 167.

EXPRESS

Another delight of the prisoners was the arrival of express, or packages over the size of the common letter. The "Express," as the prisoners called it, would be full of provisions from friends mainly in loyal states. It was fairly unusual to receive packages from the south, or "Dixie Express" as the prisoners called it, because of the breakdown in communication between the North and the South. The express, like so many other things, would have restrictions from time to time.

The Express would create a high level of excitement. W. A. Wash recorded in his diary the joy of a package: "I, with triumphal look and feeling bore the trophy off to my room, while many a poor fellow who had no friends up North to help him looked after me, thinking, 'I wish it was I'"[195] Later he described another box. "The 29th day of July [1863] was a bright era in the history of my prison life. A nice box of provisions, anticipated for some days, made its welcome appearance that afternoon. The box contained one old ham, two cans each of butter, honey and blackberry jam, sausage, apples, maple sugar, cake, a pair of pants, shoes and daguerreotypes of my uncle and his daughter."[196]

Sometimes packages would arrive for unknown reasons. Colonel Hundley mentions: "I received a box to-day by express from some kind friend in Chicago, filled with 'good things.' Who the kind Samaritan is I know not, . . . but such surprises, I learn are common here."[197] A few days later he received "a barrel filled with hams, pickles, canned fruits etc. from Louisville, Ky. The donors are strangers to me."[198] Whether some charity organized relief boxes for prisoners or, more likely, his family had someone ship it to him from inside Union lines, is not clear.

The Express would have stoppages because of bad weather. When it became too dangerous to cross the bay to the island, Express packages would pile up in Sandusky. Colonel Inzer noted in the winter of 1864 that the Express has not been delivered in twelve days.[199] During weather-related stoppages, everything compounded. Firewood became scarce, letters would not arrive to warm their hearts, and the Express, on which so many depended, would halt.

One prisoner stated in his diary, "you are compelled to pay from 25 cents to $2.00 for each package to defray the expenses from Sandusky to the island."[200] Whether this was an isolated case or common practice is not known, as his diary was the only one

---

[195] Wash, W. A., *Camp, Field and Prison Life*, 111.

[196] Wash, W. A., *Camp, Field and Prison Life*, 128.

[197] Hundley, D. R., *Prison Echoes of the Great Rebellion*, 94.

[198] Hundley, D. R., *Prison Echoes of the Great Rebellion*, 103.

[199] Inzer, John Washington., *The Diary of a Confederate Soldier: John Washington Inzer 1834–1928*, 114.

[200] Webb, R. F. "Prison Life at Johnson's Island." *Histories of the Several Regiments and Battalions from North Carolina in the Great War 1861–65*, 669–670.

found mentioning an extra price. The other prisoners may have just not mentioned it but that is unlikely.

Just like everything else in the prison, Rebels were always suspicious of the Yankees. For example, Colonel Hundley had a very low opinion of the Express handlers. He stated: "One Frank Burger, a low, squat-built Dutchman, who formerly lived in Richmond, and is said to be a deserter from the Southern Army, superintends the delivery of the 'Express,' and is said to make a very handsome sum by peculation, by bribery, and by confiscating all the wines, brandies, etc., which are declared to be contraband articles. Frank confiscates these articles, and turns them over to Foster, the Hospital steward, who brings them in privily [sic] and sells them to those who will pay for them in Greenbacks."[201] Another prisoner, Henry Shepherd, accused the guards of taking the hams out and then "the empty box [was] carefully delivered to me at my quarters."[202]

In retaliation to treatment of Union soldiers in the camps of the Confederacy, Colonel Hoffman, Commissary-General of Prisoners, ordered new rules on August 10, 1864 regulating what prisoners could receive, via Express, from outsider friends. The first order dealt with food. He mandated only in case of illness, near relatives, not friends, could send articles of food, but the surgeon in charge of the hospital must approve of the application. He specified all such packages be addressed to the surgeon of the post and then distributed by him. He further stipulated clothing could be shipped by relatives only in the case of extreme need. Clothing packages must be approved by the commanding officer of the post. Hoffman then eloquently stated this action was in retaliation, and when Union troops at Richmond are permitted to receive articles so will the Confederate captives.[203] This increased the pressure on the prisoners who were receiving bountiful Express boxes to fight off hunger and cold. Colonel Inzer of Alabama had made an application to receive a box of provisions and because of bad health the request was approved. He logged in his journal: "Box came in this morning's express . . . My name through mistake was not entered on [Dr.] Everman's books, so I will have to make application for it." The next day he was approved and picked up his package with over 50 lbs. of food stuffs.[204]

An excellent account of this examination method was recorded in V. S. Murphey's diary:

> When a man is sick . . . you are permitted to write a short letter to some relative requesting certain designated articles of provision which are necessary to the health of the subscriber. The quantity is limited and never exceeds over 10 pounds of any article except flour and bacon which is 25 pounds.

---

[201] Hundley, D. R., *Prison Echoes of the Great Rebellion*, 82–83.

[202] Shepherd, Henry., *Narrative of Prison Life at Baltimore and Johnson's Island*, 14.

[203] *War of the Rebellion: A Compilation of the Official Records of the Union and Confederate Armies*, Series II, Volume VII, 573–574.

[204] Inzer, John Washington., *The Diary of a Confederate Soldier: John Washington Inzer 1834–1928*, 104.

Every Monday evening the chief medical officer of the Post, holds his levee at the hospital for the purpose of passing judgment upon the merits of the various applications. These levees are numerously attended. You advance and deliver your letter, enveloped and stamped to the Surgeon, who asks you several questions in regard to his malady and then you are dismissed. Frequently the Surgeon is very impertinent and at times insulting in propounding these questions.

These letters he retains and on returning to his office re-examines them and determines which he will mail. A printed order, declaring under what restrictions provisions are admitted here is enclosed with the fortunate letters and mailed. When this letter reaches its destination the party has to carry the printed order to the nearest Provost Marshall and obtain his permit and when the box is shipped the permit with the printed order is again placed in it, so the prisoner can receive it here on its arrival. You can receive provisions and clothing only from relatives and you can imagine how fast our kindred multiply and increase. In obtaining supplies of clothing you have to pass through another circumlocution office. You address the communication to the [Superintendent of] Prison detailing the fact that you are destitute and asking permission to receive from your relative, the following articles of inferior quality cloth of grey.[205]

This method proved to be rather difficult for the prison officials to regulate and smuggling was a persistent problem. Lt. Colonel Scovill (USA) detailed in an correspondence to the Commissary-General of Prisoners, his proposal of a new method: "Instead of permitting prisoners to receive clothing by express from relatives and sick prisoners eatables, allow nothing but money to come to the commanding officer, and permit the sutler to sell such articles . . . , and on surgeon's certificate to sell a few articles of diet. My reasons for the change proposed are that there are constant and persistent attempts to smuggle in money and contraband articles, which even the most minute examination of the packages cannot always detect. It would also do away with the attempts at contraband correspondence."[206] The idea was rejected by Colonel Hoffman as no change in the system occurred until tension eased in 1865.[207]

The prisoners received many contraband items through the Express. Many articles were shipped to the prisoners that were not allowed, such as alcohol. W. A. Wash mentions Foster, "a Yankee of small caliber but wonderful pretensions had a rich time confiscating liquors and other forbidden things, but still much contraband slipped

---

[205] Murphey, V. S., *Diary*, 104–107.

[206] *War of the Rebellion: A Compilation of the Official Records of the Union and Confederate Armies*, Series II, Volume VII, 1025–1026.

[207] *War of the Rebellion: A Compilation of the Official Records of the Union and Confederate Armies*, Series II, Volume VII, 1051.

in."[208] Friends concealed forbidden articles in every possible way to get them by the inspectors, or bribed guards overlooked the regulations for some prisoners, as many forbidden items were at Johnson's Island.

Many grumblings from the prisoners came from the way the Express was so strictly handled. Lieutenant-Colonel Palmer (USA), who briefly took over the camp while Colonel Hill was away in late 1864, had the Express boxes of the sick opened outside the pen to be searched for contraband. Palmer was accused of confiscating about half of the articles that were previously approved. At the same time, Dr. Eversman, the assistant Yankee surgeon of the post, was also accused of only accepting one-fifth of all applications for packages.[209] Whether Lt. Colonel Palmer was pressuring the surgeons, Doctors Woodbridge and Eversman, to deny claims or if some other circumstance caused the happening is not known. One prisoner, V. S. Murphey, stated his confusion: "I applied to Surg. Woodbridge for permission to receive some vegetables, sugar, and coffee from a relative . . . He assured me my permit had been forwarded but after retaining it 5 days my application was returned this morning disapproved. Why he should tell me a falsehood I cannot imagine."[210]

In early 1865, with the war near conclusion, the Express rules were relaxed, in line with a general relaxation of the sterner retaliation rules of 1864. Prisoners could even receive "Dixie Express." Colonel John Inzer noted in March 1865 that eleven boxes of Dixie Express were distributed in one day, but there are 227 boxes that had not passed inspection waiting outside.[211]

Conclusion

The average day for a Confederate prisoner on Johnson's Island was very much like a town or military camp. The only noticeable differences would be the restricted freedoms and the increase in leisure time. The day started with breakfast, roll call, and the daily paper. Once that was completed, the soldiers would grocery shop at the sutler or go to work on mess detail or any another enterprise. They would spend the extra time with activities like playing ball, watching plays, or studying foreign languages. The prisoners would attend church meetings and write to love ones at home. This was all accomplished by the men themselves and shows the resourcefulness of the prisoners to maintain a somewhat normal life even if within the confines of Johnson's Island

---

[208] Wash, W. A., *Camp, Field and Prison Life*, 202.

[209] Hundley, D. R., *Prison Echoes of the Great Rebellion*, 180.

[210] Murphey, V. S., *Diary*, 156.

[211] Inzer, John Washington., *The Diary of a Confederate Soldier: John Washington Inzer 1834–1928*, 130.

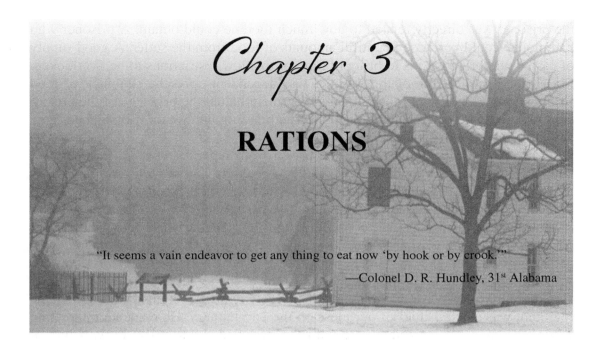

Chapter 3

RATIONS

"It seems a vain endeavor to get any thing to eat now 'by hook or by crook.'"

—Colonel D. R. Hundley, 31st Alabama

FOOD

The prisoners on Johnson's Island had to sustain themselves on the food that was allowed to pass through the main gate of the prison. They drew rations from the government, bought food from the sutler, and had food shipped to them from family and friends. The quality and quantity of the food varied from time to time. At first, food was relatively plentiful, but because of political decisions from Washington, the supply of food from all sources was restricted in 1864. Eventually, the food supply was so scarce that most prisoners had to eat rats in order to survive.

The good health and proper diet of the prisoners were dependent upon several factors. The first factor was the quantity and quality of the rations issued by the federal authorities at the prison. The supply of food was plentiful at first but later diminished as reports filtered north from Union prisoners of the starvation at the hands of the Confederates. The second factor was the condition of the soldier when he was captured. Most prisoners came from the battlefield where they had been living on meager rations for quite some time and were malnourished when they arrived at the island. Some had suffered starvation in long sieges such as Vicksburg. A fortunate minority were well fed and in good overall health. The third factor was the intermittent availability of food from the sutler. The sutler could sell vegetables and a host of other eatables until the sale of these items was restricted by Washington. Fourth, the financial position of the prisoner was directly related to how much food he could obtain. A prisoner who had money could purchase bountiful amounts of food from the sutler. A good supply of cash could bribe guards to bring in food or to allow restrictions to be overlooked. Fifth, the general health of the prisoner was dependent upon the shipment of food from outside friends. Until the federal government halted the privilege of the prisoners to receive these gifts, in 1864, friends, both North and South, had shipped large amounts of food to the prisoners.

Rations were distributed inside the prison from federal stores in the following manner: The rations, brought in daily, were inspected by Colonel John A. Fite of Tennessee, who acted as a supervisor of the distribution of the rations.[212] The food was then divided into thirteen parts for the thirteen blocks. Each block had two men, heads of their respective messes, who took the rations and divided them into smaller sub-messes. Six to eight prisoners usually composed a mess. The food was then cooked and evenly distributed to the small group.[213]

Distributing and preparing the food was one of the job duties the prisoners usually shared. W. A. Wash explained how "Judge Breare, Lieutenant of an Alabama regiment was elected chief of our mess on the 26th January. He made an interesting witty little speech, assumed the official robe, and waded into active duty. 'Chief of Mess' is one of those offices full of labor and responsibility, with no pay and but little thanks, but Breare was eminently 'the right man in the right place,' enjoyed his authority, and gave satisfaction."[214] The cook or "caterer" duty was to prepare the "food for each meal, taking it to the kitchen, going after it when cooked, setting the table and cleaning up after the meal." Colonel Nisbet stated, "In our mess this duty would come around every 8th week."[215] The wood for cooking the food and for heating the blocks was also distributed in the same manner. An ax and a bucksaw were delivered and then collected back at evening. If the tools were not returned, no wood or food would be delivered to the offending mess. One prisoner stated this "happened once during my stay; but private enterprise looking to escape, of a few, had to give way to the public [welfare], and the ax and saw showed up." Another prisoner recollected, "the most fatiguing duty, as I remember it, was sawing wood—not that there was so much to saw, but that most of us were not used to it."[216] Of course, wealthier messes would hire others to cook, clean, and cut wood for them.

---

[212] Nisbet, James Cooper., *Four Years on the Firing Line*, 226.

[213] *Confederate Veteran* IV. 438; XIX 532.

[214] Wash, W. A., *Camp, Field and Prison Life,* 196.

[215] Nisbet, James Cooper., *Four Years on the Firing Line*, 226.

[216] Knauss, William H., *The Story of Camp Chase*. Nashville, 241.

During the early years of the prison, from 1862 to early 1864, food was abundant at Johnson's Island. During this time, the prisoners were issued the same ration as Union soldiers. W. A. Wash stated that our "rations were the same as issued to the Federal soldiery consisting of baker's bread, beef or bacon, coffee, sugar, rice, hominy, vinegar, soap and candles. Whatever extra articles we got from the sutler we cooked for ourselves, and according to our notions, many a savory dish did we prepare."[217] Lieutenant O. E. Mitchell, 128th Ohio Infantry (USA), stated, "I know that the prisoners had an abundant supply of good, wholesome food, and fared equally as well as their guards. Fresh bread from our government bakery was issued to them daily, besides pork every other day, alternating with fresh meat."[218]

In addition to the ample rations, the prisoners could purchase a host of other eatables from the sutler. They could also add items to their table that were shipped from the outside. John Dooley noted how some of the prisoners fared: "Our mess having plenty of money live as well in the way of eating as we ever did, and I strained every nerve to enjoy the bountiful supply."[219] The cuisine was generally good for the prisoners who had money during 1862 and 1863. Lieutenant Cunningham noted, "our food was abundant owing to our ability to purchase from the Post sutler and the [delivery wagon] who came into the prison daily, besides which many were in receipt of supplies from friends and relatives in the North, and hence were entirely independent of the prison rations and fed on dainties not found on the prison menu."[220] All this led to one prisoner's stating, "If a body couldn't live easy, laugh and grow fat here he ought to die, for we have nothing to do but to eat, drink, sleep and be merry."[221]

During these good times, prisoners who had a proficiency in cooking would sell their culinary creations to the other prisoners. A Lieutenant McLoughlin, of Alabama, "set up an oyster saloon in Mess No. 1, of [Block 4], and for a while drove a thriving trade."[222] The most curious report found in a diary was the attempt to open up a restaurant called Johnson's Ranche. Whether this was a prisoner named Johnson or if it was the Leonard Johnson, the owner of the island and the sutler, is not known. It was located at the south end of Block 4, in shed extension built on to the block. Reverend Thrasher stated the restaurant was being constructed when the sutler "took his leave"

---

[217] Wash, W. A., *Camp, Field and Prison Life,* 88–89.

[218] Mitchell, E. O., "Johnson's Island: Military Prison for Confederate Prisoners." *Sketches of War History,* 121.

[219] Dooley, John., *John Dooley, Confederate Soldier: His War Journal,* 138–139.

[220] Knauss, William H., *The Story of Camp Chase.* Nashville, 248.

[221] Wash, W. A., *Camp, Field and Prison Life,* 122.

[222] Wash, W. A., *Camp, Field and Prison Life,* 219.

and "Johnson's base of supplies was destroyed by an unexpected and unavoidable attack of the enemy."[223] It appears the restaurant never opened, but this brings up unanswered questions. Was the construction of the shed and the running of a restaurant authorized and approved by the authorities? What happened to the shed after the failure?

Other prisoners, those forced to live solely on the government rations during that same period, did not have the same hearty opinion of camp rations. Captain Barziza stated, "our rations were very scanty, and those who were not so fortunate to have friends and acquaintances in the North, often went to bed hungry. They pretended to issue us meat, sugar, coffee, rice, hominy or peas, and candles. The hominy or rice they occasionally gave us was almost invariably musty and half-spoilt, while the apology for coffee was very unwholesome."[224] An inspection report during these "plentiful times" stated that the official rations were in sufficient quantity, with the exception of vegetables. The inspector recommended that two rations of cabbage or onions be issued each week to prevent scurvy. The report stated that a declared case of scurvy had not surfaced, but "a majority of the prisoners, are more or less strongly tainted with it."[225] Another prisoner, Henry Shepherd, noted that each prisoner received "one-half loaf of hard bread, and a piece of salt pork, in size not sufficient for an ordinary meal. In taste the latter was almost nauseating but it was eagerly devoured because there was no choice other than to eat it, or endure the tortures of prolonged starvation. Vegetables were almost unknown."[226] Later, when the issued rations were reduced in quantity and quality, the men who had to sustain themselves solely on government rations were the ones who suffered the most.

During the "plentiful times" of 1862 to early 1864, there were interruptions in the issuing of rations. Inclement weather would sometimes prevent the delivery of provisions and Express packages from friends to the island. The sutler's services were also stopped on several occasions. The stoppage of the sutler's services would last from a day or two to sometimes a month at a time. Again, the prisoners who suffered the most from these interruptions were the poorer prisoners.

By December 1863, tales about Union prisoners starving in the hands of the Confederates were filtering north from southern prisons. Many felt that the prisoners at Johnson's Island must suffer the same fate. Retaliation started sporadically, but gained momentum. The first retaliation was on December 1, 1863, when the Commissary

---

[223] Thrasher, Robert Mullins., "Prisoner of War." *The Register*, June 5, 1938.

[224] Barziza, Decimus et Ultimus., *The Adventures of a Prisoner of War, 1863–1864*, 77.

[225] *War of the Rebellion: A Compilation of the Official Records of the Union and Confederate Armies*, Series II, Vol. VI, 827.

[226] Shepherd, Henry., *Narrative of Prison Life at Baltimore and Johnson's Island, Ohio* (Baltimore: Commercial Ptg. & Sta. Co., 1917), 14–15.

General of Prisoners, William Hoffman, ordered all sutlers to close immediately.[227] The sutler was not allowed to reopen until the end of January 1864.[228]

In March 1864, the sutler was issued orders that rations could be sold only to prisoners who had received permission from the surgeons to purchase extra food.[229] At the same time, the issued rations for prisoners were reduced to levels below those prescribed for a Union soldier.[230] The prisoners could still receive Express packages from friends outside the prison, and these prisoners had to survive on the reduced issued rations supplemented by the Express deliveries. From that time, issued rations for prisoners began to decline in quantity and quality. For some reason, in mid-April 1864, no meat was issued to the prisoners for four days.[231] This may have been due to a supply problem, or rations were withdrawn on purpose. Major Caldwell recorded in his diary, "There has been much complaint of late concerning the insufficiency of our rations." He then added "I have been hungry: in fact, when I have had nothing more than the rations, I am almost always so." Caldwell believed that petitions had been sent to the authorities, notifying them of the shortages.[232] The prisoners complained to the commandant about the poor rations. Inspectors came in and examined and weighed the bread issued. They found that the issue of bread was too small for good health. To improve the rations, a few days later the quantity of bread was increased and potatoes were also issued.[233]

In June 1864, Colonel Hill announced another round of reductions on the Rebels. The War Department ordered all issuing of coffee, sugar, and candles to cease. A few diaries mentioned that potatoes and bread were reduced by the same order. Colonel Inzer recorded the reason for this reduction was because the prisoners "have been defacing the barracks by cutting windows and cutting tunnels and not reporting on each other."[234] Another diary said it was in retaliation for the treatment of Union soldiers in the hands of the Confederates.[235] Whatever was the case, this order made all of those who needed the caffeine or sugar rush to function curse the cruel Yankees.

---

[227] *War of the Rebellion: A Compilation of the Official Records of the Union and Confederate Armies*, Series II, Vol. VI, 625.

[228] Blackman, Felix Hays, *Letters to Maggie Sexton*, January 28, 1864.

[229] Wash, W. A., *Camp, Field and Prison Life*, 212.

[230] *War of the Rebellion: A Compilation of the Official Records of the Union and Confederate Armies*, Series II, Vol. VII, 183.

[231] Patterson, Edmund Dewitt., *Yankee Rebel: The Civil War Journal of Edmund DeWitt Patterson*, 161.

[232] Caldwell, James Parks., *A Northern Confederate at Johnson's Island Prison: The Civil War Diary of James Parks Caldwell*, 91.

[233] Wash, W. A., *Camp, Field and Prison Life*, 209–211.

[234] Inzer, John Washington., *The Diary of a Confederate Soldier: John Washington Inzer 1834–1928*, 82.

[235] Wash, W. A., *Camp, Field and Prison Life*, 232–233; Patterson, Edmund Dewitt., *Yankee Rebel: The Civil War Journal of Edmund DeWitt Patterson*, 171.

By mid summer of 1864, the reduction in rations was starting to affect most of the men in the prison. The men who were surviving on the government rations alone were the hardest hit by the reduction in rations. Colonel Hundley stated that "there are hundreds of poor fellows in here who have eked out a miserable existence on government rations for more than twelve months. They look very lean and hollow with shriveled yellow skins, and eyes dim and glazed."[236] Hundley continued: "It seems that the Yankees are determined to starve us to death. Colonel Hoffman has issued an order forbidding any more boxes of supplies to be received by prisoners, and forbidding sutlers to sell any other articles than combs, soap, tobacco, writing materials and the like."[237] The order to cut off Express boxes caused more suffering. Only the sick could receive Express packages (see Chapter II). W. A. Wash told of one tactic to receive food: "We had to resort to all sorts of tricks to evade the cruel and unnecessary restrictions of the powers that were. If we could not be sick ourselves we could get some fellow who was sick to assume our name long enough to get a permit for a box of good things from home or elsewhere. Lieutenant Clark, who was so bony and ugly that he always looked sick, played one off on the Yankee doctor, in my name, with a bogus case of chronic dysentery, and got an order to send to one of my friends for some needed restoratives."[238] All prisoners knew that their survival now depended almost exclusively on the issued rations from the government.

The prisoners looked for ways to supplement the rations issued by the Yankees. Because vegetables were lacking in the issued rations, some prisoners planted gardens with the hopes of reaping the benefits at harvest time. J. T. Norman commented: "Many flourishing little gardens green with growing vegetables adorn the open ground between the houses & the lake."[239] In a letter home, Captain Felix Blackman stated, "Many of them for the sake of vegetables have dug up a small plot of earth and sown as many varieties of seed as [anyone] would think of. They have spent hours bringing water during the dry weather and many consultations have been held as to the possible yield. Since the reduction of rations eatables are of vital importance and well might they speculate as to what kind of harvest they will reap."[240] The prisoners gained "green corn, tomatoes, potatoes (Irish), beets, cabbage, and turnips."[241] Lt. Colonel Inzer had a meal of turnips for dinner from Lt. Wood's garden and then tersely stated: "Rations are short."[242] These gardens did not produce sufficient vegetables to relieve the prisoners' starvation.

---

[236] Hundley, D. R., *Prison Echoes of the Great Rebellion*, 83.

[237] Ibid., 115.

[238] Wash, W. A., *Camp, Field and Prison Life,* 258.

[239] Norman, James., *Southern Letters and Life in the Mid 1800s*, 245.

[240] Blackman, Felix Hays, *Letters to Maggie Sexton (1863–1865)*, July 3, 1864.

[241] McClung, R. L., *Diary*, 24.

[242] Inzer, John Washington. *The Diary of a Confederate Soldier: John Washington Inzer 1834–1928*, 97.

In September 1864, the federals replaced beef and pork on occasion with white fish. The substitution was a cost-saving measure because white fish was cheaper than pork.[243] The ration was one half a fish per man per day.[244] One Confederate soldier noted, "The rations consisted of poor pickled beef and salted white fish alternating three and four days of the week."[245] Many prisoners despised the white fish as unpalatable.[246] The prisoners complained that the fish had to be boiled as it was so dry it would not fry.[247] In October 1864, the authorities substituted white fish with codfish. Major Caldwell noted, "The dried lake fish were bad and disgusting enough, but this is one step beyond."[248] Captain Bingham showed his disgust for the fish, which was delivered "for 122 men . . . in a gallon jug. I wanted to throw jug & all out of the window & some others did but others did not & so they went dividing it up."[249]

The prisoners felt that the rations were of poor quality and quantity. The prisoners felt that the beef in particular was low quality and the other eatables insufficient in quantity. A prisoner noted that the beef was "always the fore quarter and neck. The bread, while good, amounted to not more than one double-thick slice a day to a man, rice, hominy, or beans to no more than a handful, and potatoes and one onion to each prisoner, and they [were] unsound frequently."[250]

Reverend Thrasher had a conversation with the Yankee wagon driver about the beef. One morning when the wagon brought the beef to Block 13, Mess 1, Thrasher, being on mess duty, went out to receive the tub of beef. Being in a mischievous mood he asked:

"You have the most singular cattle up north that I ever saw."

"Why?" The Yankee corporal inquired.

"Because," Thrasher said, "they are all necks, shoulder blades, and shank bones."

"Well." He said. "You don't expect us [guards] to give you the hind quarters and the fellows outside the forequarters, do you?"[251]

---

[243] B. W. Johnson, "Record of Privation in Prison," *Confederate Veteran,* Vol. IX (1901), 165.

[244] Inzer, John Washington. *The Diary of a Confederate Soldier: John Washington Inzer 1834–1928,* 97.

[245] W. Frazer, untitled, *Confederate Veteran* ,Vol. IV, 438.

[246] Johnson, "Record of Privation," 165.

[247] Inzer, John Washington. *The Diary of a Confederate Soldier: John Washington Inzer 1834–1928,* 98.

[248] Caldwell, James Parks., *A Northern Confederate at Johnson's Island Prison: The Civil War Diary of James Parks Caldwell,* 153.

[249] Bingham, Robert, *Diary,* D2, 46.

[250] H. W. Henry, "Experiences on Johnson's Island," *Confederate Veteran,* Vol. XVI (1908), 644.

[251] Thrasher, Robert Mullins., "Prisoner of War." *The Register,* June 19, 1938.

An official inspection of December 1864, found that the beef was poor and sour. On many occasions, the prisoners returned the beef as unfit to eat. The Inspector found that the contractor supplying the prison with the beef was at fault. He stated that attention had been given to prevent a reoccurrence. The quality of the beef improved.[252]

Because of the meager rations, the prisoners were more attentive to the distribution of the rations. Each prisoner wanted to make sure he received his fair share of the short rations and eagerly devoured them. One prisoner noted that "every man gathered around his mess chief to see that he got his share of the grub. The long fellow got as much as the short one, the fat fellow as much as the lean one, and the hungry ones got just the same. Here was equality. The general didn't get any more than the lieutenant."[253] Another eyewitness stated that the "prisoners gathered around hungry and lean, and nothing was allowed to go to waste. Every bone and shred of meat, bean, grain of rice and hominy were carefully gathered, and the prisoners would rake the slop and garbage of the cook house and gather every scrap that showed any sign of nourishment. It was a regular rule to boil all the bones until not an eye of grease would rise on the water; and when the bones had passed through all the proper stages, they were soft enough to be chewed up and swallowed."[254] One prisoner, P. O. Olivier, would be so hungry that on "Saturdays a double ration (for Saturday and Sunday) was served at noon, I was so tortured by hunger, that as a rule, I devoured both before the setting sun and from then until Monday next, I existed without a morsel to eat."[255]

By the end of 1864, the prisoners were all severely malnourished. Normal avenues for obtaining food were closed except for the scant rations issued. Colonel Hundley described the hopelessness of obtaining extra food: "It seems a vain endeavor to get any thing to eat now 'by hook or by crook.' Awhile back, one could bribe the Yankees to bring in coffee, sugar, and such little delicacies, 'underground,' but not now. [W]e see nothing before us for some time now but starvation . . . we must endure all the horrors of a neverceasing hunger."[256] John Dooley stated that there was "continual suffering among the prisoners. Many go to the slop barrels and garbage piles to gather from the refuse a handful of revolting food."[257] In his diary, Edmund Patterson described the condition of himself and his fellow prisoners. He wrote, "I go to bed and get up hungry, and go hungry through the day and at night dreaming of something to eat. Men go about looking

---

252 *War of the Rebellion: A Compilation of the Official Records of the Union and Confederate Armies,* Series II, Vol. VII, 1186–1187.

253 Johnson "Record of Privation," 165.

254 Henry, "Experiences," 644.

255 Olivier, P. D. *What the Confederates Endured on Johnson's Island,* 4.

256 Hundley, D. R., *Prison Echoes of the Great Rebellion,* 179–180.

257 Dooley, John., *John Dooley, Confederate Soldier: His War Journal,* 165.

cadaverous, with their sunken cheeks and thin blue lips, that it is fearful to look at them." Patterson noted that food was the main topic in each room he visited.[258] One prisoner, Colonel Nisbet, tried to help his fellow man: "I had boxes nailed up at each block, with a written request attached to every box, that they be made receptacles of meat and bread for the starving. Each day I went around and collected food from the boxes and gave it to those who needed it most. They scrambled for it, poor fellows!"[259] In response to the fear and anger of starvation, the commandant "in answer to complaints from the inside as to what we were given to eat, and the small quantity of it, from a stairway inside the prison overlooking quite a crowd of us, Col. Hill, commander of the post, said he knew our complaints were just, that we were not being given enough to eat but he was power-less to do more than he was doing."[260] Only when the war looked won, and the exchange system was restored did the food supply get slowly better in the spring of 1865.

Not all of the prisoners suffered from hunger equally. The circumstances of the sit-uation determined to what degree they suffered. A prisoner who arrived at Johnson's Island after months of starving at the front, and, in addition, arrived at the prison with no money and no generous friends, had the roughest time. The well-fed, wealthy offi-cer who was sent to Johnson's Island had a reserve of previous good health plus the money and or friends to obtain additional rations. This class of prisoner did not suffer as much as his poorer inmates, but toward the end of 1864 and into 1865, the prison-ers' fortunes were equalized and the rich officer found out what hunger pains felt like.

RATS

By the summer of 1864, hunger had become prevalent within the prison. The reduc-tion in federal rations below subsistence levels, the restriction of purchasing eatables from the sutler, and the stoppage of Express packages from outside the prison forced the Confederate soldiers on Johnson's Island to look to other sources for extra food. Desperate situations call for desperate measures. These prisoners recognized a source of easy meat on the island—rats. Their instinct for survival overcame their pride and normal aversion to eating these vermin. The gentlemen of the South caught and killed these rodents to supplement their meager rations.

The first prisoners who started eating rats, perhaps even before rations generally became low, were the prisoners from Vicksburg and Port Hudson. They had suffered greatly during the sieges of those areas. At these battles, the Confederate soldiers were reduced to eating mule meat and rats.[261] When they arrived at Johnson's Island, they

---

[258] Patterson, Edmund Dewitt. *Yankee Rebel: The Civil War Journal of Edmund DeWitt Patterson*, 201.

[259] Nisbet, James Cooper., *Four Years on the Firing Line*, 223.

[260] Sidebottom Conf Vet, IX, 114.

[261] Wash, W. A., *Camp, Field and Prison Life,* 127.

were already starving, and some started eating the rats that abounded. These prisoners were already eating rats and informed the other prisoners that the disgust in eating rats was mere prejudice, as they tasted like frog legs and chicken. They even preferred to eat the rats to the tainted meat that was being issued from the federals.[262] These starving prisoners were the first to see the rats as a way to stave off starvation. The prisoners that had depended solely on government rations were the first to join the Vicksburg and Port Hudson prisoners in their dining habits. The idea of eating rats expanded as more and more prisoners began to suffer from the reduction in rations.

During the good times of 1862–1863, when food was relatively plentiful, the rat population swelled by eating the scraps left over from the prisoners. Upon one prisoner's arrival at Johnson's Island, he noted the large population of rats. He wrote, "My first night in prison was disturbed by a grand-drill of wharf rats, my bed being on the floor. The rats formed at the far end of the building and rushed to the other, then wheeled and returned. The rats ran over me roughshod, as I occupied a part of their former drill ground. These rats later, when rations became scarce, were trapped and went cheap at ten cents a rat."[263] This large number of rats helped supplement the insufficient rations that the soldiers were issued in the later part of 1864 and early 1865.

As rations were cut and the food supply dwindled in the summer of 1864, the less fortunate prisoners were compelled to catch and eat the large number of rats that abounded on Johnson's Island. John Dooley stated, "there are numbers [of rats] in the drains and under the house and they are so tame that they hardly think it worth while to get out of our way when we meet them. Rats are found to be very good for food, and every night many are captured and slain. So pressing is the want of food that nearly all who can, have gone into the rat business, either selling these horrid animals or killing them and eating them."[264] Colonel Hundley explained the level of desperation to which some of prisoners had sunk. "To assert that the rebels on this island are hungry, however, would be to speak rather too tamely; it would be more fitting to declare that they are famished. [My] fellow prisoners have discovered that the bull-pen is filled with a species of game . . . and the vogue now is to hunt, kill and eat the same. I witnessed a grand hunt today for this much coveted game, and I could but smile sadly as I beheld many noble gentlemen engaged with all a sportsman's keen relish in the chase after—rats."[265]

Edmund Patterson stated, "For several days some of the boys have been killing and eating rats, of which there are thousands in the prison. I have often been hungry

---

[262] Trimble, Isaac Ridgeway., "The Civil War Diary of Isaac Ridgeway Trimble." *Maryland Historical Magazine,* 17–18.

[263] J. J. Richardson, "Experiences on Johnson's Island," *Confederate Veteran,* Vol. XIV (1906), 60.

[264] Dooley, John., *John Dooley, Confederate Soldier: His War Journal,* 163.

[265] Hundley, D. R., *Prison Echoes of the Great Rebellion,* 120–121.

all day long, indeed so hungry that I felt sick, and still I could not screw my courage up to the point of eating rats." But after eating his rations and still having an insatiable appetite, he was forced to try a mess of rats. "My friend, Jones, had been very lucky and had captured a sufficient number of rats to make a big stew and invited me to try them. I cannot say that I am particularly fond of them, but rather than go hungry I will eat them when I can get them. They taste very much like young squirrel and would be good enough if called by any other name."[266] A great number of the prisoners recorded in their diaries that they were forced to eat rats in order to survive on the reduced rations.

At first, the rats were plentiful and easy to catch. A prisoner noted that in a "rat hunt we caught about five hundred wharf rats, piled them up and divided them out, then cooked and ate them."[267] The rats could be caught inside the blocks at first with deadfall traps or putting forks on broom handles to spear their pray.[268] A "Rat Club" was formed to catch the vermin. Sometimes up to twenty prisoners were deployed, each armed with a club, hunting for the rats. The zeal with which these rats were hunted quickly reduced their numbers. Colonel Hundley noted the scarcity. "It seems that, having torn up all the sewers and bridges, and dug out every rat that could be found, they are now forced to many cunning stratagems to secure their game." The "Rat Club" had obtained the help of a black terrier dog named Nellie. The dog would help rustle up rats for the prisoners. Hundley continues: "I encountered two hungry rebels, one of them holding Nellie, while the other concealed himself until a rat ran out from underneath the adjacent buildings, when he proceeded immediately to 'flank' it, his confederate at the same time turning loose Nellie and hieing her on to the chase. This party thus gobbled up two fine fat long-tails, while engaging in their nightly perambulations in the moonshine."[269] The demand for rats became so high prisoners "offered to exchange gold dollars for rats—a dollar each—but could not buy them."[270]

The large number of first-hand accounts of rat eating demonstrates conclusively that the prisoners on Johnson's Island were not supplied with sufficient nutritional quantity or quality during their last year of captivity. These "Gentlemen" were reduced to eating something that in ordinary circumstances would have revolted their delicate palates. Major Caldwell commented on how repulsed he was over the thought of eating rats: "Those who are less fortunate eat rats, but nothing short of absolute starvation could induce me to overcome my repugnance to these creatures which feed

---

[266] Patterson, Edmund Dewitt. *Yankee Rebel: The Civil War Journal of Edmund DeWitt Patterson*, 194–195.

[267] McClung, R. L., *Diary*, "Prisoners on Johnson's Island," *Confederate Veteran*, Vol. XV (1907), 495.

[268] Confederate Veteran, XXII,I 472.

[269] Hundley, D. R., *Prison Echoes of the Great Rebellion*, 131.

[270] McClung, R. L., *Diary*, "Prisoners," 495.

on the most loathsome garbage. Were they <u>barnfeed</u> I should not long resist temptation of getting one 'good meal' more."[271] A starving prisoner that had partaken of rat
flesh stated: "When prejudice is overcome by gnawing hunger, a fat rat makes good
eating, as I know from actual and enjoyable mastication."[272] In the book, *Rebels on
Lake Erie*, by Charles E. Frohman, eating rats at Johnson's Island was dismissed as
being done merely for curiosity. He gave two examples from diaries that they had
eaten a rat simply to see how it tasted; ignoring the fact that many more diaries give an
opposite opinion, that it was consumed from necessity. If people are well fed in their
position, like a wealthy mess with friends on the outside, then they might have eaten
rats out of a curiosity rather than necessity and to see what others were experiencing.
This does not dismiss the ten-fold number of prisoners with severe hunger pains being
pushed to the breaking point of existence. This degradation overshadowed all of their
experiences in the war. The bitterness of starving in a land of plenty was to be passed
on to future generations. More than 100 years later, the only story about his ancestor's
Civil War experience passed down to the author, a descendent of prisoner Felix Hays
Blackman, was of his starvation at Johnson's Island and the degradation of eating rats.

THE SUTLER

At Johnson's Island, there was a general store called the sutler shop functioning similar to a Post Exchange (PX) on military bases. This was where the prisoners could
purchase items that were not issued to them by the federal authorities. The prisoners
could buy food, newspapers, tobacco, clothing, and a host of other things as long
as the items were not considered contraband. From time to time restrictions were
placed on what the sutler could sell and were constantly in flux. On several occasions,
because of a variety of reasons explained below, the authorities removed the sutler
from the prison.

   The sutler was instrumental in maintaining the health and general well-being of
the prisoners. From the very beginning, issued items were scant and the prisoners had
to procure additional items from the sutler. Colonel Inzer acknowledged in his diary:
"My mess is living very well, but we get it from the Sutler."[273] Another inmate related
in his diary that without "the sutler's establishment (from which we can supply ourselves with butter, vegetables, molasses, sugar, etc.) and the boxes received by express,
we would find existence in this place upon our present rations almost insupportable."[274]

[271] Caldwell, James Parks., *A Northern Confederate at Johnson's Island Prison: The Civil War Diary of James Parks Caldwell*, 148.

[272] Dunaway, Wayland Fuller., *Reminiscences of a Rebel*, 113–114.

[273] Inzer, John Washington. *The Diary of a Confederate Soldier: John Washington Inzer 1834–1928*, 72.

[274] Hundley, D. R., *Prison Echoes of the Great Rebellion*, 83.

In 1863, the sutler was able to sell almost anything to the prisoners except contraband items. Every morning the prisoners would swarm the sutler's shop, located just inside the gate, to purchase goods. W. A. Wash describes the daily routine of the sutler shop. "[F]rom eight A. M. to five P.M. four clerks are kept busy in the sutler's store. The first thing there is a rush for the morning papers of which we soon eagerly devour the contents. In the next place, butter, onions, beans, cabbage, and potatoes must be secured in time for dinner, provided a fellow has the checks. Then the day is consumed in selling wearing apparel and notions of that sort."[275] He continued: "Our sutlers are driving quite a brisk trade just now. Twice each day they bring in a wagon load of vegetables, provisions and all kinds of stuff, and at night all is gone."[276]

Ice was also brought in and sold to the prisoners, on occasion. The prisoners would use this ice to refresh themselves on warm summer days. W. A. Wash described in his diary: "One the 19th [of June] the ice wagon began its summer visits, and we gladly welcomed it. We got ice at five cents per pound, and from five to eight pounds daily was enough for a mess of from six to ten men. The larger messes of from twenty to fifty kept their water in barrels, and brought ice accordingly."[277] Whether the sutler sold ice or if it was an outside vender is not readily apparent. If one considers that cash was officially forbidden and sutler checks were the medium of exchange, it is assumed that he was an agent of the sutler.

When a prisoner entered Johnson's Island, all the money in his possession was turned over to the commandant. The commandant kept an account of each prisoner's money, releasing the money only when the prisoner wanted to make purchases from the sutler. The sutler would receive from the prisoner a signed note from the post commandant for a particular sum; the sutler would then give the prisoner the equivalent quantity of checks.[278] Any money mailed to the prisoners was also confiscated and credited to the prisoner's account. These checks looked like currency with different denominations on them. The sutler's checks became the medium of exchange in the island prison. With these checks, inmates paid off gambling debts, paid for services of other inmates and paid for purchased goods from the sutler.

The commandant wanted to keep cash out of the prisoners' hands for several reasons. One was to keep the prisoners from bribing the guards. Another was to prevent a prisoner from having money upon his escape. Cash that was smuggled into the prison was held at a premium. With cash, inmates bribed guards for contraband material or for looking the other way on escape attempts.

---

[275] Wash, W. A., *Camp, Field and Prison Life,* 129–130.

[276] Ibid., 122.

[277] Wash, W. A., *Camp, Field and Prison Life,* 235.

[278] Wash, W. A., *Camp, Field and Prison Life,* 122.

Whether the sutler acted as a pawn broker or traded items with the prisoners is not clear. One prisoner, W. A. Wash, noted that "I put my watch, my only relic of home, in pawn with the sutler for some things we wanted, with the privilege of redeeming it as soon as I got money from home."[279] It is assumed that others pawned items at the sutler, but it is not mentioned in any other journals.

During 1863, the sutler, Wiley & [Joseph E.] Reynolds, had few troubles and made huge profits.[280] The prisoners seemed to be willing to spend their funds because prisoner exchanges were still taking place. The prisoners spent freely to make their stay as comfortable as possible until they were sent south. A prisoner noted, "Our sutlers are quite obliging especially when a fellow has a smart chance of funds to his credit. As we have no other source of procuring what we want, they charge us to the limit of their conscience, and in some cases it seems wonderfully elastic."[281] With business booming, the sutler expanded his shop in August 1863 by building an additional department. One department sold dry goods and the other sold groceries and vegetables, with two clerks each.[282]

The sutler had few interruptions in his brisk trade in 1863. For most of that year, he sold a wide range of articles. However, in August of that year, the War Department forbade the sutler to sell boots to the prisoners and also expanded the list of contraband items. The prisoners could still get items that they wanted, contraband or not, because the sutler was not inclined to turn down a sale. W. A. Wash bluntly stated that "when a fellow has the shinplasters a Dutch Jew sutler don't stand very heavy on orders."[283] The prisoners bribed the sutler with cash as well as sutler checks for contraband materials. After August 1864, bribing the sutler with checks was limited because all orders had to be processed through the commandant.[284]

The sutler was removed from the prison in November 1863, by order of the Commissary General, Colonel Hoffman, in retaliation for the suffering of Union prisoners in the South.[285] Also that month, a plot of a planned attack on the island to rescue the prisoners was discovered. The sutler was closed during the scare stemming from that plot. The Rebels had no idea why the sutler was removed but "grape" took over. Captain Bingham explained the rumors circulating through the prison: "The sutler was ordered away & all the checks (our currency) must be invested or redeemed & there was fears that they would

---

[279] Wash, W. A., *Camp, Field and Prison Life*, 93.

[280] Archer, J. J., "The James J. Archer Letters." *Maryland Historical Magazine*, 357; McClung, R. L., *Diary*, 14.

[281] Wash, W. A., *Camp, Field and Prison Life*, 122.

[282] Ibid., 162.

[283] Ibid., 161.

[284] Hundley, D. R., *Prison Echoes of the Great Rebellion*, 83, 111.

[285] *War of the Rebellion: A Compilation of the Official Records of the Union and Confederate Armies*, Series II, Vol. VI, 759.

not be redeemed, every body [sic] rushed to buy things as he needed, rumors were rife that the sutler's shop was to be broken up as a measure of retaliation & it would be severe too—another that he had been arrested for aiding the rebels in plans of escape—another that an exchange was effected & that this was a Yankee trick to effect a sale of the sutler's wares [etc.]—but whatever may be the cause every body [sic] rushed up & bought every thing [sic] that could be had."[286] The shop remained closed until January 1864.

Quite some commotion between the War Department and the Commissary General occurred over the sutler at Johnson's Island. A War Department letter was sent to Hoffman asking why there was no sutler at Johnson's Island when the other camps had sutlers. Even though Hoffman ordered the sutler out in December, he responded that the control of the sutler was entirely in the hands of the post commanders. Hoffman then explained that he did not have enough inspectors to discover this problem and was too busy to inspect himself. He then said the problem arose from the "inefficiency of the commanders."[287] Hoffman was very displeased with Colonel Pierson for a variety of reasons, which were discussed in Chapter I.

While the sutler was closed because of the fear of a raid, a Union soldier acted as a sutler for the prisoners. Bingham explained that "a little corporal sells stationary & tobacco—at prodigious rates—takes orders on Col. P[eirson] for $2 no less—so one must buy that much or none—& I can't get stamps except in change—I do not want paper or tobacco & so can't get stamps at all."[288] Even though Captain Bingham had problems, Colonel Pierson must have known that to stop letter writing and tobacco straight out would have destabilized the prison.

The island's owner, Mr. Johnson, became the sutler in January 1864. Mr. Johnson was not very well liked and is condemned in many diaries. One prisoner noted, "I heard but few fellows bless him, except with execrations."[289] Almost one month later, some prisoners broke in and stole some items from the sutler in retaliation for "high prices and meanness."[290]

The sutler, Mr. Johnson, came up with an idea to make extra money off the prisoners in January 1864. Mr. Johnson had "gone to the expense of getting a lithographic view of the prison, Sandusky and vicinity, expecting it would take like hotcakes among the prisoners."[291] He refused to sell anything to the prisoners unless the purchaser first bought a lithograph that depicted the island and Sandusky at the inflated price of three

---

[286] Bingham, Robert, *Diary*, part 2, 10.

[287] *War of the Rebellion: A Compilation of the Official Records of the Union and Confederate Armies,* Series II, Vol. VI, 701–702.

[288] Bingham, Robert, *Diary*, part 2, 32.

[289] Wash, W. A., *Camp, Field and Prison Life,* 197.

[290] Wash, W. A., *Camp, Field and Prison Life,* 197.

[291] Wash, W. A., *Camp, Field and Prison Life,* 197.

dollars. One prisoner, Captain Bingham, implicated Colonel Pierson in the enterprise with his January 28, 1864, entry: "So a general order appeared on the bulletin board to this effect, that each rebel must report immediately to the sutler & procure a picture—& if any one refused that the $3 [would] be taken [from] his funds outside anyhow, as the picture was gotten up at huge expense for the sole benefit of the rebels—signed by order Col. [Pierson]"[292] Mr. Johnson continued this blackmail until the post commander, Colonel Bassett (USA), discovered the plot and forced him to refund all money collected for the purchases of the photo.[293]

There seems to be conflicting reports on who was the sutler in 1864. Mr. Johnson was hated, and in many diary entries he was replaced with the brother of General Terry, the commandant of the prison. Many stated "Sutler Terry" arrived for the first time March 16, 1864.[294] Many other diaries stated Johnson & Finnegan (May 1864) or Mr. Johnson (August 1864) as the sutlers. It is curious that an inspection report noted an unnamed sutler but did not question the fact the sutler might be Terry's brother.[295] To further confuse the issue, another prisoner, Hundley, who kept a very detailed diary and newly arrived at Johnson's Island in the summer of 1864, stated that Johnson was removed as sutler in August.[296] The prisoners may have had such animosity for Johnson, and the use of clerks may have confused and twisted the real situation.

From early 1864 until close to the end of the war, the list of items the sutler could sell was continually modified or reduced. In March 1864, one of the prisoners, Captain G. S. Markham, released his frustration when he assaulted a sutler clerk, Billy Patterson. The captain broke a lamp over the sutler's head when Billy sold him the lamp, then told the Captain that he could not sell lamp oil to the prisoners.[297] That same month, an order was given that food was to be sold only on recommendation from the surgeon. Many inmates applied, complaining of sickness in order to get permission to purchase food.[298]

In April 1864, a prisoner noted that the sutler brought in an unusually large stock of goods. A crowd of prisoners squeezed into the store to make purchases. Total sales for the sutler that day were $2,000. The sutler had smuggled in brandy and sold it for $5.00 per

[292] Bingham, Robert, *Diary*, 2, 64.

[293] Patterson, Edmund Dewitt. *Yankee Rebel: The Civil War Journal of Edmund DeWitt Patterson*, 157.

[294] Wash, W. A., *Camp, Field and Prison Life*, 212, 215; Caldwell, James Parks., *A Northern Confederate at Johnson's Island Prison: The Civil War Diary of James Parks Caldwell*, 98.

[295] *War of the Rebellion: A Compilation of the Official Records of the Union and Confederate Armies*, VII, 485

[296] Hundley, D. R., *Prison Echoes of the Great Rebellion*, 111.

[297] Inzer, John Washington. *The Diary of a Confederate Soldier: John Washington Inzer 1834–1928*, 66; Wash, W. A., *Camp, Field and Prison Life*, 210.

[298] Wash, W. A., *Camp, Field and Prison Life*, 212.

quart.[299] This was a rare occurrence for the sutler to have so many items for sale, including contraband liquor. The sutler allowed sub-sutlers to sell to prisoners in each block. They would buy from him wholesale and then sell at retail making a profit and providing the prisoners with a convenient way to purchase goods.[300] The prisoners did not seem to mind—as W. A. Wash stated in his journal, "For some cause no sutler had been in the prison for several days, but it did not much matter for a half dozen subsutler shops, kept by rebels, were open, and there was a great rivalry among them for the trade."[301]

In June 1864, the War Department issued an order allowing the sutler to sell only the following items: writing materials, postage stamps, tobacco, cigars, pipes, matches, combs, soap, toothbrushes, hair brushes, clothes brushes, scissors, thread and needles, handkerchiefs, towels, and pocket looking-glasses.[302] An inspection report in July to Colonel Hoffman (USA) notified him that the sutler's prices were exorbitant.[303] Prisoners frequently complained of high prices, but with the items for sale more limited, the sutler may have inflated the price even more to keep profits rolling in. The prisoners could see that without the sutler selling food to supplement their rations, they were going to have a tough time surviving in the prison. For the inmates with money, the sutler's disappearance from the prison cut off one of their keys to comfort. These privileged prisoners were going to feel the same hunger as their less fortunate Rebel brothers.

In August 1864, a flurry of diary entrees was recorded about the sutler. In an effort to control what the prisoners acquired and to cut down on bribing the sutler and thus obtaining contraband material, a new system was enacted on August 12th. Major Caldwell explained: "A new sutler has come in, & a new system is adopted, whereby we are deterred of the use of any kind of currency inside—this sutler using no checks." Colonel Hill had all the men assembled at roll-call to explain the intricate manner of receiving funds under the new system."[304] Luther Mills went into detail of this new system: "When a prisoner wished to purchase anything he made application to the commandant of the post, asking that the sutler be ordered to sell him such and such articles. If the commandant approved the application, his bookkeeper would send the prisoner a 'schedule' showing the amount due him and ordering the sutler to sell him the articles.

---

[299] Ibid., 215.

[300] *War of the Rebellion: A Compilation of the Official Records of the Union and Confederate Armies,* VII, 485.

[301] Wash, W. A., *Camp, Field and Prison Life,* 217.

[302] *War of the Rebellion: A Compilation of the Official Records of the Union and Confederate Armies,* Series II, Vol. VIII, 573-574; Patterson, Edmund Dewitt. *Yankee Rebel: The Civil War Journal of Edmund DeWitt Patterson,* 188.

[303] *War of the Rebellion: A Compilation of the Official Records of the Union and Confederate Armies,* Series II, Vol. VII, 485.

[304] Caldwell, James Parks., *A Northern Confederate at Johnson's Island Prison: The Civil War Diary of James Parks Caldwell,* 135.

The purchases were entered on the 'schedule' and receipted for by the prisoner. The sutler then carried the 'schedule' to headquarters and drew his pay."[305] Eight days later another round of entrees surfaced. Edmund DeWitt Patterson noted in his diary the order from the War Department that now limited articles sold by the sutler to stationery and tobacco. All Express boxes were not stopped. The prisoners were very frightened by this restriction and feared the suffering this would cause for a winter surviving only on limited government rations.[306] The prisoners made an official complaint to Colonel Hill, who told the inmates he was "simply obeying orders from headquarters."[307]

The sutler was apparently arrested on November 19, 1864. The Yankees came in, arrested the sutler, placed his assistant placed in confinement. Major Caldwell simply put in his journal: "General explanation is that he has been guilty of bringing in useless old things."[308] Whatever the official response was and if he was fined or imprisoned is not known.

The sutler was of little consequence until February 1865 when the sale of eatables to the prisoners was restored. Hoffman, now a Brigadier General, issued an order on February 13, 1865, directing that the Secretary of War permitted sutlers to sell vegetables "in such quantities as may be necessary to their health." Hoffman then added that commanding officers are "held responsible that this privilege is not abused." [309] Colonel Inzer, on February 22nd, noted that the sutler was selling potatoes, beans, onions, turnips, and cabbage.[310] The decision to re-establish the sutler's sale of eatables was made only to prevent disease.[311] On March 12th, several prisoners wrote in their diaries that the Department of War had allowed the sutler to sell anything not contraband of war.[312] The general feeling from Washington was that the South was beaten and retaliation was no longer so important a factor. The end of the war was near and the exchange system was re-established. Also, the public demand for revenge for the mistreatment of federal prisoners was waning. The prisoners fared better because once again they could purchase additional food from the sutler.

---

[305] Mills, Luther Rice, *Papers*, 3.

[306] Patterson, Edmund Dewitt. *Yankee Rebel: The Civil War Journal of Edmund DeWitt Patterson*, 188.

[307] Conf Vet IX, 165

[308] Caldwell, James Parks., *A Northern Confederate at Johnson's Island Prison: The Civil War Diary of James Parks Caldwell*, 161.

[309] *War of the Rebellion: A Compilation of the Official Records of the Union and Confederate Armies*, Series II, Vol. VIII, 215.

[310] Inzer, John Washington. *The Diary of a Confederate Soldier: John Washington Inzer 1834–1928*, 126.

[311] Inzer, John Washington. *The Diary of a Confederate Soldier: John Washington Inzer 1834–1928*, 129.

[312] Caldwell, James Parks., *A Northern Confederate at Johnson's Island Prison: The Civil War Diary of James Parks Caldwell*, 187; Inzer, John Washington. *The Diary of a Confederate Soldier: John Washington Inzer 1834–1928*, 129–130.

WATER

One of the ironies of Johnson's Island was the problem of fresh water. The island was surrounded by fresh water but the delivery system was too inadequate to meet the needs of 2,500 prisoners. The prisoners were supplied water from two wells in the main street and from two pumps on the bay side of the enclosure.

The wells could be dug only to a depth of five feet because of the solid rock that was below the prison grounds. A prisoner had to be first in line in the morning to get decent cooking or drinking water from the wells. Captain Barziza of Texas wrote about the daily routine of procuring water: "As soon as reveille sounded crowds would collect around the pumps with buckets, canteens, &c., and in an hour the [pump] wells would be exhausted. I have seen scores of men standing in two ranks by these pumps for hours exposed to rain, snow, sleet and wind, waiting for the water to rise at the rate of about a green bucket full in half an hour."[313] The water that seeped through was usually contaminated with natural lime and the filth of the nearby sinks. Colonel Hundley discussed the poor condition of the water: "The water from the wells seeps through the ground, and is impregnated with the filth of the sinks and the sewers."[314] Even the officials admitted the poor character of the well water. In a July 24, 1864, Inspection report Major Scovill informed his superiors at Washington that the "wells inside are a failure; the water is unfit for use."[315]

The well water was mainly used for washing, because of the inferiority of the quality. Prisoners would wash their clothes in the yard, where at "almost any hour of the day can be found from twenty to fifty men, with sleeves rolled up, going [to work] into a tub of clothes with as much grace as though they had been brought up at the calling."[316] Prisoners could also carry buckets of water into the blocks to wash clothes, which led to filthy conditions inside the blocks.

The other source of water was from the two pumps connected by pipe to the fresh water of the bay. Captain Wash lodged in his diary, "The pump man from Sandusky repaired our old pump and put in a new one close by, watered by a leaden pipe extending out into the lake, so now we can get lots of good water without waiting long and our water is cooler, purer, and better than might be imagined."[317] Colonel Hundley stated "the water from the lake, is not much better, since it is from the harbor. Every time the wind blows, the filth from the bottom of this harbor is stirred up."[318]

---

[313] Barziza, Decimus et Ultimus., *The Adventures of a Prisoner of War, 1863–1864,* 78.

[314] Hundley, D. R., *Prison Echoes of the Great Rebellion,* 78.

[315] *War of the Rebellion: A Compilation of the Official Records of the Union and Confederate Armies,* Vol VII, 492.

[316] Wash, W. A., *Camp, Field and Prison Life,* 129.

[317] Wash, W. A., *Camp, Field and Prison Life,* 148.

[318] Hundley, D. R., *Prison Echoes of the Great Rebellion,* 78.

Colonel Hundley was one the few prisoners to complain about the quality of the lake water. Most prisoners complained about the quantity of water. The pumps were of an inferior quality and broke down often. In the winter, the pipes froze and it became even more difficult to get fresh water. Captain Barziza stated: "Two pumps with pipes, extending to the bay, furnished us with water. But early in the winter these pipes became chocked with ice, and rendered the pumps useless. Two holes about eight feet deep were then dug in the yard, and pumps were put in them, and these afforded the only sources of water for more than twenty-five hundred men. I have many a time been actually painfully thirsty, and yet in sight of an ocean of fresh water."[319]

The second water pump was installed at the prison in August 1863 and caused quite a commotion shortly after its installation. W. A. Wash recounted the story: "Along about midnight the sentinel on post number five cried out. 'Halt! Who goes there?' There being no answer, he challenged a second and a third time; click, click, then bang went his fusee, his heart perhaps nearer his mouth than the bullet went to the object aimed at. So his neighbor on post number six cracked away with the same result. The corporal of the guard who came promptly took a lamp and marched up to the figure—our new pump put in the other day. The boys christen the affair 'the skirmish with the pump.'"[320] After this incident, the prisoners laughed at the guards involved at every possible occasion.

The situation somewhat changed when General Terry took over command of John-son's Island in 1864. General Terry allowed the prisoners to go out to the bay, under guard, to cut holes in the ice and bring water back.[321] W. A. Wash stated in January 1864, "for some time we had been suffering from scarcity of water, but now an arrangement was made leaving the big gate leading to the lake open four hours each day, and we could get plenty of crystal ice water."[322] Captain Bingham noted this about the security for the water fetching parties, "They opened the gates yesterday & today—had 10 sentinels between the fence & the lake on each side—one every 10 feet—4 on the fence & a camp & batters at each end of the fence—they must think the rebels are dangerous."[323] This allowed water to be brought in, but it was at more effort than pumps with more exposure to the elements. Colonel Inzer complained that when he arrived back from a water trip to the lake, he had a significant chill.[324] Men were allowed to go out to the lake to bathe in the summertime, but this is not mentioned as a source of water. As bathing was done by rotation with only a handful at a time, it must not have supplied water to the prison in a consistent manner.

---

[319] Barziza, Decimus et Ultimus., *The Adventures of a Prisoner of War, 1863–1864,* 77–78.

[320] Wash, W. A., *Camp, Field and Prison Life,* 156–157.

[321] Ibid., 78.

[322] Wash, W. A., *Camp, Field and Prison Life,* 196.

[323] Bingham, Robert, *Diary,* #2, 31.

[324] Inzer, John Washington. *The Diary of a Confederate Soldier: John Washington Inzer 1834–1928,* 122.

An inspection report of July 1864 confirmed that the pumps were inefficient for supplying the demands of the prisoners for water. The report recommended that one additional pump be installed and the existing pumps being replaced with better quality units.[325] At the same time, Colonel Hill sent in a proposal to install a much superior water system that would supply all the needs of the prisoners and guards. The system was to have a six-inch supply pump that fed into a reservoir 70 feet wide by 200 feet long and 7 feet deep. With this reservoir full, the whole camp would have a four days' water supply for 5,000 people. A distribution system of three-inch pipe would feed the entire prison complex, but this system was too expensive, at a cost of $7079.88.[326] Money was already allotted for other expenditures inside the prison; therefore, this system was never installed. In 1865, an inspection report again requested that the reservoir system be enacted with a steam engine and force pump to alleviate the water supply problem.[327] Even at this late date in the war, water was still officially recognized as a persistent problem.

Throughout the existence of the prison, water was always in short supply. The federal government did not want to spend the money to bring a permanent solution to the problem. Instead, they relied on a patchwork system of inadequate wells, poor quality pumps, and bucket brigades to the lake. With such a large body of fresh water only yards away, it is difficult to imagine that clean water was scarce at Johnson's Island.

CLOTHING

The obtaining of proper clothing for the Johnson's Island prisoner was similar to acquiring every other commodity in the prison. Those prisoners who had money or outside friends could provide themselves with sufficient protection from the weather. Initially, the prisoners could receive clothing from home or purchase the items from the sutler. Later, these privileges would be restricted. Just like fighting hunger, the wealthier and/or well-connected prisoners had better chances of not suffering from the pains of cold weather. Those who did not have these resources were left to the mercy of the federal government or did without. The federal government issued clothing only when it was absolutely necessary.[328]

Most of the prisoners were captured in the summer campaigns of 1863 and 1864 and therefore had only light clothing that was not suited to the cold climates of

---

[325] *War of the Rebellion: A Compilation of the Official Records of the Union and Confederate Armies*, Series II, Vol. VII, 484.

[326] Ibid., 488.

[327] *War of the Rebellion: A Compilation of the Official Records of the Union and Confederate Armies*, Series II, Vol. VII, 331.

[328] *War of the Rebellion: A Compilation of the Official Records of the Union and Confederate Armies*, Series II, Vol. VI, 759.

northern Ohio. Some prisoners came directly from the Gulf Coast with clothing that was light or breathable. As winter approached, these prisoners on Johnson's Island prepared themselves as best they could for the upcoming cold weather. Few prisoners who were captured on the battlefield did not have all of their personal gear with them as they marched into captivity with just the clothes on their backs, whereas prisoners from a group surrender, like Port Hudson for example, might have packed up all of their clothing for an orderly move into captivity.

To some prisoners, the clothing situation became critical. Clothing was being worn constantly with no rotation of what was worn. To keep clean, the clothes were being washed constantly, further deteriorating their condition. Some clothing was so soiled that washing would not make it fit to wear. Some prisoners would dye their clothing to make their appearance more presentable. One prisoner described the process: "As our clothing gradually grew worse soap and water seemed to lose their powers, and we resorted to dyeing such garments as needed renovation using for that purpose a liquid dye. You simply emptied the vial into a pot of boiling water, immersed the garment to be operated on and *voila!*"[329]

The clothing situation varied from prisoner to prisoner and from case to case. Wealthy prisoners usually had no trouble with quantity or quality of clothing. The prisoners who had money could purchase clothing from the sutler until these privileges were later restricted. One prisoner stated in an article in *Confederate Veteran*, a post-war magazine: "Those who were fortunate enough to have money bought clothing, but those who had none did without. All luxuries that I knew of were paid for by those who happened to have money, and always at double prices."[330]

V. S. Murphey commented on how the home states would send clothing to be distributed to prisoners: "State associations are formed by the representatives of the respective states to aid and assist and contribute to the wants of the indigent, and destitute. Extra clothing, small sums of money and stamps, indeed anything that will alleviate their sufferings or relieve their anxiety. These benevolent associations have caused many a captive heart to throb with delight and shield their nude limbs from the Siberian blasts of winter. They are not as liberally sustained as one would desire and their sphere of benevolence is contracted by the meagerness of the material they operate with."[331] One prisoner described how clothing was distributed from a generous donor, most likely the organization above: "Mrs. Gen. Anderson sent a box for the N. C. prisoners—containing 125 shirts, 125 drawers, 125 socks. They were for Gen. [Anderson's] brig[ade], for Petigrew's brig[ade] & for others after that. I got two

---

[329] Knauss, William H., *The Story of Camp Chase.* Nashville, 246.

[330] Conf Vet VII, 442.

[331] Murphey, V. S., *Diary*, 124.

shirts & two drawers—thick & good."[332] Colonel Murphey described in his diary his philandering when it came to clothes: "Have 2 pairs of socks gave one to Lt. Dendy 17th Ala. Received $50 from Mr. S P Johnston West Greenville Pa. Paid it all for a suit of clothes and gave them to Capt John Bolling of my regiment. He would not have received them if he knew my financial condition and my own great wants. Gave Tom O'Brien 17th one of my shirts. Have not tobacco or means to buy it. All right."[333]

Those who had friends or family outside were able, for a time, to receive clothing. Confederates who had friends or family in loyal states would have more of an opportunity to receive clothing than those who did not. General J. J. Archer noted, "Many of the officers have no money or change of clothing having no friends in Yankeydom [sic] to supply them—those who have can get whatever they want."[334] One soldier, Lt. J. R. Breare, actually wrote the Secretary of War for the Confederacy, in August 1863, with a very interesting proposal:

DEAR SIR: There are about [Censored] Confederate officers confined here as prisoners of war. About [Censored] were captured at Gettysburg, and the balance belong mostly to our Western army. This is the general depot for all Confederate officers, except those who belong to General Morgan's command. There are but few men in the crowd who have a change of clothing, and as our money is worthless here there are but few who have the means to purchase what they so much need. I would respect-fully suggest to you the propriety of sending to each officer here (if in your power to do so) one month's pay in U. S. money. It would enable each officer to purchase a supply of comfortable clothing for the cold season, which in this section is close upon us. It would also be the means of preventing a large amount of suffering, sickness, and death. In thus addressing you I am not actuated by any personal motive. I have friends and relatives in the United States who cheerfully supply all my needs. I write in behalf of my brother officers who are in need and must suffer unless something is done to relieve them. I neither ask nor desire anything for myself. Our treatment here is kind and humane. Our rations are good both in quantity and quality, and all we need to make us comfortable is a supply of clothing. Hoping that this matter will receive your attention, I am, yours, respectfully, Lt J. R. Breare

---

[332] Bingham, Robert, *Diary*, 77.

[333] Murphey, V. S., *Diary*, 152.

[334] Archer, J. J., "The James J. Archer Letters." *Maryland Historical Magazine*, 357.

The Confederacy considered it and noted that they had U.S. money in the treasury taken by Morgan during a raid, but did not believe the Union authority would actually pass the money on to the prisoners.[335]

Some inmates had an abundance of military and civilian clothing of various colors. Prisoners who had civilian clothing worried the commandant. The commandant knew that if a prisoner escaped, he could blend in with the locals by wearing civilian clothing. To reduce the risk of prisoners blending in with the civilian population, in August 1863, an order was issued that prisoners could only have one set of outer clothing, in gray color, and a change of under clothing.[336] It is not known whether the prisoners who had extra clothing had to send it home or if the excess was confiscated and issued to the less fortunate prisoners. A good number of prisoners arrived at Johnson's Island with blue Union clothing. This was also problematic, because with a mixture of clothing coming in, someone could obtain a complete blue federal uniform and impersonate a guard or hasten their escape.

An order was issued from Colonel Hoffman, Commissary General of Prisoners, on July 31, 1863, restricting prisoners from purchasing from the sutler any clothing that was not absolutely necessary. They were not permitted to buy boots and could only purchase shoes of poor quality.[337] The sutler could not sell boot polish or shirt collars as well. V. S. Murphey explained: "Blacking and shirt collars are positively prohibited the former because the sentinels and men on duty here are required to burnish their boots daily and if we would in one point correspond with their men in attempting to escape, and the latter because it is dressy."[338]

In August 1863, Hoffman ordered that clothing could not be shipped to the prisoners from friends outside unless absolutely necessary.[339] Why Hoffman made this decision is nebulous and arguable. He knew that the South was suffering material shortages, especially footwear, and that prisoners all over the North might resupply themselves with clothing from loyal states only to be exchanged and sent back into the fight with better clothing than when the left the battlefield months ago. He had also heard stories of treatment of Union prisoners in southern camps. Colonel Pierson, seeing first-hand the condition of his prisoners, requested that Colonel Hoffman remove these restrictions because many prisoners were "nearly naked." Pierson explained that if this was not done, the government

[335] *War of the Rebellion: A Compilation of the Official Records of the Union and Confederate Armies,* Series II, Vol. VI, 200–201.

[336] Wash, W. A., *Camp, Field and Prison Life,* 166.

[337] *War of the Rebellion: A Compilation of the Official Records of the Union and Confederate Armies,* Series II, Vol. VI, 161.

[338] Murphey, V. S., *Diary,* 114.

[339] *War of the Rebellion: A Compilation of the Official Records of the Union and Confederate Armies,* Ibid., 193.

would have to issue clothing, increasing operating costs.[340] Colonel Hoffman answered that if the prisoner did not have the means to purchase required clothing from the sutler, Pierson was authorized to issue undergarments and overcoats from government stocks.[341]

After this decision, to receive clothing from outside or to purchase clothing from the sutler, a prisoner had to make a request in writing. The only acceptable color of cloth was gray to easily identify the men as Confederates.[342] Permits were issued only if the prisoner proved that he needed the articles. W. A. Wash described how a friend received a permit and tricked the Yankees for more clothing: "Captain Lister . . . had sent out to the post commandant for approval, a permit to receive certain articles of clothing from a lady friend in Kentucky. In the body of the permit he left a small blank place. It came back approved, and he inserted 'one pair boots' and sent it on the way rejoicing. Before long the fellows from down East detected the *modes operandi*, and after that filled up all the open spaces with red ink lines."[343]

The government issued articles only when "the prisoner [was] not protected from suffering on the account of the cold, or when his clothing [was] so worn out as not to protect his person."[344] If a prisoner was not able to purchase clothing or had no friends to send articles to him, he was a candidate for receiving issued goods. During 1863, the federal government issued to the prisoners on Johnson's Island 1,022 shirts, 200 blouses, 270 drawers, 380 pair of socks, 13 greatcoats, and 796 pair of shoes.[345] Because the prisoners were restricted from receiving or purchasing clothing and the deterioration of existing garments, the demand for issued clothing increased dramatically in 1864. Colonel Hoffman had received so many letters of misery and want of clothing that on February 19, 1864, he asked Brig. Gen. Terry to issue clothing to prisoners who had only summer clothing or were unfit for the season. Hoffman reminded him that he had given orders previously to Colonel Pierson to issue clothing from stock, which apparently he did not think was followed.[346]

An order was given in May 1864 forbidding any new issuing of clothing until October. In that month a flood of requests for clothing poured in, which was filled in November.[347] For the month of November 1864, the federal quartermaster issued

---

[340] Ibid., 201.

[341] Ibid., 330.

[342] Blackman, Felix Hays, *Letters to Maggie Sexton*, November 2, 1863.

[343] Wash, W. A., *Camp, Field and Prison Life,* 202.

[344] *War of the Rebellion: A Compilation of the Official Records of the Union and Confederate Armies,* Series II, Vol. VI, 759.

[345] Ibid.

[346] *War of the Rebellion: A Compilation of the Official Records of the Union and Confederate Armies,* Series II, Vol. VI, 972.

[347] Inzer, John Washington. *The Diary of a Confederate Soldier: John Washington Inzer 1834–1928,* 78.

423 blouses, 465 drawers, 423 pair of socks, and 17 greatcoats.[348] This issue in a single month exceeded that of the previous year. It is hard to understand why the federal government did not allow the prisoners to furnish themselves with more clothing; this would have reduced the burden on the prison treasury. Some Confederates, like W. A. Wash, took the issuing of clothing from federal sources with humor: "Having some days previous made a requisition, and my appearance being a sufficient voucher that the articles were needed, I, on the 10th day of June, drew from Uncle Abraham's bounty a pair of pants, socks and drawers."[349]

The prisoners had to prove that they needed additional clothing and the commandant was reluctant to allow the prisoners' wardrobe to swell beyond what was absolutely necessary. One prisoner described his clothing situation: "When I was captured I had a new Confederate coat and vest. These lasted me a year and a half. I had on a half-worn-out pair of gray jeans pants, which I wore for more than a year; then I drew a shoddy gray pair of pants which soon fell to pieces, and I used the rags to patch my old pants, which I finally wore home. I drew several suits of underclothing. My overcoat lasted me through the year and a half, and I carried it back to Dixie. My shoes wore out and I went up to draw some at the distribution of clothing. Finally the distribution was over. I saw two shoes and asked for them; they were not mates. One was a number nine and the other was a number ten, both for the same foot. The nine fitted one foot and I could wear the ten on the other. I wore them back to Dixie."[350]

In October 1864, Colonel Robert Ould, Confederate Agent for Exchange, recommended to Lieutenant General U. S. Grant (USA) that Southern cotton be allowed to be shipped north to be sold, with the proceeds purchasing blankets and clothing for Confederate prisoners held by the North.[351] By mid-November General Grant and Colonel Ould had come to an agreement on the matter that 1,000 bales of cotton would be sent to New York for sale. Brigadier General William N. R. Beall (CSA) was the agent.[352] The prisoners on Johnson's Island were incorrectly told that an agent would be selected from the prison to be sent to New York on parole. This caused quite a stir as Colonel Hundley illustrated in his diary:

> We have had an unusual excitement in the prison to-day, occasioned by the election of a commissioner to go to New York . . . to procure supplies of clothing

---

[348] *War of the Rebellion: A Compilation of the Official Records of the Union and Confederate Armies,* Ibid., Vol. VII, 1186–1187.

[349] Wash, W. A., *Camp, Field and Prison Life,* 94.

[350] Richardson, "Experiences," 60.

[351] *War of the Rebellion: A Compilation of the Official Records of the Union and Confederate Armies,* Series II, Vol. VII, 1063.

[352] *War of the Rebellion: A Compilation of the Official Records of the Union and Confederate Armies,* Series II, Vol VII 1117.

for rebel prisoners. The prospect of being paroled and sent off on such an expedition was so fascinating, a great many offered themselves as candidates to fill the position, and it was determined the matter should be decided by a free ballot, which was accordingly held. Previous to the balloting, the prisoners assembled in front of Block 7, and the candidates were called upon for speeches, which were delivered somewhat after the fashion of the political stump-speeches of other days, much to the amusement and entertainment of the crowd. It was evident, from the very beginning, however, that Colonel Fite of Tennessee, would run ahead of all competitors . . . and he was elected without any trouble.[353]

The shipment of cotton was late arriving in New York and finally, in February 1865, clothing had been sent out to all of the enlisted men's prisons, like Elmira, New York, and Camp Douglas, Illinois. Why General Beall omitted Johnson's Island is not clear, perhaps he felt their supply of clothing and blankets was sufficient. There was hope that provisions would arrive as one prisoner noted in a letter dated December 18, 1864: "We are expecting however, some addition to our comfort in the way of provisions & clothing arising from the proceeds of Cotton recently sent by the Confederate Gov't to N.Y."[354] While others, like Major Caldwell, correctly noted in his diary the mood of the more pessimistic in the prison that nothing was going to change.[355]

The prisoners on Johnson's Island, in general, did not have an abundance of clothing. They were allowed clothing only when it was absolutely necessary. This deficiency was compounded by the cruel cold weather of northern Ohio. The inadequate clothing caused suffering amongst the prisoners that could have been easily prevented.

BEDDING

When the prisoners arrived, they were issued bedding and blankets for sleeping and fighting off the cold. W. A. Wash described the process: "When a lot of prison birds come in, each is given an empty straw tick, and they go out in squads to a barge of straw at the landing, and in a little while, come back with their ticks stuffed full, and in that same squad may be noticed the General, the Captain, and the private."[356] A "tick" as he called it, was a cotton mattress sack for holding the straw into a bunk form. Another prisoner lamented the poor quality of these items: "In the winter of 1863–64 each prisoner was furnished with two so-called blankets, but if any sheep ever furnished any wool that entered into the make-up of those blankets, he must have been

---

[353] Hundley, D. R., *Prison Echoes of the Great Rebellion*, 182–183.

[354] Norman, James., *Southern Letters and Life in the Mid 1800s*, 264–265.

[355] Caldwell, James Parks., *A Northern Confederate at Johnson's Island Prison: The Civil War Diary of James Parks Caldwell*, 162.

[356] Wash, W. A., *Camp, Field and Prison Life,* 155.

of a hairy description, as they were made shoddy and no wool in them. Each prisoner, when he entered that prison, was furnished with two, of such blankets, and never received any more. The bedding in the bunks consisted of about as much wheat straw as would give an ordinary cow a scant meal. Neither the straw nor the blanket were ever changed while I was there."[357]

In an official Inspection Report, dated December 4, 1864, it stated that upon inspection "four-fifths of the prisoners not supplied with straw." The report concluded the reason for the shortages was because of the recent death of the federal quartermaster of Johnson's Island and the difficulty in obtaining sufficient supplies of straw.[358] It does not appear that the problem was sufficiently remedied.

Conclusion

The men at Johnson's Island were almost completely dependent on the mood of the authorities for the quantity and quality of their provisions. The government would change from time to time what and in what quantity supplies could pass through the main gate for the prisoners to possess. The reasons for their decisions were based on security, finances, and public opinion. The restrictions based on security and finances are entirely understandable, but the restriction of food, based on public opinion and retaliation, was harsh. The prisoners at Johnson's Island had hatred installed in them because the federals had the supplies, but refused to allow the men access the bounty of a wealthy nation. Many would never forgive the North for suffering that was completely avoidable.

---

[357] Conf Vet, IX, 164–165

[358] *War of the Rebellion: A Compilation of the Official Records of the Union and Confederate Armies,* Vol 7, 1186–1187.

Chapter 4

HEALTH OF THE PRISON

"I wish I were a polar bear."

—Major Henry Kyd Douglas, Jackson's Command

HOSPITAL

Block 6 housed the prisoners' hospital on Johnson's Island. It was a two-story building, 126 feet long by 30 feet wide, and of the same type construction as the other blocks. There were four wards measuring 48 feet by 30 feet, two on each floor. A transverse hall six feet wide separated the wards on each floor.[359] The hospital also had a dispensary, morgue, kitchen, surgeon's quarters, dining room, and laundry. The building was plastered and painted, making it one of the more comfortable blocks.[360] A stove in the center of each room, heated the ward; however, these stoves were inadequate to overcome the extreme cold of the northern Ohio winters. A flue passed through each room, terminating at the roof of the block, and windows ventilated the hospital during the summer months. The normal capacity of the hospital was 60 patients, but in emergency situations could hold 75 to 80 men.[361]

The chief medical officer of the prison complex was Surgeon T. Woodbridge of Hoffman's Battalion. He took charge in February 1862. A federal inspector called him

---

[359] *War of the Rebellion: A Compilation of the Official Records of the Union and Confederate Armies*, Series II, Vol. VII, 761.

[360] Wash, W. A., *Camp, Field and Prison Life*, 355.

[361] Ibid., 356.

71

a "skillful practitioner of medicine." This inspector added, however, that Woodbridge "delegates too much of his authority to his subordinates, nurses, etc., and consequently much of the duty is carelessly performed."[362] Dr. Woodbridge was in charge of the entire prison complex, but rarely entered the bull pen. Prisoner Wharton Green stated that Dr. Woodbridge was a "kindhearted and thorough gentleman, who did all in his power to alleviate the sufferings of those with whom he was brought in contact."[363]

Dr. Eversman, who arrived in early 1864, assisted Dr. Woodbridge. By several accounts, Dr. Eversman worked to improve the hospital from its previous neglected state. Captain Bingham recorded in his diary, "The hospital is a bad one. It is attended by our own surgeons but they do not seem to think it a duty but rather a favor & so they neglect the sick."[364] Before Dr. Eversman arrived, medicine was in short supply, and it was often impossible to get such medicine to prevent an outbreak of disease.[365] General Trimble noticed the change under Dr. Eversman: "The hospital was filthy & overrun with vermin. Since March [1864], Dr. Eversman asst. surg. [was] put in charge, new equipments supplied in full, and cleanliness produced."[366] Not everyone thought well of Dr. Eversman. Wharton Green described Dr. Eversman as "cruel and overbearing . . . by nature, [and] delighted in giving needless offence." [367]

Colonel I. G. W. Steedman of Alabama was in charge of the hospital for the prisoners. He reported to the federal surgeon, Dr. Woodbridge, who remained on the outside of the pen. Associated with Steedman in ministering aid to the prisoners were Captain Locke, Captain Sessions, Colonel Christian, and Colonel Maxwell.[368] Colonel Steedman was the Confederate surgeon for most of the existence of the prison on Johnson's Island. Steedman was confined to Johnson's Island in 1862, exchanged, captured again in 1863, and imprisoned once more at the island. He remained the prisoners' surgeon until March 20, 1865.[369] An Inspection Report in 1864 noted that the hospital consisted of: 1 surgeon, 1 hospital steward, 3 cooks, and 7 nurses, all Confederate prisoners.[370]

---

[362] *War of the Rebellion: A Compilation of the Official Records of the Union and Confederate Armies,* Series II, Vol. VI, 366.

[363] Green, Wharton J., *Recollections and Reflections, An Auto of Half a Century and More,* presses of Edwards and Broughton Printing Company 1906 189–190.

[364] Bingham, Robert, *Diary,* 67.

[365] Patterson, Edmund Dewitt, *Yankee Rebel,* 148.

[366] Trimble, Isaac Ridgeway. 19.

[367] Green, Wharton J., *Recollections and Reflections, An Auto of Half a Century and More,* presses of Edwards and Broughton Printing Company 189–190.

[368] Wash, W. A., *Camp, Field and Prison Life,* 352.

[369] Ibid., 322.

[370] *War of the Rebellion: A Compilation of the Official Records of the Union and Confederate Armies,* Series II, Vol. VII, 486.

On November 16, 1864, Steedman along with other Confederate doctors at the prison, sent in a report to the commandant that the diet of the prisoners was insufficient to maintain health. In the report, Steedman drew attention to the fact that, according to the medical journal, *Dalton's Physiology*, a man needed 38½ ounces of food per day to maintain health. Colonel Hoffman's official regulations allotted 34½ ounces to each Rebel prisoner. The surgeons carefully weighed the rations issued in October 1864, and determined that it consisted of 28½ ounces for each man for a 24-hour period. That was ten ounces less than recommended by science and six less than Hoffman's own regulations. Steedman stated to the commandant that "we believe that if [Hoffman's] order be faithfully executed health can be maintained for a long while." He concluded: "As physicians, we ask you, for humanity's sake, to compel your commissary to do his duty faithfully and honestly by issuing the ration we are entitled to; as prisoners of war, we demand it."[371] The food ration did not increase.

After the war ended, Colonel Steedman released a report on the health of the prisoners on Johnson's Island. The report covered his second term as chief surgeon of the prisoners from November 1863 to March 1865. During this time span, there were 1,047 cases that required hospitalization. The crowded conditions of the hospital required that only severe cases be admitted, with milder cases left in the blocks. Steedman made an estimate of the number of sick based on prescriptions filled at the dispensary. He estimated between 150 and 200 prescriptions were filled every day, with some days the number reaching a high of 400. This tally did not include in-house use of prescriptions in the hospital.[372]

Johnson's Island had smallpox break out on two separate occasions. On August 8, 1863, a group of prisoners arrived from Alton Prison bringing smallpox with them. They were immediately quarantined "in a tent in one corner of the prison yard" to stop the disease from spreading.[373] Captain Bingham described the outbreak with a cavalier attitude: "There is a faint excitement in the camp about smallpox. Some prisoners were bro[ough]t in yesterday & put in our block—3 had the disease. The other blocks are alarmed a little, but ours takes it easy."[374] He continued on August 29: "A new case broke out a day or so ago & several have left the block—two of my mess [mates]."[375] The authorities must have offered a vaccination after the smallpox scare. Lt. Colonel Pierson notified Hoffman that smallpox has been brought to the prison from prison transfers on three occasions. He reported seven cases of smallpox at that time. Lt. Colonel Pierson

---

[371] Wash, W. A., *Camp, Field and Prison Life*, 363–365.

[372] Ibid., 364–365.

[373] Ibid., 154.

[374] Bingham, Robert, *Diary*, 37.

[375] Wash, W. A., *Camp, Field and Prison Life*, 50.

recognized the danger: "There is much alarm in the prison, and cunning men in there are pretending to be more alarmed than they are. It is one way on the part of desperate men to urge desperate attempts. I have directed the doctor to do everything in the way of purification; also to have every prisoner vaccinated as soon as possible."[376] On November 11, one prisoner wrote home: "Vaccination also gives me a sore arm . . . as we have small pox here."[377] Another outbreak occurred in December 1864 and faded by January. At least seven inmates died of smallpox at Johnson's Island.

The most widespread disease on the camp during Steedman's tenure was dysentery. There were 258 cases of the disease admitted to the prison hospital. Since only the most severe cases were admitted to the hospital and the vast majority of cases were treated in the prisoner's block, the actual number of dysentery cases is not known. Few prisoners escaped an attack of dysentery. Steedman felt the frequency of this disease was a "direct result of the prison diet, bad water and the impure air of the crowded rooms." He commented that the "only successful plan of treatment was to effect a total change in the diet and habits of the patient. Give him light, nutritious, well cooked food, composed, as far as practicable, of vegetables and fresh meat; place him in a well ventilated, quiet ward, and give him pure water from the lake" and the disease would disappear. When a prisoner was brought to the hospital and treated, he would normally recover. However, when the patient was reintroduced to the poor quality rations, he would have a relapse.[378]

The second most common illness among the prisoners was chronic diarrhea. Steedman's report shows 125 cases admitted to the hospital. Since only the worst cases were admitted into the hospital, the actual number of cases is unknown. Chronic diarrhea was an incurable disease because of the conditions of the camp. Steedman reported, "I can not say that I ever saw a prisoner recover from [diarrhea] while in prison. It very soon became the great dread and fear of the prisoner. When the physician told him his case was one of confirmed chronic diarrhea, he regarded it as equivalent to the announcement of his death penalty, if he remained in prison."[379]

The federal and Confederate governments agreed to exchange the chronically sick prisoners in the summer of 1864. Many of the prisoners who were exchanged quickly recovered once reintroduced to a healthy diet. However, some exchanged prisoners never recovered and died as a result of the bad diet of Johnson's Island.[380]

There were 56 severe cases of scurvy reported in the prison during the time of Steedman's report. There were many milder cases that were treated in the prisoners'

---

[376] *War of the Rebellion: A Compilation of the Official Records of the Union and Confederate Armies*, Series II, Vol. 6, 391.

[377] *Swift Letters,* Rutherford B. Hayes November 11, 1863.

[378] Wash, W. A., *Camp, Field and Prison Life*, 365–367.

[379] Ibid.

[380] Ibid., 369–370.

blocks. Scurvy was easily treated with medicine and an introduction of fruits and vegetables. The hospital would receive extra vegetables from the federals, but still could provide the patient only a soup bowl each day. Steedman noted that even the worst cases of scurvy would recover in a month. As a result of the effectiveness of the hospital rations, not a single prisoner died of scurvy in the prison.[381]

One prisoner was allowed to go to Sandusky to get medical attention that could not be provided at the prison hospital. A Captain Frank Crocker "was attacked by serious eruption on his lower lip." General Terry released "Capt. Crocker on parole that he might have the services of a skilled surgeon in Sandusky. Capt. Crocker had the operation and stayed at the hotel until he was well enough to return to the island."[382]

The health of the prisoners at Johnson's Island was reasonable considering the circumstances. The health of the soldiers was sometimes poor when they entered the prison, some still recovering from wounds received in battle. The poor diet of the prisoners and the extreme cold contributed to the spread of disease and sickness; however, sickness never reached epidemic proportions.[383] In Camp Douglas, Chicago, 39 deaths resulted from scurvy. At Johnson's Island, scurvy never caused a single fatality. In each case, the prisoner was nourished back to health. The hospital was always given just enough supplies and food to maintain a reasonable health level of the hospital patients.[384]

Johnson's Island was the healthiest of the major prisoner of war camps in the North. Between 10,000 and 12,000 prisoners were housed at Johnson's Island with around 272 deaths.[385] The death rate for Johnson's Island was between 2 and 3 percent. This was far lower than the average death rate for Union prison camps, 12 percent.[386] Camp Douglas, near Chicago, had a total of 4,000 deaths, or a 15 percent death rate. The prison camp at Elmira, New York, had the worst record, with a 24 percent death rate.[387] The low death rate at Johnson's Island can be explained by the fact that the majority of men confined at Johnson's Island were officers, most with money and influential friends in both the North and the South. These officers could purchase more items and have more provisions shipped to them than their enlisted brethren at

---

[381] Ibid., 370–373.

[382] Todd, Westwood, *Reminiscences of Westwood Todd,* 323–324.

[383] Wash, W. A., *Camp, Field and Prison Life,* 366.

[384] Levy, George, *To Die in Chicago, Confederate Prisoners at Camp Douglas 1862–65,* (Gretna, LA: Pelican Publishing Company, 1999), 334–335.

[385] Speer, Lonnie R., *Portals to Hell: Military Prisons of the Civil War,* (Mechanicsburg, PA: Stackpole Books, 1997), 327.

[386] Ibid., xiv.

[387] Levy, George, *To Die in Chicago, Confederate Prisoners at Camp Douglas 1862–65,* 335.

camps like Camp Douglas and Elmira. The enlisted soldiers suffered more than did the officers at Johnson's Island because the other prisons were crowded, mass camps. Johnson's Island prison was a relatively small camp with a maximum occupancy at 3,256 compared to the huge camps at Elmira (9,441), Fort Delaware (12,600), and Point Lookout (22,000).[388]

DEATH AND BURIAL

Even in death conditions were not equal. If a prisoner had connections, the body might be sent home and escape eternal rest on Johnson's Island. This option for the wealthy ended on December 17, 1864, when an "order, brutal in every respect, posted on the bulletin board not allowing the remains of deceased prisoners to be removed in future for interment."[389] The southerners saw this order as depriving loved ones at home the possibilities of being reunited with their beloved soldier.

Most of the deceased were buried on the island. The cemetery was eventually established in the northeast area of the island. At first the dead were buried at various locations and records were not strictly kept, causing some graves to become lost. Reverend Thrasher commented on the poor record keeping: "Until recently this graveyard has been much neglected—no order has been observed in the burial of the dead, graves are scattered here and there in confusion—some marked by a headboard with the name of the deceased while others have nothing by which to tell who slumbers beneath." He began digging—"when about 18 inches below the surface we came to a box which admonished us that we were intruding upon the charnel house of some brother Rebel." When a prisoner died, about fifteen or more Rebels could go outside the fence to inter the deceased. If he was a Mason, it could be as many as seventy-five. The prisoners were paroled on their honor not to try to escape and to return to the prison when the burial ended.[390] Colonel Hundley noted: "Twenty-one of us were permitted to accompany the corpse on parole not to attempt to escape, nor to hold communication with anyone outside. A few Yankee soldiers gathered about us during the solemn ceremonies of burial, as well as some half dozen women, one of whom I saw weeping with true womanly sympathy."[391] Many times there would be no guard and escape was never attempted while on parole.[392]

The coffins varied in quality based on the wealth of the prisoner. He could be buried in a cheap pine box, a walnut coffin, or a metallic casket. Captain Bingham described the

---

[388] Speer, *Portals to Hell,* 324–330

[389] Inzer, John Washington, *The Diary of a Confederate Soldier,* 114.

[390] Thrasher Diary, *Sandusky Register,* May 22, 1938.

[391] Hundley, D. R., *Prison Echoes of the Great Rebellion,* 129.

[392] Patterson, Edmund Dewitt, *Yankee Rebel,* 142.

circumstances of Lt. Blunt's burial: "He had money enough to buy a walnut coffin, but his friends wished to get a metallic burial case—but we could get neither. The ice was too thin to allow anything heavy to be brought over—& so he had to be buried in a pine box—not coffin shaped & unplanned."[393] The Masons on Johnson's Island helped buy coffins and were instrumental in keeping the cemetery maintained (see Chapter VII).

PHYSICAL LIVING CONDITIONS

Johnson's Island had constant problems with mud, trash, human waste, and lack of proper policing. The island "was horribly muddy—this is the nastiest place I ever saw any how," Captain Bingham continued, "when it rains—I am going to have me a pair of stilts made."[394] The mud was a problem because of the soil composition, a solid stratum of rock blocking drainage, and improper surface drainage to the lake. Surgeon Steedman described the drainage ditches: "The drainage of the prison is of the simplest character, consisting of a large open ditch running around on the inside of the walls, with smaller ones, from twelve to eighteen inches deep running through the yard at regular intervals and emptying into the lake, which runs very nearly up to the eastern pen wall."[395] The drainage ditches were constantly collapsing, getting filled with rubbish or spillage from the sinks. Colonel Scovill (USA), inspecting the prison, reported to Hoffman (USA) that "the sinks are very offensive, and the drains are also becoming foul from the same cause. With the ditching that is now being done more [working wagon] teams are necessary for thorough policing. The one team we have inside is employed all the time carrying away the dirt from the ditches."[396] Hoffman ordered another team to be requisitioned immediately. The problem of the poor ditches was never fully remedied as an inspection report of March 2, 1865, advised: "I further recommend that all the ditches be cleaned and boarded and braced with timber to prevent the sides from falling in as at present; and that a main ditch, similarly planked and braced or walled with stone, be made, extending entirely across the prison enclosure from north to south and as near the center from east to west as the position of the buildings will allow."[397]

The prison was in a very dirty state. Colonel Webb commented on the sad state of affairs: "I do not exaggerate when I say that it is worse than a hog pen. All kinds of filth is allowed to accumulate around the buildings. This, with the black mud,

---

[393] Bingham, Robert, *Diary,* 2, 38.

[394] Bingham, Robert, *Diary,* 2, 44.

[395] Wash, W. A., *Camp, Field and Prison Life*, 353.

[396] *War of the Rebellion: A Compilation of the Official Records of the Union and Confederate Armies*, Series II, VII, 492.

[397] *War of the Rebellion: A Compilation of the Official Records of the Union and Confederate Armies*, Series II, VIII, 331.

renders it almost impossible to get from one building to another."[398] The policing of the prison was primarily the responsibility of the prisoners themselves. "A detail for general police is made for each day from both messes whose duty it is to keep everything clean outside the quarters and here you would sometimes find your humble friend shoveling filth into a cart and a Yankee slop boy giving orders." Webb continued, "In addition to this detail, another is made from each room whose duty it is to sweep up the rooms, cut and split wood and bring it into the house."[399] Captain Barziza explained, "We had all the work about the place to do—cook, wash, scour, dig pits and ditches, and load the truck carts."[400] In September 1864, "One hundred men, prisoners, from Camp Chase, all privates, arrived here to-day. The Yankees sent them here to have them police the prison, but when the subject was broached to them, they refused to do more than their proper proportion with the rest of the prisoners. The Yankees could not understand this manly pride of free men, and threatened to bring in a guard and force them to do the work. 'Bring in your guard' was the spirited reply, 'and we'll whip them out quicker than hell could scorch a feather!' The guard was not brought in, nor will it be."[401] To encourage the prisoners to work and make sure the prison was kept in a good state, the authorities offered to pay for some extra work. Colonel Inzer reported that the "infernal yankees detailed some 25 of our men to ditch the kitchen. All justly refused to work." But a month later his attitude changed for some reason as he "took a detail and built [a gravel] road in rear of the Block."

An inspection report on July 23, 1864, put the blame of the lack of cleanliness on Major Scovill (USA). He stated, "Seeing the camp, you would not know whether to be most astonished at the inefficiency of the officer in charge of the prisoners' camp or disgusted that men calling themselves gentlemen should be willing to live in such filth. The quarters are very dirty; the kitchens filthy. Major Scovill has charge, assisted by Captain Wells. The Major is somewhat of an invalid, not, however, so sick as to be confined to his quarters at all times; judging from his appearance, able to direct. A necessity exists for placing in charge of the prisoners an efficient, practical officer, who knows what good police is, and with decision sufficient to enforce his orders. With the improvements above recommended and an efficient officer to enforce the keeping the ditches for drainage empty, the sinks clean, and the quarters properly scrubbed and swept, the camp can be brought to such a standard as will be respectable."[402] Scovill,

---

[398] Webb, R. F., "Prison Life at Johnson's Island." *Histories of the Several Regiments and Battalions from North Carolina in the Great War 1861–65,* 672.

[399] Webb, R. F., "Prison Life at Johnson's Island." *Histories of the Several Regiments and Battalions from North Carolina in the Great War 1861–65,* 668.

[400] Barziza, Decimus et Ultimus, *The Adventures of a Prisoner of War, 1863–1864,* 77.

[401] Hundley, D. R., *Prison Echoes of the Great Rebellion,* 130.

[402] *War of the Rebellion: A Compilation of the Official Records of the Union and Confederate Armies,* Series II, Vol. VII, 484.

on October 23, 1864, sent a report to Hoffman stating, "The police of quarters and grounds in the prison is good, with the exception of part of Block 10 and one room in Block 4, and measures have been taken to compel the occupants of the block and room above to have them put into order."[403]

BATHING

During the summer time, the prisoners were allowed to bathe in the lake. In many diaries, the prisoners documented that this little pleasure perked up morale. Edmund Patterson scribed on June 17, 1864, that a special order from the post commander now permits the prisoners to go out in the lake bathing, two or three times a week. This was seen as breaking the monotony of the everyday routine of prison life.[404] This meant that the prison gates were opened for bathing two or three times a week, not that each prisoner bathed that often. The bathing occurred one block at a time, which meant the prisoner would get a lake bath once a month. Major Caldwell commented on this same day he took a "Glorious bath in the lake."[405] W. A. Wash described the delight of the privilege: "The 2nd day of July [1863] we were allowed to go swimming in the lake. The water was clear and pleasant, and one hundred yards from the shore was not over waist deep, which made it delightful bathing. A guard was placed on the bank to watch us, and pop a fellow if [he] proved too good a swimmer, and made off for the mainland."[406]

PARASITES

The prisoners at Johnson's Island were constantly battling the infestation of lice, also referred to as the foot soldier's unwelcome companion. For this reason, whenever new prisoners were brought into the compound, a scrutinizing inspection for lice was required prior to their entering their assigned block. They would have to go through a rigorous delousing procedure. The inmate was ordered to scrub in scalding hot water while his clothes were boiled in the very cooking vats in which their meals were prepared.

Captain W. Gart Johnson describes his first memories of Johnson's Island and the de-lousing procedure:

"After handshakes and greetings one of them yelled out: 'Say, Johnson got any bugs about your clothes?'

---

[403] *War of the Rebellion: A Compilation of the Official Records of the Union and Confederate Armies,* Series II, Vol. VII, 1025–1026.

[404] Patterson, Edmund Dewitt, *Yankee Rebel,* 172.

[405] Caldwell, James Parks, *A Northern Confederate at Johnson's Island Prison,* 122

[406] Wash, W. A., *Camp, Field and Prison Life,* 103, 156.

'Of course. What else could you expect from a fellow who has been lying around for a month in the same clothes and with no chance to wash?'

'I thought so. Right this way to the washhouse before you go into any of our rooms. See that kettle of boiling water? Off with your duds, except hat and shoes. Pile them in there. See that tub? Get into it and scrub.'"[407]

Delousing was a very tedious and frustrating procedure. The lack of pesticides to completely eradicate the pest made the task practically impossible. The boiling process was very labor intensive, and the lice were a very resilient foe. Another prisoner, Captain Bingham, had to go through this process twice because of an error. "I preformed quite a feat in the washing line—today—took off my shirt & drawers after breakfast washed & boiled them & had them on again before dinner. They were dried on the grass which is full of lice . . . [and] . . . they were [re]infested." He went through the process again without drying his clothes on the ground and stated in his diary "they are clear of inhabitants, much to my relief." Upon occasion the blocks would be scoured with boiling water to neutralize the problem, which was quite a task.[408] Block 13 waged a constant war with the lice. It was the worst of all the blocks as new prisoners usually arrived there first and the large open overcrowded rooms offered perfect breeding grounds for the pesky parasites.

Bedbugs were another pest the men of Johnson's Island had to endure. Captain Bingham noted "when it gets warm the bedbugs come out from their hibernation & make rapid & destructive raids on poor defenseless men."[409] The common remedy was the same treatment as the lice. Colonel Hundley said, "By scalding our bunks once a week, we ought to get rid of the troublesome bedbugs altogether."[410] Luther R. Mills made reference to the infestation in his diary: "Any description of JI, which does not contain no mention of bed bugs would be very incomplete. The barracks were ceiled, and were several years old. During cold weather the bugs did not trouble us much, but toward the latter part of May they became terrible. My bunk was papered with Harper's Weekly, and if at any time I struck the walls with any object, a red spot would appear as large as the object striking the wall. We left the barracks and slept in the streets."[411] These hungry parasites added to the boundless obstacles and discomforts in which the inmates had to combat on a daily basis.

---

[407] *Confederate Veteran II.,* Nashville, Tennessee, 242.

[408] Bingham, Robert, *Diary,* 38.

[409] Bingham, Robert, *Diary,* 2, 45.

[410] Hundley, D. R., *Prison Echoes of the Great Rebellion,* 108.

[411] Mills, Luther Rice, Papers, Ohio Historical Society, 7.

COLD WEATHER

The prison on Johnson's Island was situated on the northern edge of Ohio off the shores of Lake Erie. The government wanted this prison far from the action in the South. They feared raids and rescue attempts from the Confederate forces in Kentucky. As a consequence of this decision, the Confederate soldiers were placed in a bitterly cold climate. The prisoners were not accustomed to this degree of cold and were unprepared for the constant below-freezing temperatures. The island acquired a reputation for its cold temperatures and bitterly cold gusts of wind. These two characteristics combined to create hardship and discomfort among the prisoners.

Many of the southern prisoners perceived the selection of this location as intentionally cruel. Prisoner Henry Kyd Douglas stated: "I do not think any fair man of the North will attempt to defend the selection of Lake Erie as a winter prison for Southern soldiers, any more than he would have excused the selection of the malarial regions of southern Florida or Louisiana as a summer prison for Northern troops."[412] He continued, "Johnson's Island was just the place to convert visitors to the theological belief of the Norwegian that Hell has torments of cold instead of heat."[413] The prisoners could not stay huddled inside their blocks all day. Each morning, every prisoner had to muster outside for roll call, sometimes standing in the snow and freezing wind for up to an hour. These outdoor roll calls were enough to chill the prisoners to the bone. This chill added to the misery of the winter days. At night, all fires had to be extinguished, Pierson's Rule #6, which just added to the misery of the unrelenting cold nights.

One of the coldest days in the prison was New Year's Day of 1864, when the thermometer reportedly fell to 28 degrees below zero.[414] One prisoner, in a letter written on that bleak day, stated his dislike of the weather when he wrote across the bottom, "I wish I were a polar bear."[415] Felix Hays Blackman wrote of his unfamiliarity with the cold of that New Year's Day: "The weather has been so excessively cold that one could scarcely keep warm. I thought I had some idea of cold weather but since feeling the [cold] or rather trying to keep from feeling the cold, I am satisfied there is more [truth] in Sunny South than I ever dreamed."[416]

The federal government made an inspection and report in March 1865 because of the accusations of the prisoners of the extreme cold on Johnson's Island. The report

---

[412] Douglas, Henry Kyd, *I Rode with Stonewall*, 262.

[413] Ibid., 260.

[414] Douglas, Henry Kyd, *I Rode with Stonewall*, 261.

[415] Douglas, Henry Kyd. *Letters.*, December 31, 1863, Copy at Rutherford B. Hayes Library.

[416] Blackman, Felix Hays, *Letters to Maggie Sexton (1863–1865)*, January 4, 1864.

stated that the federal government had been accused of inhumanity in putting prisoners of war so far north and wanted to give temperature reports of that area. These statistics were to give evidence that the climate was not extreme, quoting average temperatures to be 28.08°F for January, 29.47°F for February, and 34.72°F for March.[417] This report failed to acknowledge the important deficiencies of the camp, such as inadequate shelter, fuel wood, clothing, and food. Nor did it take into effect the fact that the men were used to the warmer winter temperatures of the South. One member of the Hoffman's Battalion, the guard unit at the prison, acknowledged the conundrum: "The rigor of our Northern winters had, no doubt, its effect on Confederate prisoners, and colored somewhat their impressions of prison life and treatment."[418]

It was very common for Sandusky Bay and the lake to freeze. Colonel Murphey commented that "it is a grand view to look upon the lake. As far as the eye can extend it is one unbroken sea of ice, so brilliantly white when the sun is shining as to be painful to the naked eye."[419] When the bay froze over, prisoners would have to walk across the ice, which was difficult for those who had no experience with ice. Lieutenant Phillips (USA) related a story of the southern gentlemen crossing the ice: "The bay had frozen over, but not hard enough to bear teams [of horses]. The ice was smooth and treacherous. Some of the poor fellows were without overcoats, and none of them appeared to be accustomed to ice. Many grew cautious as their experience increased, and before the crossing was accomplished it was not uncommon to see them on their hands and knees slowly but safely making their way across suspiciously smooth stretches."[420] The cold would stop the delivery of wood. Once the wood supply diminished, a dual problem emerged: First, the fires in the stoves would eventually burn out, causing the temperature to drop inside the blocks to the same temperature as outside. Second, the food could not be cooked, so the prisoners would have empty stomachs in which to fight the incessant cold.[421]

Because of the poor construction and maintenance of the blocks, these buildings did not give much protection from the cold. One prisoner stated that "snow would filter through the roof and cover the bunks and blankets with a layer of snow."[422] Henry Kyd Douglas stated that "on cold nights two men would squeeze into one bunk so as to double blankets, would wrap themselves up head and feet, and in the morning break through crackling ice, formed by the congealing of the breath

---

[417] Frohman, Charles E., *Rebels on Lake Erie*, 34–35.

[418] Phillips, George M., *Glimpses of the Nation's Struggle*, 246.

[419] Murphey, V. S., *Diary*, 121.

[420] Phillips, George M., *Glimpses of the Nation's Struggle*, 246.

[421] Patterson, Edmund Dewitt, *Yankee Rebel*, 146.

[422] Knauss, William H., *The Story of Camp Chase*, 241.

that escaped, as one has seen on the blankets of horses in sleighing time."[423] Some men would put on all their clothes, wrap themselves in blankets and never leave the bunks. Others would walk briskly up and down the halls trying to warm their bodies through exertion. Major Caldwell added that the ice would find its way inside: "The bay was frozen over solidly and exhaling a steamy vapor from its entire surface. My ink froze, in a stoneware bottle, forced out the cork, and found its way over my best pair of breeches." He noted the thermometer outside of the block was at 20 degrees below zero.[424]

Every room was supposed to have a stove for warmth. This was not always the case. Several prisoners complained of a lack of stoves in their respective rooms. Colonel Inzer noted in his diary the problem with stoves, "Yanks brought in two stoves to the Block. We got stove pipe today but no stove." After waiting twenty-four days for their promised stove, Inzer and his roommates took matters into their own hands by building a chimney, or fire place that produced a pleasant fire.[425] Captain Bingham reported on October 7, 1863: "It is cold & cheerless outside—& cold and cheerless inside. The stoves are on the way, but have not come. They were ordered some time ago the Yankees say."[426] The problem was not resolved by November 1864, even though the daily temperatures were becoming more frigid. A prisoner noted in his diary that many rooms are still without stoves.[427]

The stoves located in the center of each room were inadequate to handle the massive drop in temperatures. Felix Blackman described how the stoves did not keep the blocks warm and heated rocks were distributed to his mates: "I was sitting up with a sick friend a night or two since and while he slept I attempted to write. But when I would write a sentence my fingers would ache so with cold that I was forced to stop and hold them to the red hot stove before I could proceed. This with frequent calls for hot rocks I concluded it was a serious job and decided to wait for warmer weather. Poor excuse . . . but it has been really so cold that a master effort was required to remain from the stove or out of bed long enough to write even a page."[428]

To compound the problem of cold weather, wood was not consistently issued. Firewood was issued and the prisoners were allowed, on occasion, to go out and chop down some trees for themselves. Colonel Webb wrote in his diary, "wood is hauled

---

[423] Douglas, Henry Kyd, *I Rode with Stonewall,* 261.

[424] Caldwell, James Parks, *A Northern Confederate at Johnson's Island Prison,* Jan 1, 1864. Page number.

[425] Inzer, John Washington, *The Diary of a Confederate Soldier,* 102–106.

[426] Bingham, Robert, *Diary,* 77.

[427] Caldwell, James Parks, *A Northern Confederate at Johnson's Island Prison,* 157.

[428] Blackman, Felix Hays, *Letters to Maggie Sexton,* February 19, 1864.

from the outside every day at the rate of one four-horse load to each block, which is equally divided according to the number of stoves."[429]

Regardless of this policy, wood was always in short supply. Anything was fair game for a source of firewood when the issued stocks became exhausted. The Confederate officers "by cutting stumps and a few trees in the yard have a small stock of wood on hand." Because the "mean yankees refuse to issue wood for two weeks."[430] When it became extremely cold, tables, benches, and anything made of wood were in danger of being thrown into the fire to meet the increasing demand for wood.[431]

DEPRESSION

The inmates at Johnson's Island suffered from boredom, loneliness, the lack of privacy, nostalgia, and depression. Like any prisoner in confinement with limited access to the outside world, time seemed to move slowly with the uncertainty of when they would be released to the outside world. They needed to regain some control over their life and their actions. Being predominantly the upper class of the South, these men were forced into an unfamiliar predicament of being at the mercy of other men. It was unusual for a southern officer to be out of a position of power. From his home plantation life, to commanding men on the battlefield, the Confederates now found themselves enslaved by a Yankee master. Without feeling the guilt of a criminal, these men felt that their confinement was unjust.

Other than the occasional event, most prison life at Johnson's Island was marked by the repetition of continuance. Jans T. Norman tersely stated. "Our life here is very monotonous, no variety of scene & action. The history of one day is the history of all."[432] After the time used for roll call, dining, and chores, all that was left was the monotony of disposable time. There were just not enough new events to distract from a sedentary life. At night they were not allowed to move about or visit friends. On cold or rainy days the prisoners huddled inside. Even if the weather was nice, conditions might prevent freedom of movement. Captain Barziza noted, "The yard was one vast mud-hole, knee deep, and consequently, we could take little or no exercise."[433] Because of never ending boredom, men could feel their mental state slipping. Lieutenant Houston noted: "I was so unfortunate as to fall asleep. Far from being refreshed by the nap, I never felt more worthless, more completely prostrated, than the present

---

[429] Webb, R. F., *Histories of the Several Regiments and Battalions from North Carolina in the Great War,* 668.

[430] Inzer, John Washington., *The Diary of a Confederate Soldier,* 108.

[431] Patterson, Edmund Dewitt., *Yankee Rebel,* 147.

[432] Norman, William M., *A Portion of My Life,* Jans, 231.

[433] Barziza, Decimus et Ultimus, *The Adventures of a Prisoner of War, 1863–1864,* 81.

time. Everything seems to be wrong side up—ideas running riot and [my] brains dashing themselves out against [my] skull."[434]

Each night, at half past nine, all lights had to be extinguished inside the prison blocks. This was when loneliness engulfed the prisoner the most. A prisoner noted that after lights-out, "All within our walls [was] dark and silent, save the rays of a dozen lamps reflected over the prison yard and the lonely tread of the sentinels on the parapet."[435] Captain Barziza noted that "the most heavy and lonely hours I ever passed were during the winter nights. In the dark, around a smoldering fire, some of the most restless ones would sit and talk and smoke and chew, and lamenting their hard lot, watch the creeping hours as they would be called out by the sentinels. Visions of home and loved ones, of comfort, liberty, and plenty would crowd into the bosom, and oppress the sad captive. Many a time have I with others, sat up, hour after hour, thus in the dark, and longed for the morning to come."[436]

The inmates were lonely in the crowded rooms because they dreamed of being in happier places and with familiar faces. The prisoners wanted to see their old friends and their families and be surrounded by loved ones. W. A. Wash composed this eloquent synopsis of daydreaming: "many one of us gave up the day to reflections concerning home, the happiness once experienced there and the prospect of ever again greeting the loved ones and finding such a home as we once had with little effort one can forget passing events and fall into a reverie to rehearse and pass before the vision of imagination the panorama of past life. As in a dream, the joys are sometimes almost real, but alas: something startles us from the reverie to find only fleeting phantoms where was once genuine life and happiness."[437]

The irony of the prisoners' loneliness was that a crowd of inmates constantly surrounded each one. The prisoner could not roam anywhere within the pen without being in a crowd of inmates. The very circumstance of never being alone caused the feeling of isolation to increase. Edmund Patterson noted the worst feature of prison life was that it was impossible for one to get away from the crowd and the bustle of prison life. He believed that there was not a spot within the walls of this prison to have a quiet moment for contemplation.[438] Many letters and diaries have entries regarding the lack of privacy and the continual interruptions. Felix Blackman asked, "Why don't others enjoy their own thoughts and allow me to the bliss of my own?"[439] Instead of

---

[434] Houston, Thomas D., *Prisoner of War Letters : 1863–1865. From Johnson's Island.* 37.

[435] Wash, W. A., *Camp, Field and Prison Life*, 154.

[436] Barziza, Decimus et Ultimus, *The Adventures of a Prisoner of War, 1863–1864,* 81.

[437] Wash, W. A. *Camp, Field and Prison Life*, 90–91.

[438] Patterson, *Yankee Rebel*, 171–172.

[439] Blackman, Felix Hays, *Letters to Maggie Sexton (1863–1865),* November 8, 1863.

being intentionally interrupted, disturbance continuously got in the way as Captain Bingham related in his diary, there are "40 or 50 men in our room & there is scarcely a moment when someone is not tramping over the floor—it shakes very much."[440] There was virtually no escape from the crowd. One prisoner, who was becoming a recluse and living in the attic of Block 3, stated how pleasurable it was to get away from the crowd: "One who has never been constrained to herd promiscuously with hundreds of his own sex for any length of time, deprived of all privacy, of all uninterrupted freedom of thought, can form no adequate conception of the satisfaction and downright happiness which the poor comforts of even a garret . . . can bestow."[441]

On almost a daily basis, the prisoners contemplated their fate. They felt they were useless. They wanted the opportunity to be on the battlefield defending their homes, yet found themselves imprisoned among the people they despised. Colonel Lewis, a Confederate preacher, stated, "Who can know, save those who were there, how the heart sunk . . . at the contemplation of our home and loved ones given to merciless aliens and strangers, and we unable to raise an arm to save those precious treasures."[442]

Many young men could see that they were becoming embittered by their fruitless existence: "I am worn out with this prison life. I feel that I am growing old before my time. My disposition has become soured against the world generally, and I am afraid that if a change does not come over the spirit of my dream, that I will soon get to be a very unlovable object." The prisoners worried that they were being permanently changed by their prison experience and questioned if their loved ones would even want them once they returned home.[443] As time wore on, the prisoners' mental health sunk lower and lower. Captain Barziza described how time wore heavily on the prisoner's mind. "He who has been in confinement knows that the longer he remains so, the more irksome it becomes. One becomes perfectly miserable; the mind cannot be fixed upon the same subject any length of time; restlessness, anxiety and dejection fill the breast, and one becomes almost cowered."[444]

The lack of privacy, the loneliness, and the feeling of uselessness caused the inmates to fall into spells of depression. These factors all compounded to create hate. Most of the prisoners resented what was happening to them and felt that the Yankees were to blame for their misery. Colonel Hundley, who had turned into a recluse, stated his contempt for Yankees and the world: "I have with great egotism constituted myself a judge, and the

---

[440] Bingham, Robert, *Diary,* 32.

[441] Hundley, D. R., *Prison Echoes of the Great Rebellion,* 147–148.

[442] Wash, W. A., *Camp, Field and Prison Life,* vi.

[443] Patterson, *Yankee Rebel,* 189.

[444] Barziza, Decimus et Ultimus, *The Adventures of a Prisoner of War, 1863–1864,* 81.

world has been summoned to appear before my august tribunal to be judged. And this is the wise decision I have rendered: That it is a very hollow world, a very cruel world, a very shallow world, a very deceitful world, a very vain and selfish world."[445] Another inmate released his frustration in his diary, "I am fully of the opinion that the Yankees are the meanest people on earth. Was always a despiser of the North, but now I live to hate Yankees. I am willing to spend my days in killing Yankee vandals."[446]

The depression and anger at being held captive led to poor social conditions inside the bullpen. Colonel Webb of North Carolina described the mental conditions of the camp. "The moral and social condition of our men is deplorable. I have not heard as much profanity in my regiment as I have heard from the officers in my little room here. With this there is very little dignity or self-respect. Politeness or chaste conversation is out of the question. Selfishness predominates, and many bitter words and angry looks are exchanged."[447]

FIGHTING

The pent-up frustrations of prison life, stress from bad news from home, and the deteriorating situation at the front created tension among the prisoners. This tension escalated itself into fights between inmates. To do so put both participants in danger of being shot by the sentinels under Pierson's Order #7, which prohibited fighting. Not very many fights were recorded in diaries in 1862 and 1863, but as the time dragged on and the prospect of exchange disappeared, fights began to break out in 1864 and 1865. Several fights resulted in Rebels being admitted to the hospital. Colonel Murphey showed his disdain for his comrades' actions: "Two Rebs had a severe fight resulting in one having cut the other. It is ridiculous and shameful."[448] On February 19, 1865, a prisoner, Harmon W. Morgan, died in the hospital. He was stabbed by Thomas F. Berry several days before. Both of the men were from Kentucky. Major Caldwell noted that "Berry has been ordered into close confinement (irons, some say) & will be tried."[449] In Block 5, a Lieutenant Black was struck by a chair on the side of his face. The blow fractured his jaw and endangered his eye.[450]

---

[445] Ibid., 141.

[446] Inzer, John Washington, *The Diary of a Confederate Soldier : John Washington Inzer 1834–1928* 68.

[447] Webb, R. F., *Histories of the Several Regiments and Battalions from North Carolina in the Great War,* 672.

[448] Murphey, V. S., *Diary,* 198.

[449] Caldwell, James Parks, *A Northern Confederate at Johnson's Island Prison : The Civil War Diary of James Parks Caldwellh,* 183.

[450] Patterson, Edmund Dewitt. *Yankee Rebel: The Civil War Journal of Edmund DeWitt Patterson,* 185.

Conclusion

Despite the starvation and the cold weather, the overall health of the prisoners at Johnson's Island was reasonably good. The hospital was kept at a level that would maintain minimal health of the prison. A sick prisoner would be given just enough care to return him to the prison population. As a result, the death rate at Johnson's Island was far less than the other northern prisons. The prisoners' physical health was maintained but their mental health was left to their own resources. Most of the prisoners suffered from bouts of depression, but lived to recover after their release.

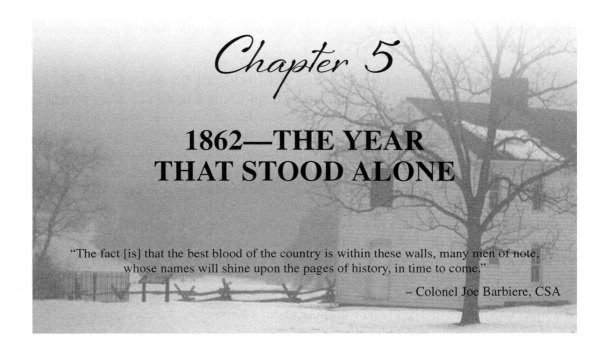

Chapter 5

1862—THE YEAR
THAT STOOD ALONE

"The fact [is] that the best blood of the country is within these walls, many men of note,
whose names will shine upon the pages of history, in time to come."

– Colonel Joe Barbiere, CSA

THE BEGINNING

The year 1862 was a unique time for Johnson's Island. This was the first year of operation for the camp and the first year of almost continuous battles for the Civil War. The leadership skills of Major Pierson, which Colonel Hoffman questioned, would be tested for the first time. Would he pass the test? Hoffman's Battalion would see their baptism by fire, not by the roar of cannons, but by the influx of thousands of captured prisoners. Would they do their duty professionally and proficiently?

The residents of Sandusky were anxiously awaiting the arrival of the first Rebels. The *Sandusky Register* on March 12, 1862, gave notice to the citizens that any day now, Rebels would be brought to the prison, and it would become operational. The article stated, "the next thing we know, the Secesh will be upon us. All we have to say is—let them come. We can stand it. If they never had any idea of a stiff northern breeze, the first thing they know, after they get to their quarters over there, their neglected education will be completed."[451]

On April 10, 1862, the first railroad train of captured Confederates arrived in Sandusky with the final destination of Johnson's Island. They were marched, under guard, to the wharf to board the steamboat to take them to the island. As they marched

---

[451] Frohman, Charles E., *Rebels on Lake Erie*, 7.

through town, curious residents gawked and jeered the captured Rebels. The *Sandusky Register* reported on the event:

A special train on S[andusky] D[ayton] & C[incinnati] RR arrived at 6 P.M. yesterday with about 200 rebel prisoners from Camp Chase. . . . They were clad variously. Some had the characteristic butternut color, and some did not. Some wore blue coats with brass buttons; others had on coats of no particular color, and as for buttons, we saw none. We learn that they are all officers, and conclude that they were not in full uniform yesterday.

Some of them had something of the bearing and carriage of gentlemen and some had a different carriage. Some had the "don't care a dime" swagger of bloods, some were sullen in appearance, while others seemed to forget themselves in their curiosity to see the sights. Some of them were tall and some of them were short, and most of them were more short than tall. Some tried to be jocose. Some were sullen some were mischievous.

Taking an average of them, we should have a man about 30 years of age, 5 feet 9 ½ inches in height and weighing about 140 pounds. An average of their features would be marked with a case-hardened sort of expression, shaded with a malicious frown. We suppose they represent the flower of the chivalry of the South. If there was anything about them superior to the greasy mechanics of the North, which they affect to despise, we could not see it.

We suppose they are men after their sort, and have some of the feelings belonging to mankind generally, and had they, together with all of their kind, had more good sense and less chivalry, we presume they might be at home, attending to their affairs, and our country would have escaped one of the saddest wars of modern days.[452]

The prisoners made the quick trip across the bay. Ahead lay the island that would be their home for an indeterminate amount of time. Their feelings were mixed with foreboding, excitement, and anxiety over the conditions they might encounter. To impress upon the prisoners that their situation was beyond their control until the authorities decided to release them, the prisoners "were marched between files of soldiers from the boat landing up to the gates of the prison." Flavel Barber of Tennessee was one of the first to arrive from Camp Chase, as "the gates were thrown opened and we walked into a large enclosure of twelve acres surrounded by a high plank wall. In this enclosure were built, eight wooden blocks of Barracks, four on each side of the street, [plus a hospital barrack]."[453] Colonel Barbiere described the examination of

---

[452] *Sandusky Register*, April 11, 1862.

[453] Barber, Flavel C., *Holding the Line: The Third Tennessee Infantry*, 49.

clothing: "Upon entering the prison a sergeant approaches and desires to know if any are suffering for clothing and, if a candidate responds in the affirmative . . . furnishes a new pair of pants, a light blue blouse, a little cap, a pair of drawers and a shirt. There are but few of us who 'got the blues' . . . and not over a half dozen became ornamented with what we deemed badges of servitude."[454]

The men were then assigned to a block, one man to each bunk. Blocks 1 through 9 were available and were filled first. Blocks 10 through 12 were in the final stages of construction when the prison was opened and were "left vacant for future inmates, the results of future Federal victories."[455] Block 13, the crudest block, was built last. Prisoners, about 200 at a time, started arriving "every few weeks, some from Camp Chase, some from Pea Ridge and Missouri, some from Shiloh and Corinth, some from Huntsville, Alabama, some cavalry from Lebanon and other points."[456] By mid-July, prisoners could move into Blocks 10, 11, and 12. Flavel Barber and friends "procured permission from Major Pierson to occupy a vacant room in number twelve."[457] They hoped to have a little more privacy, but prisoners continued to arrive and fill all the blocks. In August, all prisoners had to move out of blocks 11, 12, and 13 to make room for 300 to 400 political prisoners from Kentucky and Tennessee.[458]

Once the prisoners were situated in their quarters, they noticed their surroundings and the beauty of the island. Major James Poe described his view: "To the east my eye beholds nothing but the broad waters of the lake. The sun rises as from a watery bed, but sets behind the thick timber of the Island, the western portion being thick, heavy timbered with sugar trees and sugar maple, ash, walnut, and buckeye trees."[459] Flavel Barber spent many an hour watching the activities of the bay: "The view from the lake was always novel to me. Sometimes the water was smooth as glass, again the waves were dashing furiously against the shore; sometimes half a dozen steamboats were ploughing their way in as many different directions, leaving behind them great trails of thick black smoke [and] . . . at the edge of the horizon, . . . the bare masts of some schooner stood straight up against the sky like the skeleton of some phantom ship."[460]

---

[454] Barbiere, Joe., *Scraps from the Prison Table, At Camp Chase and Johnson's Island*, 193–194.

[455] Barber, Flavel C., *Holding the Line: The Third Tennessee Infantry*, 54.

[456] Ibid.

[457] Barber, Flavel C., *Holding the Line: The Third Tennessee Infantry*, 54.

[458] Poe, James T., *The Raving Foe: The Civil War Diary of Major James T. Poe, CSA*, 49–50.

[459] Poe, James T., *The Raving Foe: The Civil War Diary of Major James T. Poe, CSA*, 39.

[460] Barber, Flavel C., *Holding the Line: The Third Tennessee Infantry*, 53.

ACTIVITIES AND INCIDENTS OF 1862

A daily routine was established with "breakfast at six, dinner at half-past eleven, and supper at half-past five, P.M. We retire to our quarters at 'retreat,' and blow out our lights at 'taps,' the former being beat at sundown, the later at ten P.M. and then all is quiet, until the treadmill of daily movements begins with the next day's sun."[461] Another prisoner related his experience of his daily routine: "We rose every morning about seven o'clock, ate breakfast very soon after, answered to roll call at eight. At nine the newspapers came in and the next three hours were spent in reading and discussing their contents. At twelve we had dinner, then we took our siesta, and lay about in the shade."[462]

The prisoners on Johnson's Island in 1862 had the best food of all the years at the prison. R. L. McClung commented: "We were very well fed, got plenty to eat and drink and were permitted for a good while to purchase anything we wanted from the sutler."[463] Major Poe thought the prisoners got "plenty to eat here such as it is, viz, loaf bread, beef, pork, coffee, sugar, and sometimes dried beans. We get very tired of being confined to one diet. If the question was asked what we will have tomorrow, for dinner, we can easily tell for we know that it will be the same old diet."[464] Colonel Barbiere described the dining arrangements: "In our room, there are ten bare, plank tables, each adorned with ten tin plates, an equal number of tin cups, two-pronged forks, a dull knife, and an iron spoon, a chunk of bread about the size of your fist, to each plate, which allowance is all you get at that meal. In the center of the table is the meat allowance for ten men, seven and a half pounds of fat if bacon, and twelve and a half pounds of mostly bone if beef."[465]

The milkman usually arrived after breakfast. Colonel Barbiere described the spectacle: "This arrival creates some excitement, as the supply rarely equals the demand and all those who desire the fluid are compelled to place their vessels in a line, beginning at the post at the guard-line in front of the big gate. The vessels, present amusing spectacle, canteens, preserve jars, bottles, jugs, cups, pitches, bowls and crocks of all shapes and size; each officer on the alert to see that some other individuals vessel is not slipped nearer the milk-cast." He continued: "At 8 A. M., the vegetable man comes in, with a dray load of onions, beets and potatoes. He is immediately surrounded by the prisoners who have the money to buy with, and sells out by nine."[466]

---

461 Barbiere, Joe., *Scraps from the Prison Table, At Camp Chase and Johnson's Island*, 106.

462 Barber, Flavel C., *Holding the Line: The Third Tennessee Infantry*, 55.

463 R. L. McClung, "Prisoners on Johnson's Island," *Confederate Veteran*, 6.

464 Poe, James T., *The Raving Foe: The Civil War Diary of Major James T. Poe, CSA*, 40.

465 Barbiere, Joe., *Scraps from the Prison Table, At Camp Chase and Johnson's Island*, 105.

466 Barbiere, Joe., *Scraps from the Prison Table, At Camp Chase and Johnson's Island*, 126.

Food was not the only important commodity to arrive during the day; mail was eagerly awaited. After lunch, the mail arrived for the prisoners at Johnson's Island. The chief of each mess received mail in bundles for his men. He would stand at the foot of the stairs and call out the lucky ones who received mail from home with "anxious faces" hoping to have his name called. With the chance of receiving a letter, "all are keenly alive to hear the news from home and the loved ones. Some are made happy, others go back to their rooms disappointed."[467]

The prisoners had to find ways and means to pass the time. Captain Drummond commented: "We have gone through our regular routine of only playing Ball, Cards, Dominoes etc. etc. anything to pass away time."[468] The prisoners would go for walks, read, play poker, and watch the guards outside, anything to keep themselves occupied. Baseball was another favorite. On July 5, a match game of two teams and eleven players each was played. Men who had known the adrenaline rush of battle had a hard time living a sedentary life in confinement. This inactivity created a dirt clod throwing battle, which broke out on June 25. Colonel Joseph Barbiere described the combat:

> The amusement of the sham fight on the Campus, is one of the most exciting of the many efforts, to while away the time, and break the monotony of our confinement. The fortification consists of a wood-pile, with a crest of sticks. The engagement generally opens not by knocking a chip off an antagonist's shoulder, but by throwing several chips at the enemy, who is admirably poised upon a billet of wood, awaiting the attack and the opening of the foe's batteries, which are masked. The attack is frequently violent, and the character of the missiles effective, and if the shot are not hot, the work is. Lieutenant McWhorter, brother of Captain McWhorter, who is one of the most valiant of the combatants, and hurls his projectiles like he had a sling of the ancients, and uses his forces with the power of Archimedes. Mac, as we term him, is a gallant young man, and the life of the upper part of . . . Block 1. He is the most terrific of the battery corps, and is as good as a baker's dozen in the evening attacks, always sustaining his ground in the many combats in which he has participated. The fight draws to a close, with a single combat, between Captain Leslie Ellis, of the Tenth Tennessee, and Lieutenant Andrews, of Alabama. All others cease hostilities, and leave to these two representatives of the opposing hosts. Lieutenant Andrews makes a happy "hit," and . . . Ellis retreats, to a flight of steps, he again returns to the attack, anticipating a scarcity of ammunition, on the part of his adversary, who is beating a hasty retreat, the captain feeling his want of [clods], is furnished by an ambushed friend, with a new shell, with

[467] Ibid.

[468] Drummond, Edward W., *Confederate Yankee: The Journal of Edward William Drummond: A Confederate Soldier from Maine*, 85.

which he now pursues his fleeing enemy, who seems aware of the character of the missile, brought to bear upon him . . . the shells still flew around the head of the merry Andrew, until an unlucky one, with well-directed aim, struck the devoted youth upon the most exposed part of his person, forcing an exclamation. He was seriously, but not dangerously, wounded, a few moments serving to recuperate him, and the attack was renewed. A well-directed shot, from Lieutenant Andrews, struck the rear of Captain Ellis' fortifications, rendering him hors du combat, for the time being an armistice was agreed to.[469]

Periodically, a novel sight would bring on onlookers to break up the routine. Drummond explained: "We have today had an opportunity of watching the process of mowing with a machine, a sight unseen by many a one here before."[470] A social club, the Muggin's Club was established, the initiation fee was one cent. The President was Captain Thompson who was "one of our most erudite and finished scholars."[471] The purpose of the club is not clear other than to have camaraderie with a select group of their choosing.

After dinner and lights out, the prisoners had to entertain themselves without leaving the blocks. Captain Drummond wrote:

"Imagine the imitation of voices of all the Beasts and fowls in the world among over one thousand men. As soon as dark sets in some dog will bark that wakes up the fowls and such a general cackling and crowing you never heard. There are men here that can imitate anything from a Jack Ass to a sparrow. Whenever something good comes out a shout goes up from the whole garrison which shakes the air and has so terrified the Guard that they have got reinforcements.[472]

In addition to these artificial animals, there were real pets that the prisoners cared for on the island. Lieutenant Rankin had a cat to keep him company, while others in the prison cared for two ducks, two dogs, a hen, and her hatchling.[473] By order of the Quartermaster-General, the prisoners "may be permitted to engage in any occupation which they can make profitable and which will not interfere with

---

[469] Barbiere, Joe., *Scraps from the Prison Table, At Camp Chase and Johnson's Island*, 101–105.

[470] Drummond, Edward W., *Confederate Yankee: The Journal of Edward William Drummond: A Confederate Soldier from Maine*, 88.

[471] Barbiere, Joe., *Scraps from the Prison Table, At Camp Chase and Johnson's Island*, 94.

[472] Drummond, Edward W., *Confederate Yankee: The Journal of Edward William Drummond: A Confederate Soldier from Maine*, 76–77.

[473] Barbiere, Joe., *Scraps from the Prison Table, At Camp Chase and Johnson's Island*, 258–259

their safe-keeping."[474] The prisoners engaged in business to have funds to purchase from the sutler. Some prisoners cooked, cleaned, and did laundry for prisoners wealthy enough to hire this work out. One of the most profitable enterprises was ring making. Prisoners would purchase buttons to carve finger rings. This was not a small initiative, as Colonel Barbiere points out "twelve hundred dollars [has been] spent for buttons to make rings, which are sold to prisoners as high as one dollar and a half each." The rings were also sold in Sandusky by the guards for a portion of the profit. Joseph Barbiere continued about business: "The tailoring department of our prison, is an extensive one. We have two shops. The business of this department amounts to about fifty dollars per day. Our shoemaker shop turns out three pairs of boots per week. The barber shop is constantly filled. We have an ice cream and lemonade establishment whose net receipts are six dollars a day. Two pie establishments, and a ginger-cake department, under the control of a captain, who seems more affected by the fluctuations of flour, than the fortunes of the Confederacy. Two laundries, price of washing five cents per garment. The entire summing up of our expenditures, four hundred dollars per day, quite a business tone for a population of one thousand one hundred and fifty souls."[475]

One of the simple pleasures the Rebels experienced in 1862 was to go bathing in the lake. About five hundred prisoners were allowed to go out of the pen at a time under guard to bathe, swim, and collect water. In July and August the prisoners were allowed to go bathing in the lake, which according to W. H. A. Speer, was "delightful."[476] Lieutenant Montfort of Georgia would try his hand at fishing. While the other prisoners bathed, he fished, and his fishing outfit, collected from the prison, was most curious. An old slouch hat on his head, a shirt and soldier's backpack covered the upper part of the body. He went without pants, with his bare slim legs showing under the tails of his shirt. Confederate brogans, a high lace-up shoe, were on his feet. On one arm he carried a basket of bait, and with the other he carried his rod and line purchased from the sutler. He would walk out away from the bathers to try and his luck with the native fish. None of the prisoners ever heard of a fish being caught or even a bite.[477] The prisoners were allowed to go out under a pledge from Colonel Battel and other officers that the Rebels would "not attempt to swim out, and seize the little boat and twelve pound howitzer [guarding the island], capture Hoffman's Battalion, or do any of these desperate deeds, that have made rebels so famous."[478] While the prisoners were out bathing in the lake, sightseers would still come out to

---

[474] *War of the Rebellion: A Compilation of the Official Records of the Union and Confederate Armies,* Series II, Vol. 3, 123.

[475] Barbiere, Joe., *Scraps from the Prison Table, At Camp Chase and Johnson's Island,* 145.

[476] Speer, Lonnie R., *Portals to Hell: Military Prisons of the Civil War,* 6.

[477] Olmstead, Charles H., "The Memoirs of Charles H. Olmstead." *The Georgia Historical Quarterly,* 195.

[478] Barbiere, Joe., *Scraps from the Prison Table, At Camp Chase and Johnson's Island,* 84.

see the Rebels. Captain Drummond noticed that "it seems to be great pleasure for the Ladies to look at a naked man for today about twenty came down in full view of us[;] all seemed to enjoy the different attitudes taken by us in the water as much as our selves."[479] When the time allowed had expired, the guards would start to check for hidden Rebels in the reeds. Colonel Barbiere stated: "Now the harpooning commences, the fun being strictly on the side of the guards. After all are in, as supposed, the sentinels, with their bayonets, walk leisurely along the edge of the water, and like the whaler, who longs for blubber, with harpoon in rest, launches it out at the mighty leviathan of old ocean, so do these harpooners of rebels, dash their bayonets into the weeds and brush that line the shore, certain to pin a poor fellow, should he be indirect enough to imagine he could escape in that way."[480]

Sightseers came to see the Rebels confined on Johnson's Island. The same boat that transported the prisoners to the island brought tourists to gawk at their southern cousins. The *Island Queen* would steam slowly in front of the prison so the onlookers could get a good look at the "Sesech." The steamer came by on June 26 and played "Hail Columbia" and "Yankee Doodle" with "both sexes vieing [sic] with each other in displaying their contempt" for the prisoners.[481] She made another visit on the 28th and played "Dixie," which made the Confederates rally outside of their blocks with hearty shouts and much fanfare.[482] Obviously, this was a trick to get the Rebels out of their blocks so the passengers could get a good view of a thousand shouting Johnny Rebs. The Confederates must have realized the demeaning nature of these jaunts and the trick that was played on them, for when the boat returned on July 4th, the Rebels "hide out of view and the boats left."[483] One prisoner noted that sometimes the prisoners would wave flags out of their windows at the tourists. Some waved the black flag, meaning no quarter for the enemy. With these excursions arriving every few days, the prisoners started "treating them with silent contempt."[484]

Visitors were officially forbidden; however, there seemed to be exceptions. "There have been several Ladies come here to see their husbands." Major Poe noted, "[Then] their husband is taken out of the prison and permitted to converse with their wives, sometimes for 3 or 4 hours." Another Lady "at a cost of sixty dollars travelled some six

---

[479] Drummond, Edward W., *Confederate Yankee: The Journal of Edward William Drummond: A Confederate Soldier from Maine*, 90–91.

[480] Barbiere, Joe., *Scraps from the Prison Table, At Camp Chase and Johnson's Island*, 84.

[481] Barbiere, Joe., *Scraps from the Prison Table, At Camp Chase and Johnson's Island*, 146.

[482] Drummond, Edward W., *Confederate Yankee: The Journal of Edward William Drummond: A Confederate Soldier from Maine*, 77.

[483] Drummond, Edward W., *Confederate Yankee: The Journal of Edward William Drummond: A Confederate Soldier from Maine*, 77.

[484] Speer, Lonnie R., *Portals to Hell: Military Prisons of the Civil War*, 109.

hundred miles. She was only permitted to remain with her husband two hours, then left to travel over the same long and lonesome road."[485] On July 19th, a rare event occurred. A woman entered the bull pen, which was as Captain Drummond noted: "the first that has ventured inside since our arrival. We suppose she was a Lady, although we must acknowledge she did not display the qualities of one by being so bold. Men when shut off from the world usually do not take so much pains to keep themselves tidy as at other times. This did not frighten her, as she and her escort marched down the Yard and back taking a general survey."[486] Colonel Hoffman found out that exceptions were being made on visitations and demanded Major Pierson adhere to this order not to allow any visitors.[487] After the order, visitors were extremely rare for the tenure of the prison.

The Civil War was first deemed as an insurrection by traitors. The prisoners were not truly soldiers fighting for their nation in the eyes of the federals. The authorities believed the Rebels would return to their loyalties and the war would dissipate. Major Pierson "gave notice today that all that wished to take the oath to the US Government could do so and be released."[488] To recruit converts, handbills were distributed around the prison offering immediate freedom to those who would take the Oath of Allegiance. Three men from one of the border states submitted the paperwork back to the federals. As the men marched out the gate to freedom, the entire prison turned out to ridicule and admonish the men for abandoning the cause. This tongue lashing "must have remained a bitter memory for them to the end of their days."[489]

A large celebration broke out inside the prison on June 30 in response to the Confederate victory at the Seven Days Battle outside of Richmond. As the extra editions were distributed to the eagerly awaiting prisoners, an outpouring of spontaneous cheers and celebrations were seen. As more men wanted to read the news than newspapers, Captain Sims of Georgia mounted a stump and started reading the news of the great Confederate victory to the eagerly anxious men. As the hope that the news might induce an exchange, the men started "shouting & waving hats & slaping hands in a wilde [sic] inthusiasm [sic]."[490] This enthusiasm, and the defeat of the Union army, caused considerable animosity with the guards who hollered out: "Stop that yelling, you damned rebels, and clear the campus, or we'll fire upon you."

---

[485] Poe, James T., *The Raving Foe: The Civil War Diary of Major James T. Poe, CSA*, 41–42

[486] Drummond, Edward W., *Confederate Yankee: The Journal of Edward William Drummond: A Confederate Soldier from Maine*, 83.

[487] *War of the Rebellion: A Compilation of the Official Records of the Union and Confederate Armies*, Series II, Vol. IV, 215.

[488] Drummond, Edward W., *Confederate Yankee: The Journal of Edward William Drummond: A Confederate Soldier from Maine*, 85.

[489] Olmstead, Charles H., "The Memoirs of Charles H. Olmstead." *The Georgia Historical Quarterly*, 196.

[490] Speer, Lonnie R., *Portals to Hell: Military Prisons of the Civil War*, 108.

The Rebels responded: "We are not disobeying orders, or breaking rules."

The guards retorted: "Clear the campus, and dry up, or damn your rebel hearts, we'll give it to you."[491]

Major Pierson came into the prison and Captain Drummond wrote in his diary, "he had hard work to keep his sentinels from shooting into us while we were rejoicing." To prevent further celebratory activity Major Pierson did not allow any newspapers into the pen the next day.[492]

The first reported attempt to escape from Johnson's Island came on May 27, 1862. Six men who identified themselves as the Zouave Squad were Lt. Colonel Joseph Barbiere, M. Burk, Lt. John Morton, Sanders Sale, Capt. A. S. Levy, and Capt. Farabee. The men prepared themselves on that cool rainy cloud-covered night. They wore three coats to keep them dry and warm and carried crackers for hunger, cognac for drink and liquid courage, a hatchet for defense, rope and a saw to get through the fence. Burk was to crawl to the fence and saw through a few planks and then tug on the rope as a signal of success. The party "crawled one hundred and fifty yards, through the wet grass, in a drenching rain." Barbiere continued, "We crawled breathlessly, as the sentinels were ordered to fire on any one seen out after retreat. The night was intensely dark, but our wily captors had placed [lanterns] on either wall of the prison, whose rays converged, forming an unbroken line of light, and we felt that to cross it would be worse than the Rubicon." After lying in the wet grass for three hours, the cold was starting to have an effect, and an opportunity to cross the light never presented itself, the men went back to their blocks. The men of the unauthorized expedition concluded escape was impossible and to wait for exchange.[493]

The next reported attempt at escape came on July 6. This attempt resulted in gunfire from the guards. Exactly how this attempt was made is not known. W. H. A. Speer recorded in his diary that some prisoners tried to escape but were fired upon by two sentinels, both missing the men. He realized that even though the men almost got out of the prison, they almost were killed. The general sentiment was that it was foolish to try and escape. If a prisoner got out of the bull pen, he still had to get off the island to the mainland far away. [494]

On the rainy dark night of July 19, Lieutenant Green Duncan and possibly another tried to get out of the prison prematurely. Lt. Duncan had "taken advantage of a drain, which ran to the lake, and which was covered with grass. He commenced sawing one of the posts that supported the fence, when he struck a nail, and becoming excited,

---

[491] Barbiere, Joe., *Scraps from the Prison Table, At Camp Chase and Johnson's Island*, 193.

[492] Drummond, Edward W., *Confederate Yankee: The Journal of Edward William Drummond: A Confederate Soldier from Maine*, 78–79.

[493] Barbiere, Joe., *Scraps from the Prison Table, At Camp Chase and Johnson's Island*, 171–174.

[494] Speer, Lonnie R., *Portals to Hell: Military Prisons of the Civil War*, 109.

rather than wait until the tramp of the relief [guard] would deaden the sound, pulled at the plank which made a ripping sound, that vibrated from one end of the wall to the other."[495] The garrison was alerted to his actions and the guard immediately over the spot "fired twice, but fortunately they managed to get back and got to their quarters" before their identities were discovered.[496]

SHOOTINGS OF CAPTAIN MEADOWS AND LIEUTENANT GIBSON

A sense of disrespect and mistrust was apparent toward the men of Hoffman's Battalion from the southerners. The prisoners, captured in combat, were offended that they were guarded by shirkers from battle. Flavel Barber had a low opinion about the bluecoats that watched over them: "Our guards at this place were men who had enlisted merely for garrison duty. As soldiers they were much inferior to those who had guarded us at Camp Chase."[497] No prisoner was allowed to enter into a conversation with the guards. If he did try to speak to a guard, he was usually met with a derogatory nasty reply.[498] To compound this lack of respect, many prisoners had cocky attitudes and an overinflated since of superiority that would create many problems with the guards. Colonel Barbiere stated, albeit arrogantly, "the fact [is] that the best blood of the country is within these walls, many men of note, whose names will shine upon the pages of history, in time to come."[499]

The rules at Johnson's Island were much stricter than at Camp Chase where many prisoners had first been imprisoned. Some of the prisoners while at Camp Chase could even get a parole of honor to venture outside the gates and visit the nearby city of Columbus. Colonel Hoffman revoked this privilege when the soldiers were sent to Johnson's Island, making it seem that Major Pierson had disparaged their character by holding them as criminal prisoners.[500]

Pierson's Order #10 allowed a guard to shoot at any prisoner who violated any regulation. Even very petty violations could have a bullet sent in the prisoner's direction to correct the action, which enraged the Rebels at every instance. Colonel Barbiere described one such incident: "A few officers engaged in playing cribbage, were

---

[495] Barbiere, Joe., *Scraps from the Prison Table, At Camp Chase and Johnson's Island*, 255–256.

[496] Drummond, Edward W., *Confederate Yankee: The Journal of Edward William Drummond: A Confederate Soldier from Maine*, 88–89.

[497] Barber, Flavel C., *Holding the Line: The Third Tennessee Infantry*, 53.

[498] Poe, James T., *The Raving Foe: The Civil War Diary of Major James T. Poe, CSA*, 42.

[499] Barbiere, Joe., *Scraps from the Prison Table, At Camp Chase and Johnson's Island*, 267.

[500] *War of the Rebellion: A Compilation of the Official Records of the Union and Confederate Armies*, Series II, Vol. III, 574.

so unfortunate, as to neglect putting out their lights the moment 'taps' sounded, not imagining, that the dereliction of a few moments would be attended with the danger, which they found it was, as a volley came in at the window. Fortunately no one was hit; but the lesson was heeded, as no mercy could be expected, from men who are merciless."[501] Another incident of shooting by the guards was for a prisoner simply going to get water from the pump. The prisoner "took his bucket, walked to the well, some forty or fifty steps from the building, and commenced pumping. It certainly did not look like an attempt to escape." The guards hollered out "Halt!" but the prisoner calmly walked back to his quarters disregarding their warning. Several shots were fired, missing the thirsty soldier; however, "the shower of buck and ball, that ricocheted (much to the annoyance of the prisoners, who were protected only by half-inch plank,) over the campus" could have injured an innocent prisoner.

Captain Meadows, 1st Alabama Regiment, was walking near the dead line after going to the latrine and accidently strayed into the forbidden area near the fence on July 13, 1862. The sentinel of Post 13 fired at him without forewarning. The bullet passed through the meaty thigh of one leg and into the other, smashing the bone upon impact. He was badly hurt but recovered. The prisoners were angered by this shooting, and a meeting was held in Block 7 Mess 1 to discuss any planned course of action. The meeting, presided by Captain G. W. Gordon, composed a letter to Major Pierson explaining the circumstances of the shooting. The letter asked for justice and demanded if "this sentinel has shot him down in cold blood, we call upon you, to see that he receives the punishment his crime deserves, and we be secured against similar outrages."[502] Another prisoner, Flavel Barber, recorded in his journal a more radical reaction to the shooting: "an indignation meeting was held by the prisoners and a communication sent to Major Pierson, stating that if we were to be shot down in that manner we wished to know it, so that we could take measures for our own protection, and he was also assured that if such outrages were repeated we would break out and massacre the guard, even if all our lives should be the forfeit."[503] Major Pierson was told by an anonymous surgeon who had been released on June 22 that the pen was in a state of agitation and might charge the wall. Pierson notified Colonel Hoffman of the situation, where Hoffman ordered the raising of another company of guards.[504]

On August 8, Lieutenant Elisha Gibson of the 11th Arkansas Regiment was fatally shot by a guard. Almost every diary and memoir of 1862 mentions the murder with

---

[501] Barbiere, Joe., *Scraps from the Prison Table, At Camp Chase and Johnson's Island*, 265.

[502] Barbiere, Joe., *Scraps from the Prison Table, At Camp Chase and Johnson's Island*, 121–122.

[503] Barber, Flavel C., *Holding the Line: The Third Tennessee Infantry*, 53.

[504] *War of the Rebellion: A Compilation of the Official Records of the Union and Confederate Armies*, Series II, Vol. IV, 87–89.

a few minor variations.[505] Lieutenant Gibson was visiting friends in another block, thought to be Block 13, and decided to go back to his bunk for the night, perhaps he forgot the time, but it was after curfew of 9 o'clock. At 9:30 he left his friend's block and started walking down the avenue toward his own block. He was told by a guard on the parapet to go back to his quarters, at the same time leveling his rifle. Gibson told the guards he was heading home and continued in the same direction. The guard stopped him and told him to turn around immediately, which he did and headed to the nearest block. As he was entering Block 11, the guard fired. The guard had a double load, which was a one ounce ball and then buckshot loaded into his weapon. Gibson was hit in the right breast with the ball, which passed through his chest and exited at the cross of his suspenders. Two pieces of buckshot hit him in his left arm. He must have turned to face the guard as he was shot through the front to exit in his back. His orientation placed him where the ball lodged into the block. He fell instantly. No one was allowed to come near him. The guard was raised, reinforcements arrived on the wall, and the cannons were manned and pushed into firing position. A full fifteen minutes passed before the prisoners were allowed to come to his aid. He was carried inside the block where he died shortly afterward. Major James T. Poe carried the lifeless body into the block: "I and others washed and dressed him, then sat up with the corpse through the night. I feel much wearied this morning having no rest last night."[506]

After news of the death of Gibson, the prisoners were quite angry and threats to storm the wall were quite vocal. W. H. A. Speer recorded that there was a stong desire to break "down the plank fence & take the gards [sic] guns & try to secure the block houses & take the cannon." He realized however, to a "man of good Sence [sic] it was an act of rashness to Self destruction." He understood that to take the garrison was the easiest phase, but how would they accomplish the difficult task of getting off the island?[507] Captain Drummond wrote: "I believe at a moment's warning the whole guard would have been killed."[508] Colonel Olmstead was worried about revolt as the prisoners were like a "seething pot" all the next day. All over the bull pen, men gathered in small groups and lamented over the event with blood boiling with rage. A cry of "we had better die like men than be shot down like dogs" permeated the air. The

---

[505] Olmstead, Charles H., "The Memoirs of Charles H. Olmstead." *The Georgia Historical Quarterly*, 194; Poe, James T., *The Raving Foe: The Civil War Diary of Major James T. Poe, CSA* 110; Barber, Flavel C., *Holding the Line: The Third Tennessee Infantry* 58; Drummond, Edward W., *Confederate Yankee: The Journal of Edward William Drummond: A Confederate Soldier from Maine*, 93–94; [505] Barbiere, Joe., *Scraps from the Prison Table, At Camp Chase and Johnson's Island*, 265. 198–199.

[506] Poe, James T., *The Raving Foe: The Civil War Diary of Major James T. Poe, CSA*, 45.

[507] Speer, Lonnie R., *Portals to Hell: Military Prisons of the Civil War*, 110.

[508] Drummond, Edward W., *Confederate Yankee: The Journal of Edward William Drummond: A Confederate Soldier from Maine*, 94.

atmosphere was toxic for bold action.[509] Colonel Avery approached Colonel Olmstead and suggested the men were going to make a break for it tonight. Since they could not in all likelihood stop them, "so we must lead them."[510] Olmstead did not like the proposition of leading 1,200 unarmed men against a fully reinforced stockade with fortified cannons. He realized the attempt would be futile. A meeting was arranged with all the high-ranking Confederates. Colonel Avery made a case for an attack, while most of the others, including Col. Olmstead, Col. Battle, and Col. Quarles, argued against an uprising. In a unanimous vote, all the officers in attendance decided to calm the other prisoners and "quiet the excitement." Fortunately, by the time the meeting was over, passions had settled and docility prevailed. Two years later, in 1864, Colonel Olmstead met Colonel Quarles during the Tennessee Campaign and reminisced about the shooting. Colonel Quarles commented that nothing had alarmed him more in the war than the possibility of "that wild uprising on Johnson's Island."[511] Colonel Battle wrote a letter to the U.S. Secretary of War explaining the situation and demanding an investigation. The letter was signed by all of the high-ranking officers and sent out. Nothing more was heard of the letter and many doubt that it ever left the island.[512]

Elisha Gibson was buried the next day on the Island. All of the prisoners from Arkansas, about thirty, were allowed to attend the funeral. Prisoners noted that "four ladies from out side went to the Grave with them, something that has not happened before!"[513]

EXCHANGE AND ARRIVAL

As the cartel to exchange prisoners worked on a general exchange, certain groups were the first prisoners to leave the island. The first group to depart was surgeons, as they were granted a full release. Fifteen Confederate surgeons departed Johnson's Island for the South on June 22.[514] The second group to leave were the chaplains. Captain Drummond explained, on August 4, "the Chaplains went off this morning. They are turned loose and have to find their way back at their own expense."[515]

---

[509] Olmstead, Charles H., "The Memoirs of Charles H. Olmstead." *The Georgia Historical Quarterly*, 194.

[510] Ibid.

[511] Olmstead, Charles H., "The Memoirs of Charles H. Olmstead." *The Georgia Historical Quarterly*, 194–195.

[512] Olmstead, Charles H., "The Memoirs of Charles H. Olmstead." *The Georgia Historical Quarterly*, 195.

[513] Drummond, Edward W., *Confederate Yankee: The Journal of Edward William Drummond: A Confederate Soldier from Maine*, 94.

[514] Drummond, Edward W., *Confederate Yankee: The Journal of Edward William Drummond: A Confederate Soldier from Maine*, 74.

[515] Drummond, Edward W., *Confederate Yankee: The Journal of Edward William Drummond: A Confederate Soldier from Maine*, 92–93.

In July, Colonel Hoffman arrived at Johnson's Island in order to "classify the different ranks of the prisoners and making necessary arrangements for an exchange should such be effected."[516] This was a good sign to the prisoners that the exchange system was being created. Hope reached a zenith that the end of their confinement was coming to an end. The happy day arrived as an order was given for the military prisoners on Johnson's Island be prepared to depart on Friday, August 29. The majority of the prisoners left on Monday, September 1, 1862, via Cairo, Missouri, to Vicksburg, Mississippi, to be returned to their own army.[517] One prisoner noted: "We were treated with great civility in Sandusky and in fact all the way through."[518]

A small scandal occurred as these prisoners departed Johnson's Island. It was discovered that the prisoners "obtained 500 new suits made of gray drilling goods, cut in military style and trimmed with military trimmings." The prisoners were allowed to send off patterns to northern manufacturers and resupply themselves using loyal companies to help outfit Confederate soldiers. The authorities also discovered that large amounts of U.S. marked property was taken with them off the island. Notice of this outrage was passed on to the Secretary of War and Colonel Hoffman, with a demand that if the federal officers "had knowledge of and gave assent thereto then they are unworthy of government employment and confidence."[519] No action was known to be taken.

As Johnson's Island was emptying, it was decided to make the depot the only western prison for the non-military prisoners. Guerrillas, bushwhackers, spies, and disloyal citizens were ordered to Johnson's Island.[520] The compound, with everything designed for a large number, did not prove manageable with a small amount. The number of prisoners got so low that Pierson rented space in Sandusky to house and guard the few prisoners.[521] This era has the scantiest information as no known diary or memoir exists from that winter. The men confined over the winter of 1862–1863 were irregular troops. This gave the authorities problems as each case was murky as to the men's true disposition. Many claimed to be Confederate officers and demanded to be exchanged.

[516] Drummond, Edward W., *Confederate Yankee: The Journal of Edward William Drummond: A Confederate Soldier from Maine*, 84.

[517] *War of the Rebellion: A Compilation of the Official Records of the Union and Confederate Armies*, Series II, Vol. IV, 421, 435.

[518] Drummond, Edward W., *Confederate Yankee: The Journal of Edward William Drummond: A Confederate Soldier from Maine*, 100.

[519] *War of the Rebellion: A Compilation of the Official Records of the Union and Confederate Armies*, Series II, Vol. IV, 591.

[520] *War of the Rebellion: A Compilation of the Official Records of the Union and Confederate Armies*, Series II, Vol. IV, 499.

[521] *War of the Rebellion: A Compilation of the Official Records of the Union and Confederate Armies*, Series II, Vol. VI, 449.

On November 19, 1862, Colonel Hoffman ordered the exchange of all military men, including bushwhackers, and for Major Pierson to determine if anyone marked citizen was actually Confederate military.[522] The numbers at Johnson's Island got smaller with this group's departure. Major Pierson complained of the wretched physical condition of the political prisoners that arrived to replace the military men. He reported that eight or ten have died and fifty had to go straight to the hospital. Not much is known about these men, but the death rate at Johnson's Island was high for that winter.[523] About sixty-six men died during this seven-month period. The death rate was disconcerting especially when the numbers of prisoners at the island got down to a low of forty men. The war intensified in the spring of 1863, and subsequently a new influx of prisoners arrived at Johnson's Island to renew the normal responsibilities of the prison.

---

[522] *War of the Rebellion: A Compilation of the Official Records of the Union and Confederate Armies,* Series II, Vol. IV, 732.

[523] *War of the Rebellion: A Compilation of the Official Records of the Union and Confederate Armies,* Series II, Vol. IV, 760.

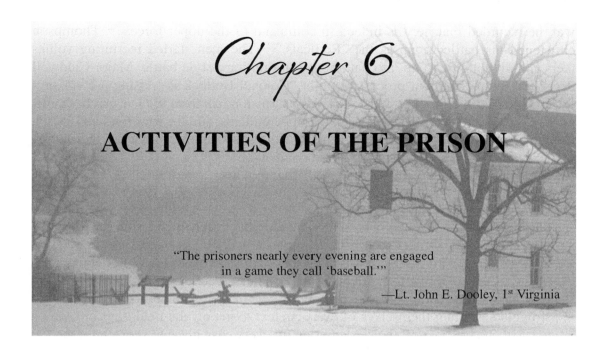

Chapter 6

ACTIVITIES OF THE PRISON

"The prisoners nearly every evening are engaged
in a game they call 'baseball.'"

—Lt. John E. Dooley, 1st Virginia

THE GREAT SNOWBALL FIGHT

After the harsh freeze of New Year's Day 1864, temperatures moderated and a great snowball battle was staged among the prisoners at Johnson's Island. It began on January 18, and ended three days later on the 21st. How or why it began, no one is sure, but the mock battle must have been a release from the boredom and monotony of huddling inside the barracks from the previous freeze. The restless prisoners always welcomed any deviation from the normal prison routine.

The mock battle was between the six upper blocks (1, 2, 3, 4, 5, and 7) and the six lower blocks (8, 9, 10, 11, 12, and 13). The leaders of the battle were mentioned in several diaries. Colonel G. Troup Maxwell of Florida commanded the lower blocks, called the "Conservatives."[524] But there was some contradiction as to who was the commander of the upper forces. John Dooley states that Major-General Isaac Trimble of Maryland was their commander. Edmund DeWitt Patterson, however, stated in his diary that General Jeff Thompson was in command.[525] In Jeff Thompson's reminiscence of the

---

[524] Wash, W. A., *Camp, Field and Prison Life*, 195.

[525] Dooley, John., *John Dooley, Confederate Soldier: His War Journal,* 158; Patterson, Edmund Dewitt., *Yankee Rebel: The Civil War Journal of Edmund DeWitt Patterson*, 157.

war, he recorded that he was indeed in command of the upper forces.[526] Thompson christened his battle group as the "Radicals."[527] The men started recruiting volunteers and dividing them up into battalions for a military-style battle. Major Caldwell described the recruitment process: tonight "Colonel Bullock is 'raising a company' for a grand battle tomorrow. Our block is to furnish a battalion to Gen. Archer's brigade in the conflict imminent between the upperendians, and the lowerendians." Each room was supposed to furnish a company.[528] Both sides put the number of their block on their hats for easy identification of the combatants.[529]

Captain Felix Blackman observed the battle from his window at Block 7 and wrote:

Our pen has been stark mad or crazy for the past two evenings snowballing. One uninitiated would really have thought so to have seen three or four hundred men Gens, Cols, Officers of every rank marshalled [sic] in combat testing the ability of each party to overpower the other with snowballs. I have not enough of the icelander in me to participate and of course became in parlance of the pen. The sham battle very much reminds one of the genuine article. To see strugglers availing themselves of every pretext to get off the field–four or five to carry one prisoner off the field hunting for every easy place to keep out of the fight. But the true veterans. The hard pressed snowballs flying in every direction–dodging–whooping—throwing (alias shooting)–Signal corpse [sic] waving their flags from every prominent point. Officers with staff and escort in the rear commanding their forces. (Men playing boys, children on sticks)–Cavalry–charging hither and thither–with a little stretch of the imagination and supplying–the necessary thundering of cannon–and the rattling popping of musketry one could have seen enacted before him the death dealing heart rendering grandeur of the actual engagement. Not much blood was spilt however, except a few bloody noses and now and then a black eye was the only evidence of the sanquirary [sic] contest. After it was over each party was drawn up for review and congratulatory orders read and speechs [sic] made to the war worn soldiers of the arctic campaign. To day [sic] one . . . deserter was taken out and shot for his crime. He fell dead upon the field not a snowball striking him–was examined by the surgeon in attendance–pronounced dead–born off the field to his last resting place–a snow bank interred and thus ended the campaign. The commander of the victorious party proclaimed an amnesty–pardon–to all except the leaders, upon taking the oath of allegiance–imprisonment or banishment to the ring leaders. All in all a farce savoring too much of truth to please those of fastidious

---

[526] Thompson, M. Jeff., *The Civil War Reminiscences of General M. Jeff Thompson*, 217.

[527] Wash, W. A., *Camp, Field and Prison Life,* 195.

[528] Caldwell, James Parks., *A Northern Confederate at Johnson's Island Prison,* 77.

[529] Bingham, Robert, *Diary,* D2, 60.

taste. It was an entertaining exhibition to all observers–Rebs and well as our Yankee guardians. I suppose so from the number assembled in the parapet.[530]

General Jeff Thompson wrote about the fight, "Each arm of the service was represented, even [the] Gunboats, and the battle lasted three days, with the usual intermissions of flags of truce, exchange of prisoners, armistice to bury the dead and political correspondence." Thompson later told of the violence of the mock battle. "Sometimes after our battles, the snow would be nearly as bloody as in actual conflict, for bloody noses and teeth knocked loose with snow balls were plentiful. We had a regular court martials, and a number were sentenced to be shot for all the various charges of desertion, bushwacking, cowardice, etc. etc., and the culprit would be taken out, blindfolded, and from ten to twenty men would knock him over with snow balls. One or two were actually buried in the snow, until another party would pull him out."[531] Thompson's chief signal officer was Captain Youngblood, who made a spyglass out of two bottles tied together. Captain Youngblood tore off his shirttail to make a signal flag to report the movements of the enemy "Conservatives."[532] Major Caldwell gave his account of the battle: "our block lost its colors early in the day (stolen). We captured two [flags] from the enemy, and never once [retreated] except when those in our flanks had given way. Exciting fight though, some hard hits were given."[533] The winner of the snowball fight was the "Conservatives" of the lower blocks when they drove the the "Radicals" from the battlefield, which was the parade ground between the blocks.[534]

The zeal with which the Southern gentleman carried on the battle showed vividly their intense desire for action, especially since many young men of Johnson's Island had lived life on the edge in combat for the past two years. Their perception was that they were wasting away in this prison. They had faced the roar of the cannons and were convinced that they were contributing to a great cause. Now they felt impotent. Many soldiers were frustrated that they could not actively participate in the war, so a war game inside the pen was their only alternative. For a time, the battle took their minds off of their boring life. While this was a mock battle with no loss of life, it represented a chance for these soldiers to participate in the arena of combat. Also, many soldiers from the Deep South had never seen such a snowfall as this northern Ohio winter brought. This snow must have been a new experience for these southerners, and they were fascinated by the experience.

---

[530] Blackman, Felix Hays, *Letters to Maggie Sexton* (1863-1865), January 22, 1864.

[531] Thompson, M. Jeff., *The Civil War Reminiscences of General M. Jeff Thompson*, ed. Donal J. Stanton, Goodwin F. Berquist, and Paul C. Bowers (Dayton, OH: Morningside House, 1988), 217–218.

[532] Wash, W. A., *Camp, Field and Prison Life*, 195.

[533] Caldwell, James Parks., *A Northern Confederate at Johnson's Island Prison*, 77.

[534] Dooley, John., *John Dooley, Confederate Soldier: His War Journal*, 158.

BASEBALL GAMES

The prisoners of Johnson's Island relieved the boredom of prison with baseball games. The Rebels had free use of the yard between the blocks and set up a baseball diamond. John Dooley noted, "The prisoners nearly every evening are engaged in a game they call 'baseball,' which notwithstanding the heat they prosecute with persevering energy. I don't understand the game but those who play it get very much excited over it, and it appears to be fine exercise."[535] One prisoner who played a game in the fall of 1863 appreciated the much-needed break from the monotony of prison life with the statement, "my ankles rather gave way, but I feel pretty well after it."[536]

Games were played as early as 1863, but with the hope of exchange dampened, the summer of 1864 saw significant organized play. It is unknown if they set up leagues or if they played a season with many teams. Only two clubs are mentioned in diaries, but whether these clubs are groups of teams or are just one team is not known. The Southern Club, whose captain and catcher was Charlie Pierce, was composed of prisoners below the rank of captain, the Confederate Club was composed of higher officers.[537]

The enthusiasm with which the Rebels greeted the games caused much anxiety to the federal authorities. The Yankees believed that the games might be a cover for a mass escape attempt. During the heavily attended games, the guards would slide open the gun ports and have cannon at the ready to quell any attempt to rush the walls.[538] On one occasion a member hallowed out for the ball club to assemble. The yell alarmed the sentinels to the point that the whole guard was assembled for action.[539]

One game was of enough importance for several inmates to write about it in their diaries. The game of August 27, 1864, was between the "Confederate Base Ball Club" (red shirts) and the "Southern Baseball Club" (white shirts). This game seems to be the most famous of baseball games at Johnson's Island. Edmund Patterson watched the game and reported the Confederate Club went ahead by three runs and held the lead until the fifth inning when the Southern Club rallied for a come-from-behind victory.[540] The final score was Confederate Club eleven, Southern Club nineteen. Colonel D. R. Hundley noted that "the crowd was pretty equally divided between the partisans of the white shirts and those of the red shirts, and a real rebel yell went up from the one side or the other at every success of their chosen colors. The Yankees themselves . . . crowded the house-tops, and looked on with as much interest almost as did the rebels themselves.

---

[535] Dooley, John., *John Dooley, Confederate Soldier: His War Journal,* 163.

[536] Bingham, Robert, *Diary,* 86.

[537] McNamara, M., *Southern Historical Society Papers,* 62.

[538] McNamara, M., *Southern Historical Society Papers,* 63.

[539] Inzer, John Washington., *The Diary of a Confederate Soldier: John Washington Inzer 1834–1928,* 88.

[540] Patterson, Edmund Dewitt., *Yankee Rebel: The Civil War Journal of Edmund DeWitt Patterson,* 190.

Some of them who had never yet visited the front doubtless congratulated themselves with the reflection that . . . they were permitted to listen for once in their lives to the famous yell of the ragged rascals of the Southland."[541] Wagering was commonplace, and a considerable amount of money changed hands after this game.[542] This was not the last game; one was expected for the next Saturday, but was never mentioned in any diaries.

RELIGION

Religion was very important to the prisoners of Johnson's Island. Captain Barziza remembered: "We had the privilege of religious exercises almost daily. All denominations were represented, and indulged in their own peculular [sic] services. We often had revivals of religion, and very many were converted."[543] The imprisoned men had time to think and reflect about their actions and their lives. They had time to reflect on life, love, and God and to do a lot of soul searching. These men had come from the field of battle, most narrowly escaping death. Now, they could do nothing for the war or their country. They felt impotent, frustrated, and depressed. They might have taken lives or done things in the heat of battle that might weigh heavily on a person. The prisoners might have Post Traumatic Stress Disorder, which was not formally acknowledged as such at the time, and religion might have been a release from a guilty conscience or a solace to a troubled soul. The Civil War era was the pinnacle of a religious revival that started with the Second Great Awakening earlier in the century. Almost every diary and numerous letters produced at Johnson's Island, and every other military post, contained religious references and quoted scriptures frequently. Religion played an important part of the prisoners' life.

The most prominent preacher was Colonel L. W. Lewis of Missouri. Colonel Lewis, a Southern Methodist and the leading Mason, was a very revered man on Johnson's Island. Soon after he arrived, he gained the respect of the prisoners by giving many religious services and political speeches. He was well liked and was mentioned in almost every diary kept during the time that he was at the prison. Edmund Patterson thought Colonel Lewis delivered the best sermon he ever heard.[544] According to Captain Wash, Colonel Lewis "was one of our most talented companions and decidedly the most interesting divine in prison."[545] Colonel Hundley stated that when he arrived on the island, that Colonel Lewis "preached an admirable sermon today from the text 'The name of the wicked shall rot.' It was delivered in the open air and was listened

---

[541] Hundley, D. R., *Prison Echoes of the Great Rebellion,* 120.

[542] Patterson, Edmund Dewitt., *Yankee Rebel: The Civil War Journal of Edmund DeWitt Patterson,* 190.

[543] Barziza, Decimus et Ultimus., *The Adventures of a Prisoner of War, 1863–1864,* 98.

[544] Patterson, Edmund Dewitt., *Yankee Rebel: The Civil War Journal of Edmund DeWitt Patterson,* 134.

[545] Wash, W. A., *Camp, Field and Prison Life,* 190.

to with profound attention by a very large assemblage of prisoners."[546] Colonel Lewis gave many speeches, including a stirring speech at the George Washington birthday rally. He normally did his preaching in front of Block 4. Colonel Lewis was sent on special exchange in September 1864, and became a Senator for the northern district of Missouri in the Confederate congress.[547] The prisoners of Johnson's Island missed him.

There were other preachers on the island, but none reached the esteem that Colonel Lewis held. During 1863, Reverend Littlebury W. Allen preached to quite a large audience in Block 5. Patterson noted that a large number attended and three men had professed to have found faith.[548] The Reverend Allen baptized a prisoner on November 8, 1863. In a letter sent home on this date, Captain Blackman noted, "I have just been standing at my window witnessing a solemn scene. The Baptism of a prisoner in Lake Erie by a minister, also one of the inmates. A goodly number have been permitted to go out and witness the ordinance. Such scenes tend greatly to lessening the horrors of prison life and is a living memento of the truth and sincerity of Christian religion."[549]

The authorities tried to send in a local preacher in the spring of 1864. Patterson reported his feelings on the subject in his diary in which he wished that no Confederate would dignify the event or bow to the Yankees by attending. Most of the men in prison felt that it was an insult to send in a northern preacher or at worse an attempt to convert them into "Yankee religion." After the service he logged in his journal that the Yankee preacher had fifty listeners.[550] He preached in Block 12. Reverend Thrasher observed the event and said that some angry rebels dropped sticks and other things through holes in the floor to the Confederates in attendance and finally a "paper with writing on it advising the congregation to go out and take the oath of allegiance" was dropped.[551] There were feelings of animosity and apprehension that this was an attempt by the authorities to propagandize religion to alter the prisoner's conceptions on a variety of matters. Whether the Yankee preacher had malicious intent or truly wanted to preach about the divine is not known; however, the literature he gave to the attendees had a Union flag on the cover. As one prisoner noted, he preferred to be preached to by southern man and one of the slaves at Johnson's Island commented to him; "It ain't our religion no how."[552] The prisoners wanted to listen to their own fellow southerners, who shared the same viewpoint

---

[546] Hundley, D. R., *Prison Echoes of the Great Rebellion,* 100.

[547] Patterson, Edmund Dewitt., *Yankee Rebel: The Civil War Journal of Edmund DeWitt Patterson*, 200.

[548] Ibid., 151–152.

[549] Blackman, Felix Hays, *Letters to Maggie Sexton* (1863–1865), November 8, 1863.

[550] Patterson, Edmund Dewitt., *Yankee Rebel: The Civil War Journal of Edmund DeWitt Patterson*, 158–159.

[551] Thrasher, Robert Mullins., "Prisoner of War." *The Register,* Sandusky, June 19, 1938

[552] Patterson, Edmund Dewitt., *Yankee Rebel: The Civil War Journal of Edmund DeWitt Patterson*, 159.

about "Uncle Abe." Luther Mills commented on the quality of the Yankee preacher: "Our little Yankee chaplain was so far surpassed that he rarely showed his face."[553] No other mention of this preacher giving a sermon was recorded; however, another incident to validate the southerners' fear of being propagandized did occur. The preachers in the Hoffman's battalion asked Colonel Lewis if newspapers and tracts could be distributed to the prisoners of "purely a religious character." A prisoner noted that the "books and papers were sent, and upon examination they were found to be abolition in character interspersed with political works. The large box containing them was sent to the gate to be returned to the Federal chaplain."[554]

The prisoners wanted to build a separate church inside the pen on two separate occasions and made several requests to the authorities. In April 1863, The Office of the Commissary General approved a request to build a chapel inside the pen, with half the funds coming from the prison funds, the other half might have had to come from local Christian groups or the prisoners themselves.[555] For whatever reason, it was not built. In September 1864, the prisoner's Y.M.C.A. appointed a committee to meet with the authorities and petition to build a church. The sermons were usually held in the open and the prisoners were afraid that the sermons would stop when the cold weather arrived. The prisoners themselves would raise the money to build the church. The idea was not accepted and the church was never built.[556] The sermons continued inside the cramped blocks that winter.

There were many other preachers at Johnson's Island mentioned in diaries and letters, but no matter how beloved, none had the fame of the aforementioned. A Reverend Samplin, who preached in Block 13, was mentioned, but since diaries and letters from Block 13, the poorest of the blocks, are rare, no further information is available.[557] In an 1862 account, a prisoner Henry Bullitt stated; "There is but one minister here—he is a very fine one . . . I think his name is Dr. Winthrop Hobson."[558]

Other prisoners complained about the lack of sanctity concerning religion. Captain Bingham lamented that "Sunday here does not differ from any other days. There is no quiet—no holy calm. The same card playing, the same novel reading, the same profanity goes on as on other days."[559] Captain Barziza complained "while the minister

---

[553] Mills, Luther Rice, Papers, Ohio Historical Society, 5.

[554] Webb, R. F., *Histories of the Several Regiments and Battalions from North Carolina in the Great War 1861-65,* 673–674.

[555] *War of the Rebellion: A Compilation of the Official Records of the Union and Confederate Armies,* Series II, Vol. V, 435.

[556] Patterson, Edmund Dewitt., *Yankee Rebel: The Civil War Journal of Edmund DeWitt Patterson,* 200.

[557] Wash, W. A., *Camp, Field and Prison Life,* 171–172.

[558] Bullitt, Henry, *Letters to Helen Bullitt,* 1862.

[559] Bingham, Robert, *Diary,* 37.

was speaking the audience were [sic] engaged in all sorts of disorder, laughing and talking."[560] When prisoners had prayer meetings in the rooms, they would have to share with others not inclined to respect their intentions. Edmund DeWitt Patterson observed the uncaring attitude of some prisoners. Patterson noted that some of the more religiously inclined prisoners were holding a prayer meeting, at the same time another group started gambling in the same room. No respect was given to the religious assembly. Profanity and curses could be heard by the prayer group every time someone from the card game lost a pot.[561] Colonel Hundley added: "Last year, several faro-banks were in successful operation inside the prison, and not infrequently one could observe in the same block a devout assembly engaged in the worship of God, while not far off a crowd of gallant fellows fought 'ye tiger' with unconquered pertinacity, and such a profusion of blasphemous expletives as one would expect more properly to hear in the [dens] of the Five Points than from the lips of cultivated Southern gentleman."[562]

MASONS

The Masons, a civic organization, were very active at Johnson's Island. At first, the acts of kindness were between individual members of the Order and not officially organized. The early living conditions in prison were beneficial enough that a support organization was not needed; however, by the fall of 1863, the situation degenerated to the point that organized assistance was desperately needed. By this time, the possibility of exchange had proven to be improbable. The prisoners knew that winter was approaching and assistance would be needed to keep the Mason population healthy throughout the severe Ohio winter. The Masons decided to organize the Masonic Association of Johnson's Island. The first meeting was held on September 11, 1863.

At the second meeting, the Masons decided to call upon "Brethren of the Federal States" to help with supplies for the hospital. The Masons never received any responses. The Masons conjectured that the letters they mailed never left the island, for brother Masons would never let another Mason down, even if a state of war existed between them. They sent letters of help to Lodges in Kentucky, a "loyal" state. A Lodge in Louisville sent the Masonic Association of Johnson's Island an Express box that consisted of 10 gallons of pure French brandy and two large cans of diarrhea medicine. Later they received a larger box with whiskey, sugar, medicine, and other articles needed for the hospital.[563]

---

[560] Barziza, Decimus et Ultimus., *The Adventures of a Prisoner of War, 1863–1864*, 98.

[561] Patterson, Edmund Dewitt., *Yankee Rebel: The Civil War Journal of Edmund DeWitt Patterson*, 131.

[562] Hundley, D. R., *Prison Echoes of the Great Rebellion*, 80.

[563] Stakes, Edward T., *The Scottish Rite Journal*, 52.

The Masonic prisoners at the camp not only assisted the sick at the hospital but tended to the cemetery. A Mason, A. J. McCreery, "was appointed visiting Bro[ther] from the hospital, whose duty it should be to go through the various wards every day, and make a report to the Chairman of our executive committee Col. J. Lucian Davis, of all sick Masons and their situation so those would not be neglected."[564] Captain Blackman wrote home that "[t]he Masons deserve a great deal of credit to the attention of the sick of their order here."[565] Another inmate noted in his diary that the Masons had caused the hospital to be more comfortable and furnished food and attention to all of the sick.[566] When a Mason died, the other Masons would try to make arrangements to have the body sent home. Sometimes they were successful. In the event that they were not able to send the body home, they would provide for his burial at the Confederate cemetery on the east end of the island. Captain W. A. Wash noted that a "Choctaw Indian, a captain in the Confederate service died in the hospital, and was buried by the Masons in a metallic case. They put a nicely painted head and foot board at his grave, with his name, rank, Masonic emblems and wild scenery carved thereon."[567]

The Masons took the lead in supervising the cemetery. They put "up neat head and foot boards of wood, with the name, rank, age, and date of death in each case."[568] Captain Blackman stated that "all prisoners have contributed to purchase lumber for the fence and foot & head stones of the graves. The fence I regret has been sadly abused but they are now preparing the simple slabs each bearing the name of the deceased. Marking out for convenience of friends the last home of the fellow prisoners."[569] If it is true that the Masons were responsible for marking the graves with headstones, then they did a great service for the prisoners that will forever remain on Johnson's Island. An accounting of Masonic contributions was made in a diary report. It counted 460 Masons present at the prison with fifteen entering apprentices to join. The group raised $670.75 total. $350.00 went to purchase metal coffins, $153.00 for walnut coffins, and $32.00 to purchase double pine box coffins. Another $27.05 went to purchase lumber for head and foot boards to mark the graves.[570]

Colonel Lewis, in addition to preaching, led the Masons at the prison. W. A. Wash wrote that "the hearts of some will swell with continued gratitude as they think again

---

[564] Stakes, Edward T., *The Scottish Rite Journal*, 54.

[565] Blackman, Felix Hays, *Letters to Maggie Sexton* (1863–1865), June 24, 1864.

[566] Hundley, D. R., *Prison Echoes of the Great Rebellion*, 79.

[567] Wash, W. A., *Camp, Field and Prison Life*, 201–202.

[568] Hundley, D. R., *Prison Echoes of the Great Rebellion*, 79.

[569] Blackman, Felix Hays, *Letters to Maggie Sexton* (1863–1865), June 24, 1864.

[570] Stakes, Edward T., *The Scottish Rite Journal*, 54.

of him who ministered to their spiritual welfare, and persuaded them to forsake their evil ways; and many a masonic brother will go back in memory and bless him for his zealous labors in their behalf."[571] Colonel Lewis was the president of the Masonic Association at Johnson's Island and gave numerous lectures on the qualities of being a Mason. The largest Masonic Celebration was held at the prison on June 24, 1864, St. John's Day. According to Edmund Patterson, the Colonel had delivered a very eloquent address to the largest audience ever assembled within the prison. Patterson continued that he was so moved by Colonel Lewis, he, and others, now wanted to join the Masons.[572] Colonel Hundley was in attendance at this celebration and stated that it was a "very feeling and eloquent address [and] . . . gave me a higher opinion of the order."[573] Felix Blackman, a Mason, was in the audience and said that the lecture was "pronounced excellent by the judges."[574] The speech detailed how the Union army, out of bitterness, had destroyed Masonic lodges in Fredericksburg and other southern places. Lewis described the northern Mason's attempt to "black ball" Rebels from joining their order. The Yankee Masons used the political view that any man who took up arms against the Union was not an acceptable addition to their organization. Also in this speech, Colonel Lewis described how the northern Masons were refusing to recognize the southern Masons as members entitled to the privileges of brother Masons.[575]

The Masons seem to have made a lasting impact on the inmates of the island. These inmates praised the Masons along with other organizations that helped the sick and less fortunate in the prison. Many prisoners were impressed by the Masons for their unselfish acts and became familiar with their workings and members. W. A. Wash records his impression of the Masons: "From early childhood I had imbibed a dislike to anything hidden or secret, for I imagined that whatever was meritorious would not suffer by being brought out into the light. But now I take it all back, and give my testimony in behalf of Free-masonry as a good and valuable institution."[576] The Masons showed that under the stressful situations of a prisoner of war camp, they could act in a charitable way. They must have attracted many prisoners to their order. To this day, the local Masonic Lodge decorates the Confederate Cemetery on Johnson's Island with flowers and flags every Memorial Day.[577]

---

[571] Wash, W. A., *Camp, Field and Prison Life*, iv.

[572] Patterson, Edmund Dewitt., *Yankee Rebel: The Civil War Journal of Edmund DeWitt Patterson*, 174.

[573] Hundley, D. R., *Prison Echoes of the Great Rebellion*, 79.

[574] Blackman, Felix Hays, *Letters to Maggie Sexton* (1863–1865), June 24, 1864.

[575] Patterson, Edmund Dewitt., *Yankee Rebel: The Civil War Journal of Edmund DeWitt Patterson*, 174.

[576] Wash, W. A., *Camp, Field and Prison Life*, 190–191.

[577] I witnessed the Masons decorating the graves on Memorial Day of 2000.

PRISONERS' COURT

The prisoners of the Island organized a court to take care of infractions of prison etiquette. The guards would not handle small infractions between the prisoners, so the B. S. C. (Block Security Court) was set up by the prisoners.[578] A prisoner could be brought up on charges and issued punishment. The Court was comprised mainly of lawyers. An inmate explained the court: "His Honor assumed as much dignity as if he had the judicial ermine about him; the senior Prosecuting Attorney, an able lawyer, stated, with great gravity, that he charged A or B with 'talking after taps,' 'washing in the room,' or 'failing to do duty as detail [mess duty];' 'all this against the peace and dignity of this room.' The sheriffs bustled about, and in loud voices ordered 'silence,' and 'hats off gentlemen;' the Clerk would qualify the witnesses with much seriousness, and all present would take intense interest in the proceedings."[579] If a prisoner were convicted, he would usually be given extra detail, such as fetching several buckets of water or other menial tasks. One prisoner, George Bethel, who at night had a bad habit of telling of his fox hunts with too much excitement, whooping and hollering and disturbing many of the men trying to sleep, was convicted of disturbing the peace. His punishment was to be reprimanded in front of the other prisoners.[580] Not much else is known about the Court.

THE PRISONERS' GOVERNMENT

With exchange or release from Johnson's Island remote, in February 1865, the prisoners organized a government for Johnson's Island to "increase the means of relieving the consequent mental and physical strain."[581] Another prisoner deemed the government for "their safety and welfare."[582] They organized a legislative, executive, and judicial department. A notice was put up on the bulletin board for the election of delegates to frame a constitution. The meetings were held in Block 4. The prisoners "considered that a good form of government would be to let each block represent one of the Southern States; that each block should have its own government as the State government; that all the States should have a government with each state represented; that a president and all other officers to complete the Confederate government should be elected, and that they should hold meetings as the Southern Congress did. It was left with each State that they could withdraw if they preferred, and generally the laws of

---

[578] Patterson, Edmund Dewitt., *Yankee Rebel: The Civil War Journal of Edmund DeWitt Patterson*, 159.

[579] Barziza, Decimus et Ultimus., *The Adventures of a Prisoner of War, 1863–1864*, 82.

[580] Dooley, John., *John Dooley, Confederate Soldier: His War Journal*, 151.

[581] Kenan, Thomas S., "Johnson's Island." *Histories of the Several Regiments And Battalions from North Carolina in the Great War 1861–65*, 691.

[582] Freeman, *Confederate Veteran*, Vol. XXI, 487.

the Southern States were carried out."[583] Since every block had two messes, and each mess had an elected representative, twenty-four men made up the legislative branch.

The prisoners decided to get official permission from the authorities to create the government. Three men had a meeting with Colonel Hill at his headquarters and informed him of the government thus created. The prisoners made it clear to Col. Hill, "no suggestion [the government] wished to have diplomatic relations with the United States or any other foreign powers." Colonel Hill stated "he had no power to grant the application, but would submit it to the War Department at Washington and advise the committee of the result."[584] As the war began to have a foreseeable conclusion rapidly approaching, no response was received from Washington.

THE Y.M.C.A.

A Young Men's Christian Association (Y.M.C.A.) of Johnson's Island was created on August 9, 1864. Edmund Dewitt Patterson was in attendance and stated that several resolutions were made that sparked a lively debate. They normally held meetings in Block 7 or Block 13. [585] The organization was created primarily to help the needy in the hospital. Irl Hicks, one of the members, recalled that "supplies were purchased by the Treasurer with funds contributed and solicited by the association, and distributed among the *most destitute* in the hospital and elsewhere by *standing* monthly committees." Hicks continued, "[T]he association attained to a degree of influence with the commanding authorities which enabled them to procure nourishments of which the sick would otherwise have been deprived." The association had weekly meetings with a requirement that at each meeting a guest speaker or an address be delivered to cultivate "religious, social, and literary interests." The last meeting was held on May 19, 1865.[586]

ORGANIZED ACTIVITIES

As the possibility of exchange grew dim in the fall of 1863, the prisoners started to accept their fate as long-term prisoners and organized activities sprang up to pass the time and entertain the prisoners. The Confederates set up clubs, classes, and entertainment groups. The prisoners were generally well educated and did not want to let their minds sit idle. Edmund Patterson noted that inside the pen were several burgeoning debating societies, which included readings, essays, recitals, and debates. Bible

---

[583] Freeman, *Confederate Veteran,* 487.

[584] Kenan, Thomas S., "Johnson's Island." *Histories of the Several Regiments And Battalions from North Carolina in the Great War 1861–65,* 692.

[585] Patterson, Edmund Dewitt., *Yankee Rebel: The Civil War Journal of Edmund DeWitt Patterson,* 192

[586] Hicks, Irl, *The Prisoner's Farewell to Johnson's Island,* 3.

classes were also popular where one could study the history and meaning of the book. For amusement, the prisoner could attend concerts, vocal and instrumental, performed by prisoners every Friday and Monday.[587] College fraternities had meetings as well. Major Caldwell noted these fraternity meetings with old associations were very pleasant and gave the prisoners feelings of brotherhood.[588] Monotony was a demoralizing force in their prison life, and these activities helped the prisoners pass the time in a constructive manner.

A society was formed called the General Assembly of Social Friends. Not much is known other than they formed up in July 1864 and had confirmed meetings until September of the same year. Edmund Dewitt Patterson was acting Secretary for the Committee appointed to draft a Constitution and Bylaws for the Grand Assembly of Social Friends of the Confederate States of America.[589]

One of the activities set up by the prisoners was a debating society. They philosophized about the situation of their country, the ongoing war, and the prospect of exchange. Their society was cut short when an order was issued in September 1863, that curtailed their subject matter. Debating societies continued to be held, but under order from the commandant, no discussion could be held about the present war or about Confederate States as an independent country.[590] The Commandant's order to cease these discussions did not stop them altogether. The prisoners continued to discuss the forbidden subject matter. However, instead of using organized groups as a medium for these discussions, the prisoners used small casual exchanges.

Upon occasion, a prisoner would give a speech to his fellow prisoners to pass the time or exchange views on news or recent events. On May 5, 1864, Captain Fellows delivered an address on the state of the Confederacy and the prisoners' duty to it. The stirring address was given in a crowded block with many prisoners intently listening to his eloquent prose. He was seen as one of the best debaters and natural orators inside the prison.[591] Captain Fellows was also one of the three individuals who gave such provocative addresses during the Washington birthday celebration of 1864 that troops had to be sent into the pen to quiet the rowdy Rebels. The prisoners could not actively help the Confederacy so they gave their all with loyalty and spirit.

Not all of the groups organized by the prisoners were successful. In early 1864, a group calling themselves the "Southern League" was established. W. A. Wash describes the short career of the group: "[T]he most prominent and ardent Southern

---

[587] Patterson, Edmund Dewitt., *Yankee Rebel: The Civil War Journal of Edmund DeWitt Patterson*, 134.

[588] Caldwell, James Parks., *A Northern Confederate at Johnson's Island Prison,* 191.

[589] Patterson, Edmund Dewitt., *Yankee Rebel: The Civil War Journal of Edmund DeWitt Patterson*, 178.

[590] Patterson, Edmund Dewitt., *Yankee Rebel: The Civil War Journal of Edmund DeWitt Patterson*, 138.

[591] Ibid., 162–163.

rights men in our prison convened and organized a society known as the 'Southern League,' intended to strengthen and make more lasting the bonds between Confederate soldiers. It flourished for several weeks then died a natural death."[592]

The prisoners also established classes that taught the inmates foreign languages and the Bible. Colonel Smith of Tennessee, Lieutenant Tobey of Arkansas, Captain W. A. Wash, and several others attended French class. The instructor was Major Mitchell of South Carolina, who had been educated in Europe. Wash remarked, "All parties took a deep interest in the study and we recited once a day wherever we could find a fitting place."[593] Other inmates studied German and Latin. Colonel Lewis of Missouri offered Bible study classes.

The prisoners who were inclined toward the performing arts set up different entertainment groups. The "Island Minstrels" was one of these groups. One of their performances included the singing of "Yellow Rose of Texas" and "Clap Your Hands for Dixie." They had a band that included T. F. Mitchell, the renowned guitarist, and J. G. Ward, an exquisite flutist. As part of the entertainment program, Charlie Stout gave a lecture about the "glorious constitution." Admission to the performance was 25 cents, reserved seats cost 50 cents, private boxes brought $5.00, children jokingly cost 12½ cents and "niggers" were seated free.[594] Known dates they played were September 12 and September 20, 1863, and October 26, 1863.[595] They had programs printed in Sandusky specifically for these events.

There was another theater group on the island called the "Rebel Thespians," who were organized after the "Island Minstrels." John Dooley stated, "This new dramatic association wishes to improve on the Minstrels by abandoning the lees of wine or the glossy black of burnt corks and performing plays worthy of the intelligence and admiration of men of education and enlightenment."[596] The "Rebel Thespians" were led by Major George McKnight of Louisiana (also known as "Asa Hartz" of poetry fame). In one program, the "Thespians" wittily boasted that "An orchestra, expressly provided at an immense expense of Sutler's Checks, has arrived from Europe and other seaboard towns, and will entertain the appreciative audience with selections from the finest music ever heard on this or any other planet."[597] Lieutenant T. D. Houston commented that they "have given a number of tolerable performances to large and highly intelligent audiences. The most feminine clothed in female garb play the part

---

[592] Wash, W. A., *Camp, Field and Prison Life*, 203.

[593] Ibid., 196.

[594] Brochure, Frohman Collection, Rutherford B., Hayes Presidential Library.

[595] Dooley, John., *John Dooley, Confederate Soldier: His War Journal,* 142, 144.

[596] Ibid., 144.

[597] Brochure, Frohman Collection, Rutherford B. Hayes Presidential Library.

of women."[598] Colonel Hundley described one of their performances: "The stage scenery was of a very unique description. On the right-hand side was a monster likeness of a Confederate colonel . . . and on the left a naked Venus, while in the rear were most preposterous flower-girls with very scanty costumes." He continued, "There was no shifting of scenes during the play, or performance rather, for there was really no play, but a secession of comic singing, dancing, Irish and negro solos, etc."[599] The Thespians were very ambitious, perhaps too ambitious, as they had decided to build their own dramatic hall at their own expense. The logistics, monetary outlay, and the subsequent need for approval from the chain of command, made this unobtainable. They then scaled down their ambitions "to erect a permanent stage for the production of [their] dramas" in Block 12.[600]

"The Rebellonians" was a theatrical and minstrel concert group that performed in Block 9. It was created and managed by Lieutenant T. D. Houston "to entertain the pleasure seekers of the fashionable summer resort" of Johnson's Island. "The Rebellonians" was to replace the "Thespians" as many of their members went on exchange to the South.[601] W. A. Wash thought well of the group: "They had displayed much talent and enterprise in getting up so creditable an entertainment under so many adverse circumstances. The house was crowded, the music was splendid, and the theatrical scenery and acting though somewhat rustic gave evident signs of genius." The price of admission in sutler checks was 25 cents, with reserved seating priced at 50 cents. There were several federal officers present and they seemed to enjoy the jokes got off on the Yankee nation.[602] How many performances they gave is not known but they did give at least one show on April 14 and another in June 1864. The entertainment was needed and welcomed by the prisoners to dispel the boredom of prison life.

BUSINESS AS USUAL

Johnson's Island became a beehive of activity as prisoners settled into the routine of being in confinement. With free time on their hands, the prisoners would find ways to occupy their time and keep their minds busy. Sometimes they would become entrepreneurs with the hopes of improving their lives in the camp with additional revenues. Colonel Hundley described the variety of ways prisoners passed their time: "Many devote themselves to making rings, breastpins, watch-chains, etc., of gutta-percha, shells, gold and silver—some of these articles being really very handsome and very

---

[598] Houston, Thomas D., *Prisoner of War Letters: 1863–1865. From Johnson's Island,* 15.

[599] Hundley, D. R., *Prison Echoes of the Great Rebellion,* 112.

[600] Dooley, John., *John Dooley, Confederate Soldier: His War Journal,* 152–153.

[601] Houston, Thomas D., *Prisoner of War Letters: 1863–1865. From Johnson's Island,* 36.

[602] Wash, W. A., *Camp, Field and Prison Life,* 221–222.

creditable as works of art; some make chairs, some shoes, some coats and pants; some cook, wash, black boots, clean up rooms, etc; some study law, medicine, divinity, and the modern languages; whilst others do nothing but idle, or spend their time to no profit, reading trashy romances and books of kindred character."[603] W. A. Wash noted, "some are making fancy canes, some stools and shelves, while others are playing cards, checkers or chess. In another quarter not far away you may find one fellow making pies to sell, while another deals in lemonade, a third sells ice cream, and a fourth has cakes and beer to exchange for sutler's checks. Two tailors are kept all the time employed, and to wind up with, we have a boot and shoe shop."[604] One prisoner somehow managed to bring in a pair of scales and "would tell any fellow his hog weight for a three cent postage stamp."[605] Lieutenant Houston playfully commented, "everything but love making is carried on here to perfection, and nothing in the world prevents the latter but the want of material."[606]

Creative arts were another medium that prisoners used to offset the boredom of prison life. Gutta-percha, a black hard rubber substance, could be bought from the sutler and carved into various designs. W. A. Wash described how some inmates would pass time: "An ingenious fellow would take a gutta-percha rule and some buttons, and a few bits of shell, silver or gold, and with no implements but a knife and file, in a little while be able to show rings and other trinkets. He would cut the shell and precious metals into squares, diamonds, hearts, triangles and other shapes, which, neatly fitted and imbedded into the face of the polished black surface, added to the beauty of both by the contrast."[607] Many prisoners made trinkets and sent them to their loved ones at home. Felix Blackman wrote to his sweetheart, "I have ready to ship you . . . a plain cross with the ends tipped with shell—and a scroll on the underside. It is plain and does not show work to advantage but I think a very pretty cross."[608] This manual labor not only passed away the hours by taking their minds off their own situation, it also gave the prisoners a sense of accomplishment and satisfaction. It also provided a way to send a little of themselves home and therefore strengthened their link to home.

Commandant Pierson allowed the prisoners to sell their products to the people of Sandusky. The guards acted as middlemen between prisoner and civilian. The guards sold the items in Sandusky, took a modest percentage, and returned the rest to each prisoner's account. These Rebel-made items became the latest fashion and demand

---

[603] Hundley, D. R., *Prison Echoes of the Great Rebellion,* 91.

[604] Wash, W. A., *Camp, Field and Prison Life,* 129.

[605] Wash, W. A., *Camp, Field and Prison Life,* 218.

[606] Houston, Thomas D., *Prisoner of War Letters: 1863–1865. From Johnson's Island,* 11.

[607] Wash, W. A., *Camp, Field and Prison Life,* 94–95.

[608] Blackman, Felix Hays, *Letters to Maggie Sexton* (1863–1865), December 13, 1864.

was substantial. The Yankees took great pride in wearing a trinket made by a "Johnny Reb" officer.[609] One prisoner noted, "My room has almost been turned into a ring manufactory, our little shelf being piled full of rude, home-made tools and material, and my companions were filing and gouging away right earnestly. Some of the prisoners have managed to procure complete sets of tools and made it pay by disposing of their trinkets at fair prices, the Yankee boys buying many of them as curiosities for their friends and sweethearts."[610]

Most of the prisoners tried their hand at carving the gutta-percha. Not all were successful. Wash stated, "my ring business proved disastrous; I lost one button [,] spoiled the second and made a botched job of the third, after which I became disgusted with the profession."[611] Joe Barbiere stated, "I tried to make a ring, and failed, but would have commenced again, (but after looking at a box and set of chess-men exquisitely carved and designed, that would take a prize at any fair in the world, made with a file and knife by Captain Wynn of the 14th Mississippi Regiment, who made it as a souvenir for his mother,) I concluded that talent must be inherent" and gave it up.[612]

The carving of gutta-percha by the island prisoners continued until it was considered contraband. On October 19, 1864, Captain Blackman wrote home and requested a slab of gutta-percha and some tools, as the sutler no longer sold those items. On December 13, he wrote that gutta-percha had become contraband and for whatever reason was no longer allowed inside the prison.[613]

During the summer months, the woodpile was raided as a source for raw materials. One prisoner even made a violin from the scrap lumber. Luther Mills commented: "I am no judge of music, but to my uneducated ear those fiddles were as sweet as any I ever heard."[614] Chairs were constructed in which the inmate would carve his name, regiment, and state. The bottom sometimes was made of old shoe soles. The leather would be cut into strips and interwoven to form a comfortable seat.[615] G. G. Westcott had a small turning lathe on which he produced chess men and sold them to other prisoners until he ran out of suitable materials.[616] An unknown prisoner hand made two sword-fighting figures that "go through the parries and thrusts laid down in the

---

[609] Knauss, William H., *The Story of Camp Chase*, 245.

[610] Wash, W. A., *Camp, Field and Prison Life*, 95.

[611] Ibid., 109.

[612] Joe Barbiere, *Scraps from the Prison Table, at Camp Chase and Johnson's Island* (Doylestown, PA: W. W. H. Davis, Printer, 1868), 267.

[613] Blackman, Felix Hays, *Letters to Maggie Sexton* (1863–1865), October 19, 1864; December 13, 1864.

[614] Mills, Luther Rice, Papers, Ohio Historical Society 5.

[615] Hesseltine, William, *Civil War Prisons*, 208.

[616] Wescott, G. G. Letter to Dr. Sereno Watson, Rutherford B., Hayes Presidential Library., October 16, 1864.

manual for sword exercise. The thing was given life and made to run by a small windmill."[617] These hand-manufactured items were highly prized by the inmates, but when the weather became chilly, many reluctantly threw these items into the stoves for warmth.

Some men, who had the ability to draw, sold their artistic talents to the other inmates. One prisoner hung out a shingle that said, "Drawing or Painting of any Description." The inmates that had such a talent would render a sketch of the island in autograph books, diaries, letters or anything else the prisoner chose.[618] Two prisoners were mentioned by name as creating portraits. Major J. C. Smith, 12th Arkansas Regiment "employs his time in painting and sketching," Reverend Thrasher noted; he can "sketch very well, and has made picture-taking of that style very profitable."[619] Captain Cox also painted portraits. He charged $3.00 each.[620] One prisoner noted that an unnamed lawyer, "partly as amusement, and partly to assist in procuring from the sutler a few luxuries that only greenbacks can supply, has devoted himself for some time to taking pencil sketches of his fellow prisoners. These sketches are admirable, and prove him to possess a high order of the native artistic merit."[621]

When men of all calibers and backgrounds are placed together, human ingenuity prevails and remarkable accomplishments are achieved. In Block 5, a prisoner set up a photography studio. Lieutenant G. B. Smith had a camera lens with him when he was captured. By bribing a guard, he procured some chemicals, fashioned a camera out of a cigar box and began photographing Rebels. He opened a crude gallery located in the attic of the block. He cut sheets from old tin oyster cans for his tintype pictures.[622] For a charge of 50 cents, a prisoner could bring back to Dixie an image of himself at Johnson's Island. John Dooley described what was involved in procuring a photo: "First we ascend a ladder nailed against the side of the house, and after reaching the rafters we crawl from one to another until we reach a kind of platform made of boards laid loosely over the rafters and joists. There is just sufficient light and no more, but notwithstanding all the disadvantages under which he labors he succeeds in taking very correct pictures."[623] With some knowledge and a little bribing, a prisoner was able to overcome the lack of appropriate supplies and facilities to produce photographs.

617 Mills, Luther Rice, Papers, Ohio Historical Society 5

618 Wash, W. A., *Camp, Field and Prison Life*, 160.

619 Thrasher, Robert Mullins., "Prisoner of War." *The Register,* Sandusky, June 5, 1938.

620 Bingham, Robert, *Diary,* 2, 60.

621 Hundley, D. R., *Prison Echoes of the Great Rebellion*, 102–103.

622 Robert C. Crouch, "Picture Made on Johnson's Island," *Confederate Veteran,* Vol. XVII (1909), 28–29.

623 Dooley, John., *John Dooley, Confederate Soldier: His War Journal*, 167–168.

Early in 1864, Captain E. A. Small established a library on Johnson's Island. Many of the officers had books sent to them by friends on the outside, with the result that a large number of books were floating around the prison. Captain Small requested that all books that his fellow prisoners had read and no longer wanted be sent to his room. He collected about 500 to 800 books, newspapers, and magazines. He set up a lending system and acted as the librarian. For every book that was donated by a prisoner, Captain Small allowed the prisoner to check out a certain number of books. If a prisoner did not have any books, he could pay 50 cents a month for the privilege of using the library.[624]

A group of men went into the laundry business and went to quite an expense in order to accomplish the endeavor. Whether they had partners on the outside or if they created this on their own is not clear. Reverend Thrasher described the operation of the laundry, which included a washing machine: "Twenty-five or 30 men are engaged in this business for the day. They can wash 200 pieces per day easily; which is worth about $12.50." The charge was five cents for washing and ironing and 10 cents to add starch. Those who could not pay washed their clothes themselves. [625]

Reverend Thrasher recorded in his diary some of the business ventures in the prison. There was a tailor shop in Block 3, run by Captain Knowles, fully equipped with a Singer sewing machine. Thrasher noted, "On the shelf is a pile of goods; and around the room hang coats, pants, and vests; some finished others nearing completion, and others but just begun." A lieutenant in Block 10 was a cobbler and repaired shoes and boots with his "coat off, sleeves rolled up, and a piece of India rubber cloth serving for an apron." As you walk in front of Block 4, "you may see at one of the middle front windows some watches hanging against the window panes" this was the wares of a watch and jewelry repairman.[626] One eccentric prisoner was known as "Old Bush." Luther Mills described him and his desire to get rich in his memoir:

He was a "Kentucky blockade runner [who] . . . made a vow not to allow his whiskers or his hair to be cut til [sic] his release. His face was [illegible word] and pinkly ugly and ended in a huge mass of sandy red whiskers. His head was covered with a tremendous mop of reddish hair from 2 to 3 feet long. Bush was an industrious jeweler, and made a great deal of money. Whenever a fresh lot of prisoners were brought in, many who were hard up would bring their watches and sell them for a very small sum of money. His wealth was estimated at a half-bushel of watches. Today before my release, I went to see him and found him alone in the Northeast corner room on the ground floor

[624] Wash, W. A., *Camp, Field and Prison Life*, 243–244.

[625] Thrasher, Robert Mullins., "Prisoner of War." *The Register,* Sandusky, June 5, 1938.

[626] Ibid.

of block 11. He had picked up the old clothes thrown away by the prisoners [before they deported], and had nearly filled up to the ceiling the large room which he stayed he was going to make big thing selling old rags in Sandusky after his release."[627]

Prisoners who were inclined to drink or feed their alcoholic needs built several stills inside the prison, resulting in drunkenness. Captain Bingham noticed "there is a good deal of drunkenness among the prisoners. They manage to get liquor and easily manage to get drunk."[628] Alcohol was a prohibited item, but the prisoners found the necessary ingredients to create spirits to supply the demand. Luther Mills noted there was a "blockade distillery which made and sold, an inferior article of corn whiskey at five dollars, in greenbacks, per quart. It was a very easy matter to get the corn meal; but I never could imagine how they could conceal the mash tubs and the still, so as to escape detection on the part of the federal officers who inspected the prison very thoroughly two or three times each week."[629] To escape detection, the prisoners either had to be very clever in hiding the operation or were bribing inspectors not to see it. At least one distillery was broken up as a prisoner "being found drunk" made the authorities investigate how he received the alcohol and "broke up the distillery."[630]

With time to think about their plight, many of the Southern gentlemen of Johnson's Island wrote poetry. Their poetry revealed their innermost thoughts about the loneliness of prison life, their longing to get off the island, and how they missed their family. The most famous poet of Johnson's Island was Asa Hartz. His real name was Major George McKnight of Louisiana. He wrote many witty poems and published them in the *New York News'* personal advertisements while in prison. One ad was for a replacement for himself in the prison. It read:

> WANTED—A substitute, to stay here in my place. He must be thirty years old, have a good moral character, A1 digestive powers, and not addicted to writing poetry. To such [a] one all advantages of a strict retirement, army rations, and unmitigated watchfulness to prevent him from getting lost, are offered for an indefinite period.
>
> Address me at Block1, Room 12, Johnson's Island Military Prison, at any time for the next three years, enclosing half a dozen postage stamps. Asa Hartz"[631]

---

[627] At that time, rags were collected and sold to make newspapers. Luther Mills Memoir, 5–7.

[628] Bingham, Robert, *Diary,* 50–51.

[629] Mills, Luther Rice, Papers, Ohio Historical Society. 4.

[630] Todd, Westwood, *Reminiscences of Westwood Todd,* 327–328

[631] Frohman, Charles E., *Rebels on Lake Erie,* 148.

Conclusion

Organized games, performances, and clubs lessened the boredom and monotony of prison life. The prisoners exercised their minds by reading books from the library and through debating societies. The confined prisoners' restless spirit was satisfied by numerous sermons preached throughout the prison. These activities became more common as the time in prison increased. Throughout the year 1863 prisoners were increasingly not being exchanged. The prisoners began to settle in to the prison routine and subsequently the amount of organized activity swelled.

Chapter 7

INCIDENTS OF THE CAMP

"The command was given to fire and the roar of the volley echoed over the still waters of the bay, the convict fell back upon his coffin, a corpse."

—Lt. Edmund DeWitt Patterson, 9th Alabama

STORMS OF 1864

High winds off the lake would routinely batter Johnson's Island. The prison buildings were only built to last for the duration of the war, so construction was cheap. This sub-par construction would reveal itself when high winds struck, which happened often. With these winds, buildings collapsed, even on the guards' side of the prison. On December 16, 1863, a heavy gale blew down a new building on which the Yanks were at work. The building came down with a thunderous crash, killing one and wounded several. The rebels gave out an apathetic cheer.[632]

Two great storms hit Johnson's Island in the late summer of 1864. The first was on August 25, 1864. W. A. Wash logged in his journal the violence of the storm that came up and pelted the creaking and rocking buildings with wind. The storm knocked over fifty yards of the prison fence on the west side. Seeing an opportunity, a "large squad of secesh threaten to charge out, but it's all smoke and no fire,"[633] as the Yankees had quickly put a sufficient force in the gap to repel the attack.[634] But this storm was just a precursor. A much larger, more destructive storm arrived a month later.

---

[632] Patterson, Edmund Dewitt., *Yankee Rebel: The Civil War Journal of Edmund DeWitt Patterson*, 150.

[633] Wash, W. A., *Camp, Field and Prison Life*, 257.

[634] Patterson, Edmund Dewitt., *Yankee Rebel: The Civil War Journal of Edmund DeWitt Patterson*, 190.

On September 23, 1864, a very large and violent storm rolled in off Lake Erie. The storm was extreme enough to be called a hurricane by some of the southern boys. Others called it a tornado, while still some described it as a bad storm. By any name, it badly damaged the hastily built buildings of Johnson's Island. J. J. Richardson witnessed the storm's destruction: "It came up about nine o'clock at night. I watched the cloud, and concluded I would not retire till after it was over. I stood beside the door and watched its approach; the lightning was constant. I saw it strike trees beyond the prison; they bent to the storm and went down. It struck the first row of buildings; the roofs of blocks four and two were carried away. It next struck block five, and the roof gave way, the building quaked, and the men who had retired leaped from their bunks and ran out of the building. The debris from block four fell in front of our building, rafters, sheeting, shingles, etc., having been blown three hundred yards."[635] A prisoner who resided in Block 5 said that he felt the building rock like a ship at sea. As the fury reached a fever pitch, a cry, "out of the Blocks for your lives," was belted out of nowhere. Edmund Dewitt Patterson, fearing the structure was about to collapse said, "I think I touched the floor once between my bunk and the door and the next jump I landed outside amid the flying timbers of Block 4, the whole roof of which was taken up and wrenched into a thousand pieces, which could be seen whirling and spinning around in the air as flash after flash of the most vivid lightning succeeded each other, casting a lurid glare over all." Some of the rafters rained down on the frightened and scurrying prisoners and were thrust into the ground as "though pitched by some unseen giant, plowing up the ground."[636] Another prisoner of Block 5, Major Caldwell, wrote this in his diary: "an Equatorial storm was accompanied by the fiercest gale of wind I ever felt; almost in an instant, Blks 4, 5, & 9 were roofless and their inhabitants flying for dear life, whether none seemed to know, for the air was filled with flying rafters & shingles. The roofs, almost entire, were moved a distance of 100 yds. The new dining room was blown away, trees fell & their branches strewed the pen. One soldier seriously injured & many sprained and bruised. Our block is still roofless, & has careened over fearfully." Luckily, Major Caldwell only suffered a bruised hip because of the ordeal.[637]

The storm was a very frightening experience for the prisoners. The men of the prison went running out of the blocks trying to find a safe haven. Shelter was taken wherever they could find it. One side of the prison wall went crashing down. The guards on top of the prison wall put up a pretty lively fire to prevent escapes. The guards fired at inmates that came too close to the collapsed fence. The sentinels were not trying to shoot the prisoners; the intention was to stop the confused prisoners from leaving the compound. The guards were put on alert and filled the gap in the

---

[635] J. J. Richardson, "Experiences on Johnson's Island," *Confederate Veteran,* Vol. XIV (1906), 60.

[636] Patterson, Edmund Dewitt., *Yankee Rebel: The Civil War Journal of Edmund DeWitt Patterson,* 197.

[637] Caldwell, James Parks., *A Northern Confederate at Johnson's Island Prison: The Civil War Diary of James Parks Caldwell,* 146.

fence. A few guards were so fearful of an uprising that they fired indiscriminately into the blocks; one shot went through the hospital and one through block five. Several inmates narrowly missed being hit by the firing.[638] One frightened Confederate ran halfway to the deadline and in the dark mistook the well pump for a guard. He yelled out, "Good Lord, Mr. Yank, don't shoot—don't shoot—I surrender."[639] One can only surmise that the pump accepted his surrender. Edmund Patterson, an Alabama officer and veteran of Gettysburg, stated that he was more frightened during that night than he had ever been in combat. He would prefer "fighting a battle every morning before breakfast" than experience a repetition of that terrible storm.[640]

As the storm decreased in intensity, the Confederates returned to their blocks. The guards kept up a constant firing of small arms to intimidate any prisoner who might try to escape.[641] And yet there was at least one attempt to escape. During the storm, a Virginian tied three planks together and made his way out onto the bay. There he tried for several hours to make his way to the mainland. The wind and waves were too much to navigate, however, and he returned to the island.[642]

After the storm, the prisoners surveyed the damage. Three blocks had their roofs completely removed and a portion of the roof to the hospital was peeled away. The roof of one of the blocks was thrown through the new dining hall.[643] The prisoners themselves were fortunate that they did not have more injuries. A rafter hit one prisoner in his thigh, ripped through his flesh, and broke his leg. Quite a number of prisoners had stepped on nails as they ran for cover.[644] All in all, the prisoners were fortunate that there was not a single fatality.

The next day, the compound was littered with all types of debris. The blocks that suffered damage had the prisoners' belongings scattered about the bullpen. The prisoners picked up their belongings the best they could, but many articles were never recovered, being either stolen or blown outside of the prison walls. The bulletin board was full of advertisements for lost articles of every description.[645]

The guards protected the debris from theft, but almost immediately the prisoners started stealing the wooden shingles, planks, and pieces of broken lumber. They used the lumber for firewood and to repair the damage made to their bunks. Some also

---

[638] Patterson, Edmund Dewitt., *Yankee Rebel: The Civil War Journal of Edmund DeWitt Patterson*, 198.

[639] J. J. Richardson, "Experiences on Johnson's Island," *Confederate Veteran*, 60.

[640] Patterson, Edmund Dewitt., *Yankee Rebel: The Civil War Journal of Edmund DeWitt Patterson*, 198.

[641] Hundley, D. R. *Prison Echoes of the Great Rebellion*, 139.

[642] W. Gart Johnson, "Prison Life at Harper's Ferry and on Johnson's Island," *Confederate Veteran*, Vol. II (1894), 242.

[643] Hundley, D. R. *Prison Echoes of the Great Rebellion*, 140.

[644] Patterson, Edmund Dewitt., *Yankee Rebel: The Civil War Journal of Edmund DeWitt Patterson*, 198.

[645] Wash, W. A., *Camp, Field and Prison Life*, 269–270.

collected lumber to build partitions and additions to their blocks. The prisoners knew that winter would be arriving soon, and filled their attics with the scrap bits of lumber. The inmates remembered well the bitter cold of the previous winter and the lack of wood for the stoves. With the prospect of exchange practically nil, the soldiers were preparing the best they could for the coming winter.

The federals brought in new lumber to repair the damage from the storm. The prisoners engineered ingenious ways to steal the lumber. One inmate would step up to a plank and pick it up. While the guard walked over to stop him, two or three others would help themselves to the rest of the lumber. The decoy kept the guard occupied for as long as possible. Many pieces of lumber were stolen in this way. The commandant then announced that anyone picking up lumber would be shot. Even this did not stop the resourceful Rebels. One prisoner would carry a clothesline and hook it onto a plank. The other prisoners would walk behind, concealing the "hooked" plank.[646] Many additions and improvements were made from the stolen wood. Even though the storm was frightening, the improvements made to the camp, with the stolen wood, made the prisoners think the storm was a blessing.

The blocks were repaired, but some of the blocks were never fully restored to original construction. One prisoner noted three months later that he expected some blocks to collapse over the winter, especially Block 5, because it was the most damaged. Because of the damage, Block 5 was routinely evacuated every high wind.[647] Another storm hit March 17, 1865, which brought back memories of the September storm. Caldwell noted the violence of the storm that shook the "old houses & demoralizing the inmates to an extent unparalleled save by the great storm of Sept. 23rd." The winds blew down nearly the whole fence on the west side of the prison.[648]

SEARCHES

The prisoners at Johnson's Island were subject to random searches by the guards. The guards would search to find contraband items or to detect evidence of escape plots. Searches have always been a normal aspect of life in both military and civilian prisons. The gentlemen of the South, however, took these searches very personally. They felt that the searches were harassing and insulting. Their honor had been insulted by the greasy mechanics of the North.[649]

---

[646] Ibid., 198-199; Hundley, D. R. *Prison Echoes of the Great Rebellion,* 146.

[647] Caldwell, James Parks., *A Northern Confederate at Johnson's Island Prison: The Civil War Diary of James Parks Caldwell,* 165.

[648] Caldwell, James Parks., *A Northern Confederate at Johnson's Island Prison: The Civil War Diary of James Parks Caldwell,* 187.

[649] Patterson, Edmund Dewitt., *Yankee Rebel: The Civil War Journal of Edmund DeWitt Patterson,* 168–169.

The federals would call the prisoners out for muster and place guards between the Confederates and the blocks. The soldiers would then make a search for contraband. On one search, an inmate noted that the guards found a wooden gun, several life preservers built out of fruit cans, a pair of muddy pants used in tunneling, and one ladder.[650] The guards would also make searches for items that came up missing in the prison, such as axes, saws, lumber, pieces of federal uniforms, and other similar items. The prisoners would use these items in escape attempts.

Edmund Patterson wrote of one search. During roll call, with all the Rebels standing in formation outside their blocks, the federals announced they were going to conduct a search for ladders. A federal guard stood at each door to ensure no prisoner went back into the blocks. While inside, the Yankee officers went through every carpet sack, trunk, and box. The southerners were insulted and questioned how a ladder could be hidden in a carpet sack. After a thorough search lasting several hours, the Yankees found a couple of Confederate flags hidden among the prisoners' possessions. The Yankees let out a hurrah over the victory. Colonel Hill made the men give back the stolen booty.[651] Since they went into the blocks without a Rebel present to watch, the prisoners accused the guards of theft of personal objects. They reportedly stole rings, money, and other items.[652] To put a stop to this alleged theft, on the next search, an inmate would "play possum" pretending he was sick. While the prisoner moaned in his bunk, he would keep an eye on the guards, deterring them from walking off with personal property.[653]

SLAVES

There were slaves at Johnson's Island. Ironically, in the land opposed to slavery and actively fighting to end the institution, victims of slavery were living among the oppressors inside the bull pen. On October 16, 1863, a detachment of prisoners arrived. Accompanying four Confederate officers were six servants. Four were black slaves and two of them were young white boys. Because of the surrender terms at Port Hudson, where the officers were captured, they were allowed to retain their servants. Colonel Pierson questioned the order but was shown Special Orders No. 240, from U. S. General Banks, which proved they were indeed entitled to bring their servants with them. Special Orders No. 240 stated that the servants could either return home or accompany their owners, at their own choice.

---

[650] Wash, W. A., *Camp, Field and Prison Life*, 230.

[651] Patterson, Edmund Dewitt., *Yankee Rebel: The Civil War Journal of Edmund DeWitt Patterson*, 168–169.

[652] Inzer, John Washington., *The Diary of a Confederate Soldier: John Washington Inzer 1834–1928*, 81.

[653] Wash, W. A., *Camp, Field and Prison Life*, 278.

Special Orders No. 240 was unusual during the Civil War, but during antebellum times this was quite the norm. Similar to the British Army's custom of a "batman," Southern soldiers joining the U.S. Army were allowed to bring a servant with them into the service, even if the soldier was stationed in lands that strictly forbid slavery. The plight of Dred Scott illustrated this peculiarity to the nation shortly before secession.

After the fall of Port Hudson, most of the servants returned home except for six who chose to go into captivity with their masters. Pierson let them enter but told them they would not receive any rations. He immediately wrote to Colonel Hoffman to confirm that the orders to withhold rations were valid. The four owners were Colonel I. G. W. Steedman, Surgeon 1st Alabama; Captain R. M. Hewit, Miles Legion; Lieutenant J. B. Wilson, 39th Mississippi; and Captain O. P. Amacker, 9th Louisiana Cavalry.[654]

The federals offered all kinds of inducements to the slaves to get them to leave their masters and take service with the Union. They refused the offers and stayed with their masters until exchange. A prisoner noted that Captain Hewit's slave, Dick, was "faithful and loyal to his master to the end. They refused to offer him any rations, but each of us divided our meager supply, which gave him a portion equal to ours. Dick was exchanged with his master only a short time before the surrender." The name of Captain J. B. Wilson's slave was John.[655] The names of the rest and the status of the white boys are not known.

AN UNUSUAL CELEBRATION

George Washington's birthday, February 22, 1864, was an unusual day for the prison camp. The day was celebrated both inside and outside the prison fence. The Yankees had a brass band playing "Yankee Doodle" and "Hail Columbia." They fired off cannons and swore allegiance to the flag. The prisoners upstaged their captors. They celebrated Washington's birthday because he was a Virginian, a slave owner, and an original revolutionary. The prisoners' band played "Bonnie Blue Flag" and "Dixie." Edmund Patterson noted in his diary the feelings of the prison that it was right and proper to celebrate this southern hero. The prisoners felt he was the original Rebel and would have sympathized with their cause. The fact the Yankees were celebrating his birthday and claiming him as one of their own was distasteful to the southerners. He was a slaveholder and fought against military tyranny and government from foreign lands, the very ideals the southerners believed they were fighting for.[656] The prisoners listened to speeches by Colonel

---

[654] *War of the Rebellion: A Compilation of the Official Records of the Union and Confederate Armies,* Series II, Vol. 6, 397-398.

[655] A. O. P. Nicholson, "Servants in Prison," *Confederate Veteran,* Vol. XIII (1905): 11.

[656] Patterson, Edmund Dewitt., *Yankee Rebel: The Civil War Journal of Edmund DeWitt Patterson,* 158–159.

Lewis, Captain Fellows, and Lieutenant Houston. The speakers pledged and vowed to live and die for Dixie. The crowd agreed and shouted loudly. Wharton Green described how Captain Fellows, the Little Giant, "mounted on a platform of an upper floor around which a crowd was assembled, and for half an hour I have never heard such a burst of oratory as escaped his lips. The crowd by this time had been augmented by almost every prisoner on the island, who vied with each other in outburst of applause. This became so great that the authorities on the outside concluded that we were premeditating an outbreak, and marched in a detachment of troops to quell or disperse us."[657]

VISITORS

Visitors were not officially allowed on Johnson's Island. William Pierson, Commandant, issued an order on April 21, 1862, that stated, "It may prevent misunderstanding and disappointment especially with persons residing at distance, to announce that no persons will be allowed to land on Johnson's Island, without the written consent of the commanding officer, previously obtained. Also, that no one will be permitted to visit, the prisoners, except the nearest relatives, in case of severe sickness."[658] How strictly the order was observed depended on the commanding officer.

Most visitors were turned away but some were allowed. Edmund Patterson, an Ohio native fighting for Alabama, had his father, sister, and uncle, all Ohio citizens, try to visit him. On the first attempt, they were able to land on the island but were not allowed inside the pen. Patterson said he was able to talk to them by climbing the steps of Block 1, the closest block to the fence, and from that vantage point he could holler over the fence to his family standing outside. He was slightly embarrassed because for them to hear, he had to talk so loud the entire bull pen could hear him.[659] A few weeks later, his father was able to visit him. The fact that his father was a loyal citizen of Ohio and tried to convince his son to sign the oath of allegiance was instrumental in procuring a visit.

Other visitors were not so lucky. The wife of prisoner Captain Charles Frazer moved to Sandusky to be close to her husband. She received a pass from President Lincoln, through a friend, to see her husband. She was allowed to land on the island but not to visit her husband. Once again the steps of Block 1 were used so they could see each other from afar.[660] Lieutenant Colonel Joe Barbiere described how one mother was turned away: "An aged mother comes one thousand miles, to see her darling boy,

---

[657] Green, Wharton Jackson., *Recollections and Reflections: An Auto of Half a Century and More,* 192–193.

[658] Frohman, Charles E., *Rebels on Lake Erie,* 10.

[659] Patterson, Edmund Dewitt., *Yankee Rebel: The Civil War Journal of Edmund DeWitt Patterson,* 125.

[660] Unknown Author, "Prison Life on Johnson's Island," *Confederate Veteran,* Vol. II (1894), 113.

a mere youth, possibly, the last opportunity he may have on Earth to receive a mother's blessing. The mother prays to the relentless fiend in charge of us, to see her son but for one moment, but is denied. The mother does not see her son."[661] Colonel Inzer also noted the anger over this rule when he wrote, "The wife of a prisoner, also the sister of one, arrived today from [New Orleans]. The inhuman brutish Yankees would not allow them to speak to each other." A month later he noticed that a group of "Ladies from the South are here to see their husbands and sons. They are not allowed to enter."[662] The parents of a Confederate soldier from a "loyal" state, Missouri, tried to see their son. They pleaded but were turned away. They sent him some clothing and money from Sandusky, the closest they could get to him.[663] Relatives from "loyal" states were more likely to get permission to visit the prisoners, but this was at the discretion of the officer in charge.

Some of the sick prisoners were allowed to have relatives visit them. One prisoner, W. A. Wash, noted in his diary the rare sight of a visitor within the walls: "Two ladies from Kentucky came on the 18th [February 1864], with a permit from the Secretary of War to see their brother, who was sick in prison; and a woman had become so uncommon a sight inside our walls that we rushed out by the hundreds to see them."[664]

One can fully understand the problems of allowing visitors. With the prison housing an average number of 2,500 prisoners, allowing visitors would jeopardize the security of the prison. Accommodations would have to be built for such a volume of visitors. The extra facilities would cost money; money the government did not want to spend. The security risk of having information passed on to the prisoners or vice versa was very real and very dangerous. The commandant feared a rising against the guards that was coordinated with an outside attack. Confederates disguised as visitors could pass on this information. The most logical way to prevent these problems was to forbid visitors, as Colonel Pierson did.

At least one prisoner was paroled to visit relatives in the North. W. A. Wash jotted down in his journal that a "Captain Jones, of Arkansas, returned from a parole of one month. He had been to see his parents, in Illinois, who were old friends of President Lincoln."[665] Of course, strings were pulled to get that rare excursion from the confines of the island.

Another type of visitor was of the unwelcomed kind. Boat cruises routinely brought eager onlookers to the waters off the island to see the Confederate soldiers. One prisoner noted: "Other steamers, loaded with excursionists, would occasionally

---

[661] Barbiere, Joe., *Scraps from the Prison Table, At Camp Chase and Johnson's Island,* 83.

[662] Inzer, John Washington., *The Diary of a Confederate Soldier: John Washington Inzer 1834–1928,* 95.

[663] Wash, W. A., *Camp, Field and Prison Life,* 98.

[664] Ibid., 205.

[665] Wash, W. A., *Camp, Field and Prison Life,* 237.

run close in, prompted by curiosity and taunt us with their shouts and jeers. Their favorite pastime was or seemed to be, the singing of patriotic songs."[666] Some locals were allowed onto the island to peer at the imprisoned secessionists. Captain Bingham gave his opinions in his diary. "Yankee girls & women most certainly like to look at naked rebels. The fence leaves a walk on the lake shore—& there it is made with bars and spaces alternating. The pumps are there & men are nearly always walking there & very near to said naked men—12 to 15 steps at most. Today, some saw a man washing & passed by & one little one about 15 was so anxious that she looked back over her shoulder till she fell into the ditch."[667] W. A. Wash also noted: "The *Island Queen*, which makes regular excursion trips, passed close round the island with a cargo of heaven's last and best creation, and they seemed to be astonished that the rebels looked so well and perfectly contented."[668]

EXECUTIONS

There were four executions carried out on Johnson's Island during the Civil War. The men executed were William F. Corbin, T. P. McGraw, Reuben Stout, and John J. Nichols. Each man's case was unique, and not all of the men were soldiers of the South.

William F. Corbin and T. P. McGraw, both of Kentucky, were convicted by a court martial in Cincinnati of recruiting for the Confederate army within federal lines and of carrying information to the enemy. They were sentenced to be shot at Johnson's Island. The men were brought out to the south side of the island on a two-horse cart. They were then seated upon their respective coffins, facing a battle line of the Hoffman Battalion. Major Pierson, accompanied by his staff, was positioned to the right of the guards. The other prisoners were restricted to their quarters with increased guard. The command was given to fire and the thunder of sixteen muskets echoed across the island. The two men fell back upon their coffins, dead. The executions took place on May 15, 1863.[669] The bodies were sent south to their families.

The next person to be executed was Private Reuben Stout of the Sixtieth Indiana Infantry. Private Stout, a Union soldier, was executed for murder and desertion. Stout had enlisted in what he believed to be a cavalry regiment. He later discovered he had been inducted into an infantry unit. He was immediately dissatisfied with the army. After a few months in the service, he was given a furlough. While on that furlough, he became ill, and his family urged him not to return to his unit. He joined a pro-South organization called the "Knights of the Golden Circle." After several months

---

[666] Carpenter, H., "Plain Living at Johnson's Island." *Century Magazine (March 1891),* 710.

[667] Bingham, Robert, *Diary,* 70.

[668] Wash, W. A., *Camp, Field and Prison Life,* 142.

[669] Frohman, Charles E., *Rebels on Lake Erie,* 58.

in hiding, he was found by two provost marshals. When they attempted to arrest him, Stout shot one of them dead. Stout was captured the next morning.[670]

A court martial was held in Indianapolis for Stout. He was found guilty and sent to Johnson's Island for execution. He arrived at Johnson's Island on June 15, 1863, with the initial execution day to be the 26th of the same month, but the execution was deferred from outside orders until October.[671] On Friday, October 23, 1863, the execution was carried out. A prisoner noted in his diary the details of the event:

> The day is cold, and dark and cheerless, fit day for the scene I have just witnessed, the execution of a deserter. At half past two o'clock P. M. the Battalion was marched down and formed on three sides of a square on the beach in front of our quarters. The convict was led out, heavily ironed, and placed within the square just at the lake shore. The execution was delayed some time while the chaplain prayed and talked with him. He was then seated on his coffin, facing his executioners. At this time the suspense became painful in the extreme. His crime for a time was forgotten, and we saw only a fellow being trembling on the verge of another world, with but a very few swiftly fleeting moments between him and eternity. A deathlike stillness prevailed, unbroken by a single sound. The command was given to fire and the roar of the volley echoed over the still waters of the bay, the convict fell back upon his coffin, a corpse.[672]

His body was buried in the prison cemetery, the only Union soldier among the Confederates.

The last person executed was John J. Nichols (also called John G. Nickell) of Kentucky. He had enlisted at the age of 18 into the Confederate Army and became a partisan ranger. On May 24, 1864, a military commission in Cincinnati convicted him of killing two men. The court ordered that he be hung at Johnson's Island on September 2, 1864. On the island a gallows was constructed especially for this occasion. The prisoner was marched out to the gallows, accompanied by a chaplain. The proceedings of the court were read, after which the chaplain read a statement prepared by the prisoner. He was led up the stairs and placed on the drop floor. A cap was drawn over his head and the rope was adjusted. The spring was touched and moments later he was pronounced dead. Colonel Webb noted the event in his diary, "I saw the poor fellow seated on his coffin in a carryall, with the chaplin administering him the last consolations of God's holy promises, and in mockery were the loud notes of the shrill

---

[670] Knauss, William H., *The Story of Camp Chase*, 200–201.

[671] Ibid.

[672] Patterson, Edmund Dewitt., *Yankee Rebel: The Civil War Journal of Edmund DeWitt Patterson*, 141.

fife and drum with the usual parade of flags, music and troop."[673] Colonel Hundley reported in his journal, "No friend was allowed to visit this unfortunate victim of Yankee tyranny, but even his enemies bear witness that he died like a man, sending word to his brother rebels that he wished them to remember that he died a true soldier of the Confederacy."[674] He was buried in the Confederate cemetery. Later, when the wooden headboards were replaced with marble, the facts were confused. The engraving on the tombstone stated John J. Nickell, a surgeon, was interned below, and in fact this should read a sergeant. The correct spelling of his name is unclear.[675]

LINCOLN'S ASSASSINATION

Abraham Lincoln was assassinated on April 15, 1865. A boat approached the island with its flag at half-mast. This caused quite the stir inside the bull pen as prisoners anticipated the news with the hopes that it was beneficial for the struggling Confederacy. When the boat docked, the guards heard the news and angrily lined the fence top and manned the blockhouses. The gun ports were opened and the canons pushed into firing position expecting to crush the celebrating Rebels. Colonel Hill came into the bull pen to inform and warn the prisoners. H. W. Henry recounted the experience: "The prisoners gathered around him and he mounted a stairway. He told us that he had some very bad news to tell us; that President Lincoln was assassinated, that the Northern people were greatly excited, and that they attributed the act either to our government in its desperation over its defeat or to some of our people wreaking revenge upon the head of the nation in the hour of its rejoicing over its victory over us. He warned us not to make the least demonstration of rejoicing, as his men were wrought up to such a pitch of frenzy that it would be hard to restrain them from firing upon us, and that any cheering or demonstration of joy by us over the event would certainly expose us to the fire of his men. Of course under the suspense of our own apprehensions and the warning of Colonel Hill we walked very carefully and refrained from anything that might have been constructed by our guardians as evidence of rejoicing"[676] Like everyone else in the nation, the prisoners were shocked when they heard the news. They assured Colonel Hill southern gentleman would not do something as dishonorable as assassination. The prisoners knew this assassination would not help improve their lot. The exchange system was in full swing and now it might be stopped. Retaliation might

---

[673] Webb, R. F., "Prison Life at Johnson's Island." *Histories of the Several Regiments and Battalions from North Carolina in the Great War 1861–65,* 686.

[674] Hundley, D. R. *Prison Echoes of the Great Rebellion,* 124.

[675] Knauss, William H., *The Story of Camp Chase,* 205, 206; Frohman, Charles E., *Rebels on Lake Erie,* 62–64.

[676] H. W. Henry, Confederate Veteran, XVII, 335.

be swift and harsh from the government. Many prisoners lost their bitterness toward Lincoln and forgave him. Colonel Hundley made this poignant remark in his journal: Before the assassination, "Mr. Lincoln had delivered his last inaugural containing those memorable words, 'with malice toward none and charity for all,' and before he had as yet laid down his life in defense of his construction of the Constitution of our common country. Believing as I do in the atoning efficacy of blood, from the moment the assassin's bullet laid low the head of that honored American chief, the writer of these pages has effaced from his bosom every trace of resentment against Abraham Lincoln."[677]

Conclusion

These are the incidents in the camp that were significant enough to be recorded in numerous diaries, official reports, and reminiscences. The majority of the incidents described were in 1864 because that was the time span from which the most prisoners' diaries have survived. Many more incidents quietly passed into oblivion.

---

[677] Hundley, D. R. *Prison Echoes of the Great Rebellion,* 235.

Chapter 8

ESCAPES

"Escape, liberation from these blank walls, is almost a fixed impossibility. The words of Dante over his inferno might with truth be inscribed over the entrance of the prison. 'He who enters here leaves hope behind.'"

—V. S. Murphey

For as long as man has had prisons, the prisoners have derived various methods to leave the confines prematurely. Johnson's Island was no exception. However, during the early history of the prison, the Rebels were for the most part content, because exchange and a return to their own lines was seen as inevitable. Only when the possibility of exchange evaporated did the prisoners invent methods for an unauthorized departure.

To escape from Johnson's Island, prisoners were faced with very formidable obstacles. Lieutenant Phillips of Hoffman's Battalion stated that Johnson's Island was "considered one of the most inaccessible and secure of the military prisons in the North."[678] A plank fence about fifteen feet high surrounded the prison. Sentinels patrolled the top of the fence with an ever-attentive eye fixed on the bull pen. The prisoners could not come within 30 feet of the fence for any reason. A series of stakes marked this point, and because a prisoner would be shot if he crossed it, this was called the dead line. Lanterns were arrayed around the fence to illuminate the area from the fence to the dead line during nighttime. The prisoners were not allowed to move from block to block after dark. If they tried, they risked catching a bullet from the guards on the parapet. Every morning the roll was called and the prisoners counted to make sure all

---

[678] Phillips, George M., "Johnson's Island and the Lake Erie Raid of 1864." *Glimpses of the Nation's Struggle.* p 243.

figures matched. Surprise searches were administered from time to time to check for escape paraphernalia. To guarantee that the outside authorities had knowledge of any escape attempts, informants were recruited to keep an eye on their fellow prisoners. Colonel Murphey, a prisoner inside the bullpen, described the impossibility of getting out: "Escape, liberation from these blank walls, is almost a fixed impossibility. The words of Dante over his inferno might with truth be inscribed over the entrance of the prison. 'He who enters here leaves hope behind.' The palisades are tall and perpendicular and no cover nor protection to advance upon them. Huge lanterns suspended from them throw a flood of light over the entire enclosure and thus you are robbed of the friendly cover of night. The sentinels are the most vigilant active and thoroughly instructed and disciplined guards I ever saw. No movement, no agitation, no assemblage of men however insignificant succeeds in eluding the lynx-eyed custodians. Upon the slightest provocation they will shoot a rebel down, and in reply to a civil question you frequently [receive] biting curses which makes your blood seethe like a caldron in your veins."[679]

If an enterprising prisoner managed to elude the guards and got on the outside of the prison fence, he still faced the prospect of getting off the island. This was a natural barrier, one of the reasons the location was selected. The island lay three miles across the bay to Sandusky and about one mile to the peninsula to the north. A prisoner that managed to escape the bull pen would have to be a good swimmer or have another plan to actually get off the island. If a prisoner did manage to prevail over these obstacles, a cannon would be fired, warning the surrounding countryside to be on the lookout for a prisoner. Usually a significant reward was offered for the capture of the escaped. A description of the prisoner would be telegraphed to neighboring towns. Needless to say, not more than a handful of Confederates made their way safely off the island.

At first prisoners were not punished for trying to escape. W. A. Wash commented on the situation thus: "At most of the Northern prisons it was a custom to punish prisoners for attempting to escape, but with us they were generally simply relieved of what they had contraband and turned loose—always inside the pen."[680] Colonel Murphey added: "Indeed our right to escape is an acknowledged one by the prison authorities. An effort for its practical execution does not incur health penalties."[681] Later, in June 1864, in the midst of an epidemic of escape tunnel construction, Colonel Hill posted on the bulletin board an order that chief of messes were now responsible for tunneling and damage to government property. If the individuals involved were not reported

[679] Murphey, V. S., *Diary*, 122–123.

[680] Wash, W. A., *Camp, Field and Prison Life*, 188–189.

[681] Murphey, V. S., *Diary*, 136.

immediately, rations are to be stopped as a punishment. If they are not reported, then all rations would be diminished or other punishment may be necessary.[682]

During the first summer of operation, 1862, the prisoners did not try very many serious attempts to break out. Exchange was seen as the easiest way to return back to their own lines. There was one person who decided to leave the prison without the approval of Major Pierson. On, September 2, 1862, a list of prisoners to be exchanged was sent to Johnson's Island. A Confederate captain, F. W. Weed of Missouri, discovered he was not on the list to leave the compound. He decided he would take matters into his own hands. The prisoners were assembled in the usual way for a roll call. The federal officers would call out a prisoner's name for exchange. The prisoner would answer "here," and walk toward the gate. As the prisoner walked toward the gate, the guard on top of the fence would signal down for the gate to be opened. The prisoner would then be escorted to a boat ready to take the prisoners to the mainland. It was raining, so the federal officers had pitched a tent near the main gate. As name after name was called, the job became tedious. The officers and guards had succumbed to the monotony of the process and were not as attentive as at first. This, combined with the heavy downpour, presented the opportunity to Captain Weed. He had noticed that the two groups of federals administering the procedure were not in direct communication with each other. The names were called and the gates opened in a rhythmic pattern. The officers in the tent came to a name that was difficult to read. As they huddled around to examine the name, Captain Weed stepped forward, called out "here," not too loudly as to draw the attention of the officers in the tent, and walked over to the gate. The gate was opened and Weed joined his compatriots in the harbor. The boat departed with one more prisoner than expected and landed in Sandusky. On the way to the point of exchange, he slipped passed the guards and headed home to fight once again.[683]

Escape attempts are recorded very sporadically in diaries and official records before late summer of 1863. The prisoners understood that to try to escape when exchange was considered highly likely was foolish and an unnecessary risk. Only when exchange broke down and became improbable did escape attempts become numerous. Captain Bingham summed up the thoughts of escape: "In fact we are ripe for any desperate project—if there be any hope of success. We have given up all hope of exchange & to settle down to a captivity as long as the war [lasts] is a terrible thought but one to wh[ich] I am accustomed & partly reconciled."[684]

Around August 10, 1863, a prisoner concealed himself in a slop barrel used to carry garbage out of the kitchens and hoped to make his way outside of the gate. He

---

[682] Caldwell, James Parks. *A Northern Confederate at Johnson's Island Prison: The Civil War Diary of James Parks Caldwell*, 119–120.

[683] Conf Vet, XII, 182.

[684] Bingham, Robert, *Diary*, 2, 48.

had enlisted the aid of the Yankee driver to haul him out. The plot was discovered and the Rebel was returned to his block. How he was discovered is not known, but the slop cart was escorted into the prison under guard for the next few days.[685]

On a dark and stormy night in October, three prisoners crept down a ditch and sawed through the planks, only to be captured by the guards patrolling outside the fence.[686] Colonel Pierson rejected the idea from William Hoffman, Commissary-General of Prisoners, for extra boarding along the inside of the fence, as the prisoners had sufficient time to saw through any type of fencing. Instead, Pierson had more lamps installed along the fence to illuminate all areas of the fence and expose any lurking prisoners. The commandant realized that the guards could not rely upon their hearing, as the noise from the waves breaking on shore could drown out any sounds of enterprising Confederates with their saws.[687]

Colonel Pierson sent a communiqué to William Hoffman, in late October, that the prisoners had "exhibited much enterprise of late in the attempts to get out. They [had] tried digging under ground from sinks; also from quarters, commencing under the buildings." He reported that none had been successful.[688] In the late fall of 1863, a party of eight men in Block 1 began to construct a tunnel to secure their freedom. They cut through the floor of their quarters using a notched case knife as a saw. They began to dig vertically for about three feet, then angled toward the fence. The digging was done with sticks, knives, plates, or whatever could be found. The dirt was dispersed under the block; the space under the block was just enough to allow someone to crawl flat on his stomach, spreading the dirt out to avoid detection. As they neared the terminus of the tunnel, they began to dig upward, encountering a tree stump. The Rebels worked their way through the branches and broke through to the surface on the night of November 3, which was a cold, rainy night. The first two prisoners crawled to the surface and ran off into the woods. The third prisoner, Captain Cole from Arkansas, who was a large broad-shouldered man, wedged himself in the hole to the point where he could not move forward or backward. He very quietly called to the rest of the party behind him to return to their bunks. He remained quiet for as long as possible to give his comrades time to make their escape. The next morning he was discovered by the guard, shivering from the cold. The guards had to use axes and saws to clear him from his trapped state. He was brought to the headquarters of General Shaler, who asked him why he did not call out for help. Captain Cole responded that that would

[685] Wash, W. A., *Camp, Field and Prison Life*, 163.

[686] Bingham, Robert, *Diary*, 74.

[687] *War of the Rebellion: A Compilation of the Official Records of the Union and Confederate Armies*, Vol. VI, 391.

[688] *War of the Rebellion: A Compilation of the Official Records of the Union and Confederate Armies*, series 2, Vol 6, 391.

have been dishonorable because two of his compatriots were on the outside of the bull pen, and if the alarm would have been raised, it would have destroyed their chances. The General was impressed and gave him some whiskey from his personal stocks. Cole returned to his block, and was given a hero's welcome. A song was sung with the verse, "And now three cheers for Captain Cole, Who wouldn't holler out when stuck in the hole." The two other prisoners were captured that same day hiding in some brush.[689]

Not until December 1863, when the island was surrounded by ice, did the number of attempts increase dramatically. On December 11, some prisoners from Block 5 tried to cut through the wall behind Block 10. Two of them made it through before the guard discovered the attempt. The alarm was raised and the whole island was searched.[690] It is not known if they succeeded. The next night General Archer and a few others had somehow penetrated the fence and made their way onto the frozen bay. The ice started to break up and they returned to the island. They were returned to the enclosure chilled to the bone. General Archer and four others tried again on the night of December 22, 1863. They had made arrangements to bribe the two federal guards that call the roll to assist them in getting out of the bull pen. The corporals reported the offer to Major Scovill, who granted permission to continue with the deception. On the arranged night of the 22nd, the guards lowered a ladder down the inside of the fence, helped the men over, collected the sum of three hundred dollars and a gold watch, and let the Rebels continue on their way. As the Rebels headed to what they thought would be Dixie, the guards rose from the bushes and apprehended the surprised men. They were kept in a prison cell until morning and sent back to their blocks, without their money. It appears from diary entries of both prisoners and a guard that the soldiers kept the bribe, with the approval of Major Scovill. This may have been to send a message to the prisoners that bribing to escape would not guarantee success, plus they would lose their money. Word of the double-cross spread through the prison, reinforcing the belief that the guards did not have any honor.[691] During this period of time, a prisoner noted in his diary that he and a friend had arranged to pay a guard eighty dollars to secure their escape. He then never mentioned it again.[692]

At the end of 1863, the weather became intensely cold. A prisoner by the name of Boyd made an attempt to escape, hoping that the cold would affect the vigilance of the guards. The cold was too intense, so he returned to the guardhouse and gave himself up. Upon returning to his room, he informed his roommates that if one can overcome

---

[689] Philpot, Conf. vet., 361–363; Rev Thrasher, 5-1-1938; Green,100; Crouch, Conf Vet, 515.

[690] Dooley, John, *John Dooley, Confederate Soldier: His War Journal*, 152–153.

[691] Barziza, Decimus et Ultimus, *The Adventures of a Prisoner of War,* 99; Patterson, Edmund Dewitt, *Yankee Rebel: The Civil War Journal of Edmund DeWitt Patterson*, 151; Sells, Hiram, December 23, 1863.

[692] Dooley, John, *John Dooley, Confederate Soldier: His War Journal*, 153.

the cold he could make his escape since the guards were not on the lookout, keeping in their houses.[693]

Several prisoners started to construct a ladder and make preparations for escape. Major Winston, Captain McConnel, Captain Davis, Captain Robinson, and Captain Stokes[694] started to round up clothing to endure the reported 27 degrees below zero.[695] The Rebels wrapped themselves in several drawers, pants, and coats. Red pepper was sprinkled on their feet, which was thought to fight off frostbite, and they put on as many socks as would fit in their boots. The party constructed a crude ladder by securing the legs of their benches using clothesline to a board that acted like a central spine with the rungs protruding from either side. They needed a person to remain behind to remove the ladder from the fence to prevent the raising of the alarm. Lieutenant Thomas White volunteered to bring back the ladder.[696] The attempt was made that night.

Darkness fell on the extremely cold night of December 31 to January 1, 1864, and the prisoners were ready for the voyage that might lead them to home or death. To avoid detection, the party crawled toward the fence, lying flat on the ground, dragging the homemade ladder. They set the ladder on the side of the fence and to their horror it was four feet too short. Major Winston leaped to the top of the fence and crossed over, jumped to the ground and hid behind a large oak tree. Captain Davis was next, followed by Captain Robinson and Captain McConnell. When Captain Stokes came over the fence and landed on the other side, he was spotted by a federal guard and ordered to halt. The sentinel thought he was another guard and so failed to fire upon him. Lieutenant White heard the challenge of the guard on the outside and created a diversion by grabbing the ladder and running back to his block. Before he entered he struck the ladder against the side of the block to draw the guard's attention.[697] Stokes eventually ran in the opposite direction from the others and crossed the bay to Sandusky.[698] Stokes had not wrapped his feet with socks for traction so he had to crawl across the ice on hands and knees. He was badly frozen and had to take refuge in the home of a Copperhead. The helpful farmer feed him and let him warm in his home. The helpful farmer then took him to the railroad station for him to proceed to Canada, but a detective, spotting

---

[693] Dooley, John, *John Dooley, Confederate Soldier: His War Journal*, 154.

[694] Captain T. Herbert Davis 1st Va. Infantry, Major John R. Winston 45th N. C. Infantry, Capt. Charles C. Robinson 9th VA Cav. Captain Stokes has also been called Stakes and Scales. A firsthand account written by a participant called him Captain Stokes.

[695] Knauss, William H., *The Story of Camp Chase*, 226.

[696] Dooley, John, *John Dooley, Confederate Soldier: His War Journal*, 155.

[697] Dooley, John, *John Dooley, Confederate Soldier: His War Journal*, 155.

[698] Knauss, William H., *The Story of Camp Chase*, 227.

his gray clothes, arrested him and returned the captain to the Island.[699] When Stokes returned to the bull pen, his hands were so frostbitten that the tips had to be amputated.[700]

The main group of four Rebels ventured across the island to the north shore. They scurried across the ice, avoiding the thin spots. A light snow had fallen and made the thin spots stand out as black voids in the field of ice. After the one mile run to the peninsula to the north, which one member called an "exciting run," the group rested on the opposite shore, and heard the sentinels call out from their posts, "all's well."[701]

At that point, the group began to walk west, down the peninsula of Marblehead. The large number of lights that were lit in the homes along the road made the Rebels uneasy, as this might be a signal system. They concluded that the lights were lit for warmth and stayed on the road. The woods were found to be a warmer avenue for their journey, so they ventured overland. With dawn a few hours away, the frozen Rebels sought the shelter of a barn. They found two horses inside the barn. They sped off to the west on the stolen horses. They all were complaining of sore feet and chills, but Captain McConnell was affected the most by the cold. He continually complained about the cold and suddenly fell from the horse groaning. The horses were also in a dismal state; their breath had congealed covered the whole front of their heads. The horses were released and headed back in the direction of home.

Back on Johnson's Island, the guards were ignorant of the previous night's proceedings. The roll callers came in and called roll as usual. Roll was called by room and the escaped party occupied the last room to be called. Some prisoners covered for the missing men, by answering for themselves then quickly and silently moving to the other side of the formation. The federal guards did not notice the ruse. The escape of Winston and his party was detected after Captain Stokes was brought back on January 3.[702] This gave the other escapees a full day's head start.

At sun-up, Winston's group went to a home and was taken in. They told the farmer that they were land speculators. The curious farmer fed them a breakfast and delivered a barrage of questions, which they skillfully avoided. After they were warmed and feed, they continued on their voyage. Avoiding the main roads, the Rebels walked through woods and fields. They continued to walk throughout the day, with the cold nipping at the ears, fingers, and toes. In the afternoon, they stopped at a home and had some much-needed rest. They continued. As the second night approached, they went to a farmer's house, but were turned away. They continued to walk westward and, by midnight, Captain McConnell's health continued to decline. He complained of heartburn and of the cold. His condition deteriorated to the point that he asked to be left at

---

[699] Dooley, John, *John Dooley, Confederate Soldier: His War Journal*, 157.

[700] Dunaway, Wayland Fuller, *Reminiscences of a Rebel*, 118–119.

[701] Knauss, William H., *The Story of Camp Chase*, 227–228.

[702] Dooley, John, *John Dooley, Confederate Soldier: His War Journal*, 156.

the next house. He was left at a doorstep, with instructions that he not knock until the rest of the party was out of sight. He was able to recover and sold his watch for a train ticket to Detroit. While on the train, McConnell was apprehended by a detective.[703] His illness may have been fabricated so that he could carry on by himself.

Captain Robinson, Davis, and Major Winston continued to walk westward ever closer to Canada and safety. They had been in continuous motion for forty-eight hours, and except for a brief one-hour sleep the first evening, they had not slept for sixty hours. Exhaustion and the bitter cold were starting to take its toll on the Rebels. The Ohio climate was succeeding in breaking their spirits. They had tried to procure food and shelter but were turned away the majority of the time. They came upon a large house and were taken in. When quizzed about their origins, Captain Robinson said that they were from New Bedford, Massachusetts. The Yankee host stated, "Ah! That's my old home," and began to inquire about some of the residents. The host was obviously trying to test the validity of their story, but Robinson was able to answer the questions because he had been a whaler for several years and was familiar with the whaling city.[704] After sleeping for some time, they left for Toledo, Ohio. They walked through Toledo, crossed over to Michigan, and journeyed to Monroe by nightfall. They found lodging at a French-Canadian's house, and had a good night's sleep.

Upon arriving at the village of Trenton, Michigan, they decided to venture out on the ice to Fighting Island (now Grosse Island) and then across the river to Canada. The ice was smooth on the short voyage to the island, Captain Robinson slipped and injured himself, but the trio continued. They walked across the island and onto the ice on the other side. The trek across this patch of ice was treacherous, as a storm had broken the ice shifting it to resemble jagged ice cliffs. Major Winston had a foot break through a patch of thin ice, he yelled out a warning but it was too late. Captain Robinson had both feet break through. Only by leaning and falling on thicker ice was he saved. Almost instantly their feet froze stiff. They reviewed their situation and contemplated heading back to avoid freezing, but this risked recapture. To continue on might mean death; however, their drive to reach the safety of Canada was too powerful.[705] They continued on, using the stars to guide them to the other shore. Clouds suddenly moved in and for a few moments they were walking by reckoning. Then they saw what they had dreamed of back at Johnson's Island, the Canadian shore and freedom. Almost like a final hurdle placed by the forces to be, the ice became very thin near the beach. The men decided to risk it, one at a time they walked over the thin ice and one by one reached firm land.

Once in Canada, they no longer had to pretend who they were, because they were in a land sympathetic to the southern cause. They went to the first house and were given

---

[703] Knauss, William H., *The Story of Camp Chase*, 229–230.

[704] Knauss, William H., *The Story of Camp Chase*, 231.

[705] Knauss, William H., *The Story of Camp Chase*, 232–233.

shelter and freshly baked pies. Their journey lasted for four days and four nights, with little food, little shelter, and an abundance of cold weather. They were told of some Kentuckians in the area. Major Winston went to investigate but found the men to be deserters with no desire to return south. The men wrote to friends and received sufficient funds to continue in modern fashion. They made their way to Montreal, where Winston wrote a letter to his fellow prisoners back on Johnson's Island telling of his success.[706] He ventured down the St. Lawrence River, by railroad because the river was frozen, to Riviere du Loup. They traveled by sled through New Brunswick to Halifax, Nova Scotia. The trio boarded a Royal Mail steamer to Bermuda.[707] The blockade runner, *Advance*, took them back to North Carolina and once again they were home, in the land of the South.[708] Captain Davis would see Johnson's Island again as he was captured at Sailor's Creek in 1865 and returned to his previous lodgings.[709]

The night following the escape of Winston and his party, more prisoners tried to duplicate their success. The night was not as cold as the previous night with guards walking their traditional beats. Many prisoners crept down ditches with ladders to scale the wall, but they were discovered and many fired upon. One prisoner did manage to knock down a guard with a block of wood and was able to scale the wall, only to be captured on the other side.[710] He was put in chains and some of the sentinels boasted that they were going to shoot him.

Escape fever spread throughout the prison. The federals were frightened at the increased activity and tried to settle the prisoners by spreading a rumor that a general exchange had been secured, but to no avail.[711] Block 12 became a beehive of activity, building ladders and plotting of a mass escape. Some 200 prisoners were involved. Rumors spread that the order to escape had come from "higher powers."[712] With so many prisoners involved and informants infiltrating all aspects of prison life, the scheme was foiled. The federals made a search and confiscated the ladders, effectively eliminating the escape attempt.[713]

The ice bridge to the mainland was too much of a temptation for the prisoners. Two prisoners, a Colonel Johnson of Arkansas and an unidentified Captain, had disguised themselves in federal uniforms. When the federals came inside the prison to

---

[706] Dooley, John, *John Dooley, Confederate Soldier: His War Journal*, 159.

[707] Knauss, William H., *The Story of Camp Chase*, 235.

[708] Knauss, William H., *The Story of Camp Chase*, 235–236.

[709] Escape of Prisoners from Johnson's Island, Southern Historical Society Papers.

[710] Dooley, John, *John Dooley, Confederate Soldier: His War Journal*, 156,

[711] Bingham, Robert, *Diary*, 50.

[712] Bingham, Robert, *Diary*, 2, 48–49.

[713] Wash, W. A., *Camp, Field and Prison Life*, 186.

pick up the axes and saws used for chopping wood, the two grabbed up a handful of tools and walked out with the legitimate blue coats. They placed the tools in the proper spot and walked onto the ice toward Sandusky. They arrived at the city, but were discovered and sent back to the prison.[714]

The prison was still in the midst of escape fever in late February 1864. On the 23rd, two rebels "tried to scale the wall in rear of block 4—both caught—one got over, but soon found himself in the calaboose."[715] A Lieutenant Colonel Lyle "went out of the gate arrayed in all the glory of a 'Yank' officer, but was detected" at the edge of the ice and returned to the pen.[716]

In May 1864, the federal authorities decided to dig a ditch on three sides on the inside of the perimeter fence. The ditch was excavated down to solid bedrock, a depth of roughly six feet, on the third side of the fence located close to the prisoners' barracks. The side near the water, and furthest from the blocks, was left unmolested as the distance from the blocks and the close proximity to the water judged it to be unnecessary. This was to prevent tunneling out of the prison as all tunnels would terminate inside the bull pen. To dig this ditch was a massive undertaking. The guards had to not only conduct their normal picket duty, but also had to facilitate other construction and improvement projects.[717] When this project was completed is not known; however, during early June, many reports of prisoners attempting to tunnel was reported in diaries and letters. On June 3, Edmund Patterson noted in his journal that on the previous night the Yankees discovered a tunnel commencing under the dead house on the side of the prison hospital and running toward the wall. The federals went straight to the spot without any guidance of reconnoitering, as if informed by a spy.[718] Colonel Webb stated: "a tunnel was cut from one of the blocks last week, a distance of some thirty or forty feet, but just about the time it was completed and arrangements made to leave, the Yankees, like magic, discovered it. Last night another attempt was made by digging a tunnel from the dead house, but this was also discovered before an opportunity was offered to use it. It is an evident fact that we have spies among us."[719] On June 6, the federals went into the prison and found twenty Rebels actively digging a tunnel.[720]

---

[714] Wash, W. A., *Camp, Field and Prison Life*, 188–189.

[715] Wash, W. A., *Camp, Field and Prison Life*. 20.8

[716] Caldwell, James Parks. *A Northern Confederate at Johnson's Island Prison: The Civil War Diary of James Parks Caldwell*, 88.

[717] The federals during this period of time had to move the fence back, dig new sinks, and dig the ditch.

[718] Patterson, Edmund Dewitt, *Yankee Rebel: The Civil War Journal of Edmund DeWitt Patterson*, 170.

[719] Webb, R. F. "Prison Life at Johnson's Island." *Histories of the Several Regiments and Battalions from North Carolina in the Great War 1861–65*, 680–681.

[720] Thompson, Mortimer C., *Letter,* June 6, 1864. USA

The federal officer went straight to the place the tunnel began, aimed his pistol into the dark and discharged it.[721] Fortunately for the rebels, no one was hit by the bullet, but the strong action of firing the pistol was meant to convey the possibility that the prisoners do so at the risk of their lives. The tunnels were plugged with rocks, boards, and anything else available to seal up the hole. By mid-June, the ditch must have been completed because tunneling attempts were drastically reduced.

Enterprising Rebels tried to use the ditch to their advantage. The night of June 29 was a dark rainy night. Two prisoners made their way down into the ditch directly under a lamp, which cast a shadow over that immediate spot. They started to dig under the fence, were caught and returned to the bull pen the next morning, wet and shivering from the cold. Prisoners, thinking they were new arrivals, greeted them with the call "fresh fish."[722]

Charles E. Grogan, of Baltimore, decided that he needed to leave the confines of Johnson's Island. One day, when a group of men were sent outside the bull pen to gather straw for bedding, Grogan, a member of that party, saw an opportunity to escape. A straw storage building was located near the federal docks among horse stables and other support facilities for the prison complex. He went inside with the group and kicked together a large pile of straw and while the guard was not looking, he crawled under the pile. He whispered to his comrades not to disturb the straw he was under. The group of prisoners under guard made their way back inside the bull pen, with the federals not realizing they were one short. When night fell, he exited the barn and began looking for ways to get off the island. He constructed a small raft and made his way onto the water. Shortly after he realized that the raft was inadequate for the voyage and returned. By this time dawn started to break and he knew he had to come up with some type of plan or he would be returned to his former accommodations. He boldly walked up to the docks and boarded the boat. The boat departed for Sandusky and Grogan was never heard of until he wrote to Colonel Pierson from Richmond, Virginia, some time later.[723]

Block 1 was very close to the fence; only about fifteen feet separated the stairway to the fence. The safety railing was on the same level as the top of the fence. Captain Robert C. Kennedy, 1st Georgia Infantry, had procured a very long plank of wood. On October 4, 1864, a dark rainy night, the prisoner waited for the guard to walk to the extreme limit of his beat and laid the board across, walked over, knocked the board to the ground, and climbed down off the plank walk. He hid underneath as the guard, hearing the plank fall, came back to investigate. The guard saw no evidence of foul play and continued on as normal. The prisoner ran over to a boat that belonged to Captain Benson of the

---

[721] Caldwell, James Parks. *A Northern Confederate at Johnson's Island Prison: The Civil War Diary of James Parks Caldwell*, 119.

[722] Hundley, D. R. *Prison Echoes of the Great Rebellion*, p87.

[723] Howard, McHenry. *Recollections of a Maryland Confederate Soldier and Staff Officer under Johnston, Jackson, and Lee*, 400–401, Sells USA.

Hoffman's Battalion and made his way to the Canadian shore.[724] The federal authorities did not discover the escape until October 15. The roll callers had counted him as present for the past eleven days. The boat was reported lost by Captain Benson, but since no prisoner was missing, the assumption was that the boat was lost or stolen by either a federal soldier or a civilian. The breakdown in the system caused an intense investigation by Major Thomas Linnell, then Superintendent of Prison. Major Linnell ordered that all involved were to be arrested. The roll caller Sergeant Hewitt and his assistant Clark were arrested for disobedience of orders. The sentinel, a member of the Sixth Regiment Reserve Corps then stationed on the island, was also arrested. The investigation found that Lieutenant Amos C. Smith, 19th Tennessee Infantry, of the same block and room as Kennedy, had been dropped from the roll and had answered present for the escaped prisoner. Sergeant Hewitt was not on duty from October 1 to 8, his assistant Clark was told to drop the names of all prisoners that had recently been removed from the prison; Lieutenant Smith was accidentally dropped from the rolls. When Hewitt returned for duty, he called the roll from the updated list supplied by Clark. All numbers matched and everything appeared correct. Smith was placed in solitary confinement with reduced rations on November 17, 1864, for answering for Kennedy. He was not released until January 1865. This was not normal; very little punishment was ordered for any prisoners attempting escape. However, Major-General E. A. Hitchcock ordered the punishment of Smith. Clark and the sentinel were ordered to be court martialed.[725]

Robert Cobb Kennedy made it to Canada and wrote to his friends letting them know he was safe.[726] In Canada, Kennedy was recruited to join the "Northwest Conspiracy" and was arrested in connection with the attempted burning of Barnum's Museum, the Belmonte and Tammany Hotels. He was arrested and hanged March 25, 1865, at Fort Lafayette.[727] A prisoner, who resided in Kennedy's old block at Johnson's Island, gave Lt. Colonel Scovill a letter, dated December 11, 1864, in the drop box.

> Sir, It having come to my knowledge recently; that one the B. C. Kenedy [sic] a Lieutenant of the Confederate Army, who escaped this prison some time since; was in N. York at the time of the burning of some Hotel which recently occurred. I having seen two letters from said Kenedy [sic] recently both of which I think can be found at any time. Kenedy [sic] is bold, and

---

[724] Mitchell, E. O. "Johnson's Island: Military Prison for Confederate Prisoners." *Sketches of War History 1861–1865*, 125–126. USA

[725] *War of the Rebellion: A Compilation of the Official Records of the Union and Confederate Armies*, series 2, vol 7, 995–996; *War of the Rebellion: A Compilation of the Official Records of the Union and Confederate Armies*, series 2, Vol 8, 41–42.

[726] Wash, W. A., *Camp, Field and Prison Life*, 277.

[727] *The Johnson's Island Plot*, 9.

acknowledges to have had a hand in the burning. He is in Toronto C. W. at present and can if desired, be induced to come to Brooklin [sic] or N. York City at almost any time where he might be apprehended if desired. Kenedy [sic] is under an assumed name which I cannot recall at present but is contained in a letter recently Received in my room. All that is in my power will be done; at your request [sic] to ferret out this or any other Similar case written my knowledge you will please let me know of this correspondence who would convey it to any of the prisoners. Should this be of any value to you, you can know the writer by posting a note on the Bullitin [sic] Marked XX in which you need not mention what subject is embraced. Loyal Prisoner

Scovill must have responded because a week later the prisoner dropped another letter in the drop box:

Sir if your notice marked XX which was placed upon the bulliten [sic] board this morning was meant as a reply, to a communication which was in the drop letter box. Last Monday morning the 12th inst, and which communication related to one Mr. Kenedy [sic] late of Johnson's Island and now in Canada. I can inform you that I was the writer I am in Block 7 Mess 2 Co 14 if you notice was not relative to the above named communication, this can do no harm as I suppose you will not allow this to be exposed to any one if the prisoners, or others who might communicate it.

Very Respectfully Yours
George W. Paul 15th Ark Inf[728]

It is not known if this led to more information for the federals or was related to the capture of Kennedy.

One of the most persistent prisoners to try to escape was Lieutenant Charlie Pierce of 7th Louisiana. Lieutenant Pierce was a very active person on Johnson's Island. He belonged to the Island Minstrels and was the captain of the Confederate Nine baseball team, but he gained the most notoriety from his persistent attempts at escape. The first attempt would be to tunnel out of the enclosure. A tunnel was begun commencing from Block 8 toward the fence. The project was abandoned because of the length, and the project was transferred to Block 1, which was closer to the fence. The project was nearing completion but was discovered by the federals and Charlie's hopes were dashed.[729]

---

[728] Scovill Papers, Western Reserve Historical Society.

[729] McNamara, M., "Lieutenant Pierce's Daring Attempts to Escape from Johnson's Island." *Southern Historical Society Papers*, 62.

An opportunity presented itself to Charlie Pierce a few weeks later. The driver of the slop cart had entered into compound under the influence of alcohol. The driver went inside Charlie's block laid down and went to sleep. Lieutenant Pierce removed the Yankee's blue overcoat without waking him, put it on, and mounted the cart. He drove the cart toward the fence in a speedy but unassuming manner trying not to look out of the normal. He passed through the gate and drove down the main road on the outside of the bull pen. The drunken soldier was found and the alarm was raised. A squad of men was sent in pursuit and Charlie was brought back inside the bull pen.[730]

Charlie Pierce and a group of prisoners made plans to make a mass run at the wall. A group of about thirty men had agreed to rush the wall behind Block 6, which was the hospital, and make an escape over the frozen ice. On the night of December 12, 1864, the men made their way to the fence; many were armed with rocks, clubs, and one or two pistols. With about a dozen ladders at the ready, Pierce, using his baseball skills threw a rock and knocked the sentinel from his beat. The men started to make their way over and firing was heard from both sides as the prisoners had secured a pistol. One witness estimated that 50 shots were fired.[731] Lieutenant John B. Bowels of Kentucky was shot dead while climbing a ladder. One of the guards charged a Rebel and put his bayonet through his coat. The stab missed his body, so the guard struck the Reb with the butt of his rifle, leaving a bad lump on the prisoners head.[732] Seeing that the raid was being repulsed, most ran back to their barracks. Three were able to get over the fence and Charlie Pierce was one of them. The guard captured two of the three prisoners that had made it over the fence. Pierce made his way onto ice. The cannons from the fort started to fire solid shot to break up the ice preventing the unknown number of prisoners that were on the ice from making it to the mainland. Pierce had made it to the mainland to the north; however, the farmers had heard the shots and were waiting with shotguns. They captured Pierce and returned him to the island. The federals were much distressed over the mass run at the wall. That night, the federals were on guard, not allowing any prisoner to go to the sinks. They were nervous about more turmoil, and readied their cannons for fire.[733] The rush at the wall had the opposite effect; one prisoner noted that the talk of rushing the wall had all but stopped.[734]

The last attempt of Charlie Pierce was hoped to bring final success and deliver him from this northern prison. He came up with a plan to get outside of the bull pen. He

---

[730] McNamara, M., "Lieutenant Pierce's Daring Attempts to Escape from Johnson's Island." *Southern Historical Society Papers*, 63.

[731] Wash, W. A., *Camp, Field and Prison Life*, 289.

[732] Mitchell, E. O. "Johnson's Island: Military Prison for Confederate Prisoners." *Sketches of War History 1861–1865*, 127.

[733] Hundley, D. R. *Prison Echoes of the Great Rebellion*, 190.

[734] Wash, W. A., *Camp, Field and Prison Life*, 290.

started to procure a blue federal uniform, which he hid in his bunk. He obtained a block of wood and started to form it into a gunstock. He constructed a barrel out of old tin cans and a lock was built from the handle of a kettle. He obtained a very rusty bayonet, which he polished to fine shining splendor. Charlie Pierce was able to stain the stock black. How he was able to do this is not known as boot polish was a contraband item. The gun looked real, especially in low light. The gun and uniform were completed; he was now ready to make good his escape. One of Pierce's friends had agreed to lure the federals into the prison. Lieutenant Long told the guard that an attempt would be made that night to escape from Block 8, the block that Pierce inhabited. The federals took the bait, and came in for a "surprise" inspection. They marched into the bull pen in full military order. They carefully inspected all of the blocks, looking for tunnels or anything out of the ordinary. Upon finding nothing suspicious, the federals formed back into marching line in the main avenue of the prison, only this time they had one more soldier that had "volunteered" to join the Hoffman's Battalion. Charlie Pierce had fallen in with the rest of the blue coats in his homemade uniform and gun. As the formation marched out, the Lieutenant of the Guard ordered an inspection of the guard. As the officer approached Pierce, he turned and said: "How is it, sir, that you have no cartridge box?"

Charlie responded, "Well, Lieutenant, we fell in outside in such a hurry, I declare I forgot it."

"Well, you are a fine soldier! No cartridge box! Suppose the Rebels were to attack us while we are in here among them? Let me see your gun, sir!"

Charlie knew it was all over, but he presented his weapon in the usual manner. As soon as the officer felt the weight of the weapon he knew he had found a Rebel. Charlie, with the fake gun, was brought to headquarters to be interviewed by Colonel Hill. Colonel Hill complimented him on his attempt, confiscated his blue uniform and the gun and sent him back to his block. Charlie Pierce had forgotten one simple article, a leather cartridge box, that he could have fabricated fairly easily, especially compared to the work on the gun. Charlie settled down and resigned himself to his fate, as a prisoner on Johnson's Island.[735]

One of the favorite ways to attempt escape from Johnson's Island was to don federal blue uniforms and walk out of the prison. This was the easiest way to escape compared to tunneling or rushing the wall. The Confederates had the advantage of having clothing of all types in the prison: civilian clothing, civilian clothing of blue cloth, which could be modified to look like issue clothing, and federally issued blue clothing.

Captain B. L. Farinholt decided to build a Yankee uniform to try and escape. He removed the stripe on his Rebel trousers and had a blue tunic custom built by another prisoner. He put the "federal" uniform over a set of civilian clothes, and then put a Confederate long coat over the disguises. He went out onto the frozen lake with a

---

[735] Lt. Pierce's attempts to escape, 65–67; *Determined to Escape*, 663–671.

water fetching party on February 22, 1864, Washington's Birthday. He took off the grey coat and managed to carefully make his way over to a group of off-duty soldiers frolicking on the ice. Farinholt then made his way over to a group of civilians and then on to the city of Sandusky itself. He peeled off his second layer to reveal an apparent civilian mingling with the citizens of Sandusky. He boarded a train for Baltimore and eventually returned to his home state of Virginia.[736]

By the summer of 1864, the use of blue uniforms to try to escape became widespread. Confederates came into the prison wearing a variety of clothing. Some came in with blue pants, a few with blue coats, and some with blue overcoats, so to collect together a full or partial uniform was not hard to assemble. In early August, an opportunity presented itself to escape using the blue uniforms. The federals started to construct cook and mess houses in the open part of the yard. Wagons of lumber and sand were constantly going in and out of the bull pen. Federal troops were not only constructing the buildings; they were guarding the lumber from theft. One prisoner noticed that his opportunity to escape was now. On August 6, Lieutenant J. B. Murphy put on a pair of blue pants, a red woolen shirt, and walked over to the work site. He rolled up his sleeves, rubbed dirt on himself, picked up a shovel, and walked out of the prison yard behind a cart. Murphy then needed to get off the island, so he proposed a bold yet simple plan; he would march up to Colonel Hill's office and personally ask for a pass to Sandusky. He put on a long face and told the commandant that his mother was deathly ill and that he must leave immediately to see her. Murphy explained that his company commander was not in his quarters so he pleaded to the colonel for a pass. Colonel Hill issued him a pass off the island. With a pass in hand signed by no less than the commanding officer, he walked up to the docks and went about the ship destined for Sandusky. A sense of horror passed over him as he saw Major Scovill on the same boat. The major looked right at him, but did not recognize the Rebel among the Yankees. Murphy eventually made it to Toronto where he wrote a letter to Major Scovill. His fellow prisoners in Block 4 covered his escape. Captain Wash described the ruse. "For several days we kept his absence covered up in this wise: When his name was called on the roll some one would say he was sick; then, after roll-call was over, some fellow would detain the federal officer till another would go and cover up in Murphy's couch, and when the roll-man would go round to see the sick man, he would find him 'mighty bad off, aching all over,' and grunting in pain." The deception lasted until the third day, when nothing but silence was heard when the name Murphy was called out. [737]

The day after Murphy's escape, more prisoners tried to make their way out of the prison. Seven prisoners had acquired blue uniforms and repeated Murphy's actions. Captain Wash stated, "The prison pen was now in a great fever for Yankee trowsers

---

[736] Long, Roger *Johnson's Island Prison*, *Blue and Gray Magazine*, March 1987, 27–28.

[737] Wash, W. A., *Camp, Field and Prison Life*, 250.

(sic). More Yankee garb was raked up than I dreamed was in prison, worn out blue pants being worth more than new ones."[738] The morning of the eighth saw twenty prisoners repeat what Murphy had done. Almost every wagon heading out of the prison had Confederate Yankees riding in the back. Reports stated that sometimes six prisoners would ride out on one cart.[739] But the prisoners went to the well once too often. A prisoner from Missouri, Lieutenant Selecman, had outfitted himself in blue and approached a sand wagon. He shoveled out the sand, creating streaks of sweat down his face. The sergeant in charge approached him and not recognizing him inquired of his unit. The prisoner stated the company and regiment to whom he belonged, but when the sergeant asked him his Captain's name, Selecman was stumped.[740] The plot was exposed and the island was immediately searched. A picket line was formed and the island was combed for Rebels. By the end of the day sixteen of seventeen prisoners were returned to the bull pen wearing gray pants. The next day, the rest of the prisoners were returned, Murphy was the only one to make his escape. An extra picket was deployed around the island to prevent any prisoners that would be lurking outside of the bull pen from making it off the island. The federals then made a thorough search of the prison for contraband uniforms, confiscating many.[741]

Colonel Hundley described an incident with one of these escaping prisoners outside of the pen: "The adventures of some of the prisoners outside were quite amusing. One of them got the negro barber outside to shave him, and during the process, he and the barber discussed the propriety of shooting all of the rebels engaged in trying to escape. The barber felt convinced they ought all to be shot. When the Yankees came in and arrested his customer, he could only exclaim in the utmost amazement, "Fo' God! An' I done shave him, too!"[742] From that day on, a squad of men was stationed at the gate with orders to only allow men with passes to exit the bull pen.[743] The next day a prisoner managed to forge a pass and exited the bull pen with the carts. He was recognized outside of the enclosure and was brought back inside.[744] On August 18, Colonel Baxter dyed a Confederate uniform blue, passed himself off as a major from New York, and went out the small gate near the water. He was detected and brought back.[745]

---

[738] Wash, W. A., *Camp, Field and Prison Life*, 251.

[739] Patterson, Edmund Dewitt, *Yankee Rebel: The Civil War Journal of Edmund DeWitt Patterson*, 187.

[740] Wash, W. A., *Camp, Field and Prison Life*, 251–252.

[741] Caldwell, James Parks. *A Northern Confederate at Johnson's Island Prison: The Civil War Diary of James Parks Caldwell*, 134.

[742] Hundley, D. R. *Prison Echoes of the Great Rebellion*, 110–111.

[743] Wash, W. A., *Camp, Field and Prison Life*, 253.

[744] Inzer, John Washington. *The Diary of a Confederate Soldier: John Washington Inzer 1834–1928*, 93.

[745] Wash, W. A., *Camp, Field and Prison Life*, 253.

Lieutenant J. G. Odom, 12th North Carolina Battalion, secured a blue uniform and a forged pass. He walked out of bull pen on the morning of September 9, 1864, with the morning roll callers, made his way down to the docks, and made good his escape to Canada. On the 16th, Odom, yet to be discovered missing by the federals, wrote his mess mates from Canada telling of the successful escape.[746] Two others, a Captain Elkins and an unknown man, both nurses at the Rebel hospital, also attempted escape in the same manner but were captured near the docks by a sergeant looking for Odom, who was just recently discovered missing.[747] Colonel Hill reportedly threatened the returned prisoners with restricted diet of bread and water for the rest of the war for forgery. He only relieved them of the contraband uniforms and sent them back inside the enclosure.[748]

Major Green collected up a full Yankee uniform, not of an enlisted man but of a major. He also secured a forged pass signed by no less than General Grant. Green thought he had a foolproof plan. He walked out of the bull pen and into the federal portion of the prison. He was overconfident; he walked up to General Terry's office and introduced himself as a member of General Grant's army. After General Terry and Major Green dined, they smoked cigars together. The illusion was soon shattered when a corporal appeared and asked Major Green, "What are you doing here?" General Terry reprimanded him for talking to an officer in that way. The corporal responded with: "He is one of our prisoners. I know his face well, as I call his name twice every day." General Terry was not convinced and stated, "You are mistaken. This is one of General Grant's officers. Go call your roll." The corporal called the roll and Green was absent. General Terry complimented Green on his clever trick, relieved him of his uniform and forged pass and returned him inside the prison.[749]

On December 24, 1864, Captain McKibbin decided that he would make a third attempt to walk out of the prison. He had tried twice before to walk out in federal uniform with the roll callers and was caught both times. He assembled a third federal uniform and had built accoutrements out of black oilcloth for a third attempt to pass out with the roll callers. To stop this type of escape attempt, Colonel Hill had supplemented passes, because of the ease in forging signatures, with a requirement that the gate keeper had to visually identify each soldier that passed out of the gate. McKibbin had figured out a way to overcome this system. He was a Mason and had found out that some of the roll callers were also Masons. McKibbin convinced a brother Mason

---

[746] Caldwell, James Parks. *A Northern Confederate at Johnson's Island Prison: The Civil War Diary of James Parks Caldwell*, 144.

[747] Ibid., Wash, W. A., *Camp, Field and Prison Life*, 264.

[748] Hundley, D. R. *Prison Echoes of the Great Rebellion*, 135; *War of the Rebellion: A Compilation of the Official Records of the Union and Confederate Armies*, series 2, Vol 7, 839–840.

[749] Philpot, Conf. Vet., 362.

on the other side to help him, possibly unwittingly, to escape. His co-conspirator had placed a large jug near the gate. As the roll callers walked out, they would turn their heads to look at the out-of-place item. McKibbin marched up to the gate in his blue uniform and just like the other roll callers turned and looked at the jug at the precise moment to obscure his face from the officer and marched on through.[750] The guards found out that McKibbin had escaped the next day.[751] Rumors had spread that he had escaped while fetching water on the frozen lake. Colonel Hill did not believe this rumor and assumed that he had walked out of the gate.[752] It is not known if his escape was ultimately successful; however, Colonel Hill stated in an official report that he did not think McKibbin would be recaptured.

Colonel Daniel Hundley was becoming a recluse, living in the attic of Block 3. He was very bitter about his captivity and decided he would break out from the prison. He tried an early attempt to escape by sneaking out of the prison. On one cold night he cloaked himself in a white sheet and hid in a latrine. He examined the situation and felt that escape in this manner was hopeless. He decided to try another method, one that had a better chance of success. He would try to walk out of the prison in Yankee uniform. He collected up a complete federal uniform. He even procured a brass US belt buckle to which he attached a handmade belt, cartridge box, and a bayonet hanger. On January 2, 1865, a severe snowstorm hit the island. The roll callers had flipped up their great coat collars and were shivering in the cold. Hundley saw his opportunity. He reported himself sick and stayed in his bunk covering his disguise with a blanket. After the roll caller had checked the rooms for the sick, Hundley marched out of his block in his blue outfit and mingled with the huddled federals. As Hundley reached the gate, some of his comrades created a disturbance in the form of a fist fight. This caught the attention of most of the federal guards. During the commotion he tried to cross through the gate with his collar covering his face as if he were protecting himself from the biting wind. The young gatekeeper ripped his upturned collar from in front of his face. Hundley gave him an arrogant stare, and because Hundley was many years his elder, the gate keeper was embarrassed for his rough actions and allowed Hundley to pass to the outside of the bull pen. He marched confidently down the main avenue of the federal post and stopped inside a federal latrine. [753]

Hundley had succeeded on making it to the outside of the prison walls, but he still had to make his way off the island and elude the authorities. The island was no longer an island, being completely surrounded with ice. With a snowstorm raging, he walked

---

[750] Hundley, D. R. *Prison Echoes of the Great Rebellion*, 198, 199.

[751] Hundley, D. R. *Prison Echoes of the Great Rebellion*, 193, 194.

[752] *War of the Rebellion: A Compilation of the Official Records of the Union and Confederate Armies*, Series 2, Vol VII, 42.

[753] Hundley, D. R. *Prison Echoes of the Great Rebellion*, 192.

across the ice toward Sandusky. He slipped and fell a few times but was so enthralled to be away from the prison he continued with a steady pace southward toward Sandusky. As he walked away from the island several Union soldiers, including one of the officers of Hoffman's Battalion, passed by on a sail-powered iceboat, not noticing anything suspicious about his presence.

He finally arrived at Sandusky, bought some apples, a rare commodity on the island, and casually made his way to the train station. While waiting, he encountered several soldiers at the train station, some from the front and others from the garrison at Johnson's Island. The Rebel-turned-Yankee started to fraternize with the soldiers as he waited for a train to Detroit. Hundley's plan was to go to Detroit and cross over to Canada. He was well equipped with a forged pass from Colonel Hill to report to Detroit. The Colonel started to doubt that his plan would work, fearing that the soldiers would be able to detect his fraudulent status. He walked out of the station and hid in some brush on the outskirts of the city. When nighttime fell, he began to follow some tracks heading to the west. The cold started to overcome him as he walked for several miles and found his right hip was beginning to ache. Colonel Hundley was wounded in the hip in 1863, and it had not fully healed. He came across a barn and slept for the rest of the night and most of the following day. When nighttime was upon him again, he continued to follow the railroad tracks west. He then found out that he was following the wrong tracks and heading southwest and not northwest to Detroit. Trying to save time, he cut north through a frozen swamp to correct his course, came across another barn, and slept through another agonizingly cold day. Hundley continued to travel north the next night finding it more and more difficult to keep up a steady pace. The southerner was cold, stiff, hungry, and tired. He struggled onward and came across the town of Fremont, Ohio. Colonel Hundley was spotted by a policeman and questioned about his condition. Hundley acted drunk, which satisfied the curiosity of the officer. He made his way to a hotel and rented a room, where he slept on a proper bed for the first time in several years. The next morning he had a full breakfast and stayed in his room all day, enjoying a dinner late in the afternoon.

Back at Johnson's Island, the day following Hundley's escape, the roll callers discovered that he was no longer in the bullpen. Colonel Hill put out a $100 reward, which was consistent with past escapees, in the local papers and notified the Provost Marshals to try to apprehend Hundley. On the fifth of January, another prisoner, Rufus C. Jones, escaped in almost the same way, with the same physical description as Hundley. Again the countryside was alerted to be on the lookout for escaped Rebels in federal uniforms.

The Provost Marshal of Fremont went to the local hotels to check for Jones. Since Hundley matched Jones description in height, eye, and hair color, the clerk told the marshal that his man might be sleeping upstairs. They had the porter go up stairs to check on Hundley and asked if he was sick and in need of a physician. Hundley knew that something was wrong. Shortly after the boy left, the marshal threw open the door and said, "You are our prisoner, sir! Your name is Jones and you are from Johnson's Island."

Hundley replied with a laugh, "Well, gentleman, if I am Jones, it is a little (strange) that I have been so long finding it out."

"Oh! there is no use in your denying it. Here is Colonel Hill's telegram, giving your description."

"Well, gentleman, allow me to assure you I was not aware until this moment there was such a man as Lieutenant Jones in existence. I confess I am from Johnson's Island, but from the outside of that bullpen, not the inside. If one of you will take the trouble to examine the side-pocket of my coat you find a paper which will convince you of the truth of what I tell you."

After the marshal read the order, he stated, "Why, this is all right. I have seen five hundred of old Hill's signatures, and this is certainly a genuine document. But how came you here? This paper orders you to report for duty in Detroit."

"Well, you see, gentleman. To tell you the truth, I have been on a *bender*. I trust you will not report me to Colonel Hill."

"How is this?" the clerk exclaimed as he held up Hundley's coat, "here are staff buttons. I'd like to know what business a *private* soldier has with such a coat as this, and these buttons."

"Oh! as for the matter of that, you know the boys will sometimes put on a little style when they get out of camps."

The Provost Marshal and the clerk decided to examine the clothing more carefully. They picked up the homemade cartridge box and belt, which made them even more suspicious, knowing that it was not federal issue. They found his wallet and upon searching inside unearthed a Confederate document that included his name, rank, and regiment.

Hundley was returned to Sandusky, turned over to Colonel Hill's command, and returned to the island. He was searched, his blue uniform confiscated as contraband, and returned to the bunk that he left five days previously. His grand adventure was over.[754]

Colonel Hill was very upset over the latest round of escape attempts. Captain McKibbin had escaped on the December 24; Colonel Hundley had passed out of the compound on January 2, 1865, and another prisoner, Rufus C. Jones, had escaped on January 5. All of these prisoners had escaped by passing out with the roll callers. In an official report to the Inspector and Commanding General of Prisoners, H. W. Wessells, Hill stated that "no escape was practical without the direct complicity or criminal negligence of some portion of the guard, and felt vexed and disgraced by

---

[754] Hundley, D. R. *Prison Echoes of the Great Rebellion*, 201–233.

these two escapes."[755] He concluded: "they could not have passed . . . if my orders to the gate-keepers to pass no one except under the immediate direction of an officer in the discharge of his duty, or where they themselves positively identified the person, who, in addition, must have the proper pass." He discovered that his orders were not being followed: "without my knowledge or authority, the assistant superintendent of the prison, intending to aid the gatekeeper, had advised him to depend upon the uniform and customary equipments of the roll-callers. Dress and trappings were noticed and personal identity scarcely regarded." Colonel Hill assured the General that the leak had stopped.

Colonel Hill was upset and nervous over the increase of escape attempts. He noted "the formation of ice around [the island] has deprived this place of its island characteristics, and knowing that the prisoners could now count upon crossing swamps, ponds, and streams everywhere with safety, and upon help from their Copperhead friends in the country, thus inducing the most ingenious, determined, and unremitting efforts at escape."[756] Colonel Hill was alarmed of a possible raid upon Johnson's Island. He stated in his report, "We are ready for them and their outside friends, whether they come from Canada or elsewhere, at any minute, day or night. Since the 13th ultimo my officers and men have regularly turned in without undressing and will continue to do so until our locality becomes an island again."[757] During January, one prisoner noted in his diary that the "Yankees are scared, they believe the prisoners intend to make their escape some night."[758] He noted, "The Yankees shoot in the prison almost every night, miserable cowards. Maybe we will get a lick at them someday."[759] The federals made a search of the bull pen on January 21, and found a Rebel digging a tunnel. He was sent back to his quarters without punishment.[760] But this would change as another escape attempt was made on January 22, 1865. Lieutenant Cross passed out with the roll callers in federal uniform. He was captured and brought back into the prison, but this time the prisoner was punished. He was made to stand on a barrel near the south gate in the cold for five hours. The prisoners were upset over this act. Colonel Inzer stated that this was "an awful outrage. Hill ought to be hung by his heels for this vile

---

[755] *War of the Rebellion: A Compilation of the Official Records of the Union and Confederate Armies,* series 2, Vol 8, 42–44.

[756] *War of the Rebellion: A Compilation of the Official Records of the Union and Confederate Armies,* 2, Vol 8, 42–43.

[757] Ibid.

[758] Inzer, John Washington. *The Diary of a Confederate Soldier: John Washington Inzer 1834–1928,* 120–121

[759] Ibid.

[760] Murphey, V. S., *Diary,* 136.

act. Hill is a coward and a scoundrel."[761] Colonel Murphey recorded in his diary: "Col. Hill endeavourd [sic] to explain away in an order this open and vindictive violation of a principle universally acknowledged but failed and increased the indignation of the pen."[762] On January 28, 1865, Captain Shorter attempted to escape, and just like Cross, he was ordered to stand for several hours on a barrel.[763] Other prisoners were put in confinement or on reduced diet for helping cover the absence of an escaped prisoner.

With the island completely surrounded by ice, the Rebel prisoners believed this to be their prime opportunity to escape. Lieutenant William Woodson, 28th Virginia, longed to be off the island. He noticed an opportunity to escape when the prisoners went out on the ice, under guard, to retrieve water. As the prisoners were on the ice, Woodson observed that off-duty federal guards were allowed to mingle with the prisoners, trading tobacco for rings and other souvenirs that the Rebels had made. Woodson decided he would put on a blue federal uniform, and during the mixture of both Confederates and federals he would slip away from his fellow prisoners. What would be needed was a Yankee uniform, to escape from the island, and a civilian suit to pass through the countryside to freedom. He had a civilian suit that he purchased while in prison. He gathered blue pants from one prisoner, and a coat from another. Cash would be needed for his voyage, so he managed to secure a few dollars in greenbacks. A forged pass was prepared if anyone so inquired. He was ready for "death or liberty."

On February 21, 1865, Woodson put on his civilian suit, then put the blue uniform on. He gathered up a handful of canteens and proceeded over to the lakeside gate. When the gate opened, he slipped the canteens over to a friend and stepped to the side, letting the mass of gray cloaked men walk out to the frozen lake. He stepped next to a guard, put a pipe in his mouth, and pretended to be a watchful guard. The federal guard beside him did not pay Woodson any mind, thinking that he was a federal, so Woodson walked causally away toward the supply boat frozen in the dock of Johnson's Island. There he turned south and took his first steps toward freedom. He then heard a firm "Halt, there." An officer of the guard demanded a pass from him. The forged pass was delivered as requested, and Woodson was free to proceed. He quickly walked over the ice to Sandusky, climbed a plank up to the wharf, and relished the fact he had finally made it off the island. His escape was not noticed the following day because his friend had answered "present" for Woodson during the morning roll call. The following day the roll callers caught the deception and put Woodson's comrade on a bread and water confinement for a week.

With almost a two-day head start, Lieutenant Woodson began his excursion south. He took his blue uniform off and continued in his civilian attire. He walked south all

---

[761] Inzer, John Washington. *The Diary of a Confederate Soldier: John Washington Inzer 1834–1928*, 122.

[762] Murphey, V. S., *Diary*, 147.

[763] Inzer, John Washington. *The Diary of a Confederate Soldier: John Washington Inzer 1834–1928*, 123.

day and through the night. He stopped at a tollgate keeper's house and dodged a multitude of questions from the curious man. With the questions bombarding him, Woodson decided to continue on his voyage. He continued to walk southward the second day, becoming tired and sore because of the hard frozen ground. He walked up to a farmhouse and was given supper and a feather bed to sleep the night. His limbs ached so much that sleep was impossible. On the third and fourth day of his freedom, his feet were sore but he had made it to Marion, Ohio, a distance of about 65 miles. There at Marion, he caught a train to Springfield, another 74 miles. He continued south, hitching rides on buggies and wagons, making it to Dayton by night. The next day, after a nice meal from the kindness of an older farm lady, he received a ride on a wagon heading to Cincinnati. That night he crossed the river to Kentucky where he met with friends. With money from his friends, he traveled by steamer up the Ohio River for forty miles. He pretended to be a teacher until his friends could arrange for a guide to take him across Kentucky and western Virginia. For three weeks he had to put on the act of a teacher, raising the suspicion of a Union Cavalry Regiment stationed in the town. The guides arrived and Woodson continued on his journey to Virginia. Crossing the Appalachian Mountains, he avoided the marauding armies of bushwackers, deserters, and robbers. He made it to Virginia and with two days' hard ride and arrived at a familiar farm and gave his dear old mother a long overdue hug, for he was home.[764]

Johnson's Island's security record speaks for itself. Out of the thousands of prisoners and the hundreds of attempts to leave the island prison, the prisoners' success rate was abysmal with about twelve successful escapes. The island was specifically selected to give prisoners the feeling of isolation, and the inhospitable surroundings made the challenge of escape almost insurmountable. The prison was well prepared and manned with a very good system in place to keep the Rebels imprisoned. This level of attentiveness of the guards and their geographical location made many mentally give up hope of leaving without approval of the authorities. This was the true deterrent to escape. Some prisoners worked diligently and devised many genius plans to escape only to be thwarted and recaptured. Many thousands more of the prisoners simply waited for the time to come when they could leave with permission to finally go home.

---

[764] Woodson, William D. *War Recollections of Lieut. Wm. D. Woodson*, 11–19.

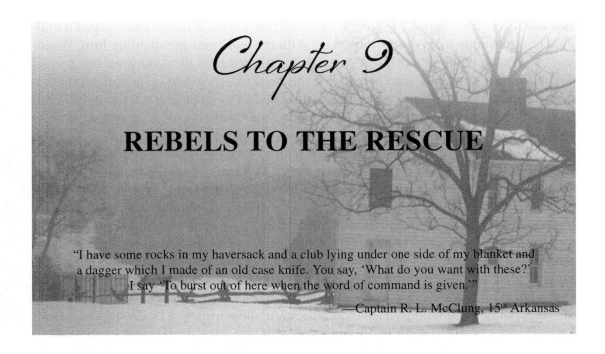

Chapter 9

REBELS TO THE RESCUE

"I have some rocks in my haversack and a club lying under one side of my blanket and a dagger which I made of an old case knife. You say, 'What do you want with these?' I say 'To burst out of here when the word of command is given.'"

—Captain R. L. McClung, 15th Arkansas

EARLY PROBLEMS

The locale and isolation of Johnson's Island was the best choice for keeping Rebels from escaping, but this isolation had a negative aspect; it put the Rebels near Canada just thirty miles away. Colonel Hoffman was concerned about a raid from southern sympathizers in Canada. Hoffman recognized this possibility on his initial visit to scout for a location in Lake Erie, but felt, despite this vulnerability, the island would still be defendable. He chose Johnson's Island because of the protection of the bay and the access to the city of Sandusky. Reinforcements could arrive quicker to prevent the prisoners from overwhelming the guard and linking up with a raid from Canada.

Canada, a British possession, was sympathetic to the southern cause. The British Empire needed cotton from the south, and a divided United States would weaken their military and economic threat. Numerous plots were hatched from Canada to attack or harass the United States. The close proximity of Johnson's Island to Canada and the two to three thousand trained Rebel officers imprisoned thereon was a tempting target for Confederate agents.

The Rush-Bagot Agreement of 1818 limited the amount of warships upon the Great Lakes. The border with Canada was largely undefended by both sides.[765] One

---

[765] www.aandc.org/research/rush-bagot_agreement.html

U. S. man of war, the *Michigan*, was stationed on the Great Lakes. The *Michigan* was an iron-clad warship launched in 1844, at Erie, Pennsylvania. She was a side-wheel steamer, 163 feet long, 27 feet wide, with a draft of 9 feet. Her armament originally was a single naval canon attached to a rotating mount. Later in 1865, she was armed with five 20-pdr. Parrott rifles, two light 12-pdrs., and six 24-pdrs. In 1905, her name was changed to *Wolverine*, on loan to the Naval Militia, State of Pennsylvania.[766]

The first rumor of a raid upon Johnson's Island came shortly after it was inhabited. On June 6, 1862, James Gordon Bennett of the *New York Herald* received a letter from an anonymous source, simply signed "Canadian." In the letter he warned about "a scheme on foot here and on the other side of the river between some Southern sympathizers and Marylanders to liberate the rebel prisoners on Johnson's Island." In the letter, he detailed their plan to purchase a sailboat, as it would not draw attention, sail to Detroit, and use it to capture a tug. The tug would then tow the sailboat to Sandusky where the prisoners would be liberated. Upon success of freeing the Rebels on Johnson's Island, they would all sail to Canada. The informant also warned that this raid would be in conjunction with an uprising of the prisoners.[767]

Colonel Pierson was warned of this plot by a telegram dated June 18, 1862, from the Secretary of War's office.[768] But Colonel Pierson, to his credit, had already caught wind of an uprising. He had already sent a few hours before a letter to Colonel Hoffman stating: "There is among the prisoners here a concerted plan for general revolt with a view of taking the island and take their chances for escape. So far as I can judge—and I have good means of knowing—this plan of revolt embraces the great body of the prisoners. We are using the utmost vigilance, and while I do not fear a successful attempt the officers as well as myself would feel better if we had another company [of guards]."[769] After reading the telegram from the War Department, Pierson requested the *Michigan* be dispatched to guard the island from an attack from the lake.[770] On June 26, Colonel Hoffman ordered a company of guards from Camp Chase, near Columbus, to be transferred to Johnson's Island immediately. He felt assured the extra guard would "overawe the reckless and encourage the well-disposed to insist on submission." Hoffman then sent a letter to the governor of Ohio, informing him of the transfer. Hoffman felt the whole story was "improbable" and

[766] Official Records of the Union and Confederate Navies in the War of the Rebellion.; Series II, Vol. 1, 143–144.

[767] *War of the Rebellion: A Compilation of the Official Records of the Union and Confederate Armies*, Series II, Vol. 3, 657–658.

[768] *War of the Rebellion: A Compilation of the Official Records of the Union and Confederate Armies*, Series II, Vol. 4, 37–38.

[769] *War of the Rebellion: A Compilation of the Official Records of the Union and Confederate Armies*, Series II, Vol. 4, 37–38.

[770] *War of the Rebellion: A Compilation of the Official Records of the Union and Confederate Armies*, Series II, Vol. 4, 42.

believed the real problem was Pierson's lack of confidence in his command.[771] Apparently the *Michigan* was not moved to Sandusky Bay and the news of a raid faded.

THE ATTEMPT OF 1863

A paroled prisoner, Y. H. Blackwell, delivered to James Seddon, Secretary of War for the Confederacy, on September 21, 1863, the following communique from General Archer, still imprisoned on Johnson's Island:

> We count here 1,600 prisoners, 1,200 officers. We can take the island, guarded by only one battalion, with small loss, but have no way to get off. A naval officer might procure in some way a steamer on the lake and with a few men attack the island and take us to Canada. C. C. Egerton, of Baltimore, would I think, furnish a fitting crew to one of our naval officers who carried your indorsement to him, and would give valuable advice regarding how to get the men armed in steamer, etc. There is no truer or more daring man in our service, and he has a large body of men sworn to obey him and help us. Lieut. George Bier or William Parker are suggested.

While this letter was being delivered, the prisoners were organizing to take over the island and link up with any help. General M. Jeff Thompson recorded in his memoir that he came up with the idea of a mass rush at the walls. The General believed there "was no difficulty in capturing the garrison, for there was scarcely two hundred of them, and they had never seen battle whereas there was twenty five hundred of us, all veterans. The question was [how] to leave the Island after capturing it. In this I saw no serious difficulty but there were others who did." Thompson's idea was for each general, in which there were five on the island, to select ten colonels who could be trusted who would in turn select ten trustworthy officers. Five hundred men would be organized to attack the guards' barracks, block houses, and capture the boats at the docks. The other 2,000 prisoners would "rush where they chose in the fight, and probably draw fire from the guards while the *details* performed their work."[772]

Captain L. W. Allen preserved a plan of the organization in his diary:

Plan of organization

Whereas the present posture of affairs in regard to the exchange of prisoners between the United States and the Confederate States governments leaves us but little hope of a speedy exchange, and whereas it is the privilege and duty of

---

[771] *War of the Rebellion: A Compilation of the Official Records of the Union and Confederate Armies,* Series II, Vol. 6, 87–89.

[772] Thompson, M. Jeff, *The Civil War Reminiscences of General M. Jeff Thompson,* 214.

the Confederate prisoners of war confined on this Island to make their escape from imprisonment, and to adopt any plan by which so desirable an object promises to be successful; and whereas for the more effectual accomplishment of the proposed plan, we hereby agree to the following plan of organization of the Confederate officers here confined:

1. The plan to be adopted shall embrace the whole or such part of the prisoners as it may be deemed necessary for harmony, efficiency and success.
2. The whole organization shall be under the command of Major-General Isaac R. Trimble, of Maryland, as commander-in-chief of all the forces thus organized.
3. Corps commanders shall be appointed to the command of the twelve blocks respectfully, viz.:
   General J. J. Archer, Maryland, to the command of blocks one, three and five; W. N. R. Beall, Arkansas, to the command of blocks seven, nine and eleven; Colonel R. S. Clarke, Eighth Kentucky Cavalry, to the command of blocks ten, twelve and thirteen. Colonel J. Miles, Thirty-ninth Mississippi, corps commander.
4. Each block shall be under the command of an officer, who shall organize companies or squads in each room or mess. Each company or squad to be under the command of a captain, who shall keep his men ready at any moment to carry out the orders and commands of their superiors in rank and position of their organization.
5. Block one shall be under the command of General J. R. Jones, Virginia; two, of Colonel D. Howard Smith, Kentucky; three, of Colonel B. D. Fry, Alabama; four, of Colonel L. M. Lewis, Missouri; five, of Colonel D. M. Shannon, Texas; seven, of A. G. Godwin, North Carolina; eight, of Captain L. W. Allen, Virginia; ninth, of General J. W. Frayser, Tennessee; ten, of Colonel R. M. Powell, Texas; eleven, of Colonel J. R. Herbert, Maryland; twelve, of Captain Johnson, Kentucky, and thirteen, General M. Jefferson Thompson, Missouri.
6. The commander-in-chief, the corps commanders, and of each block respectively, shall constitute a board of officers, who shall direct, arrange and superintend the formation of all plans and arrangements otherwise, concerning the escape of prisoners from this prison and of their return to the Confederate States, leaving all details of executing said plans to the direction of the commander in-chief.
7. Commanders of corps shall be authorized to administer to subordinate commanders the following oaths (the form of oath is not given), and they in turn shall administer them to each recruit.[773]

---

[773] Allen, Captain L. W., "A Plan to Escape" in *Southern Historical Society Papers, Volume XIX*, 286–288.

This plan is very similar to Thompson's plan, but Allen recorded that the plan was completed after the raid from Canada was discovered and halted. Perhaps he finalized the draft at that time, as Thompson stated in his memoir the plan was delayed three days and then was cancelled because the *Michigan* "came steaming into the harbor, and anchored between the Island and Sandusky" on October 24, 1863.[774] Further evidence that the Rebels were organizing came from multiple sources. Captain Bingham wrote in his diary that he "had the offer of the command of 20 select men fr[om] this room in case of a chance" to rush the walls. He continued: "I refused. Duty in the field does not regard danger—but here I expose myself upon no uncertainty. I would go to Canada & run my chances if transportation were ready."[775] Colonel Pierson, who had spies in the prison compound, sent a memorandum to Colonel Hoffman on October 1, 1863: "There is a very bad spirit among the prisoners. They have the idea that it would be a great thing for the Confederacy for them to escape, and they are talking about it being their duty to make the attempt, as they are superior in numbers to so great extent; that if they could get off to Canada their Government would be much relieved. Such things are reported to me by those who overhear."[776] The language of the letter is very similar to that of the plan, proving the plan was in existence before October 1st.

Colonel Pierson then requested the presence of the *Michigan*. Hoffman initially denied the need of the ship and the severity of the happenings. Pierson responded on the 16th: "I have the honor to acknowledge the receipt of your letter of the 12th instant, in which you state that you do not feel at liberty to either ask for the *Michigan* or for more companies here, and express the opinion that there is no danger. I feel it my duty to say frankly that I think differently. The number of prisoners is 2,452. They are a most desperate set of men, with great smartness and a conviction that their escape would be better than a victory in any battle, and that their risks would not be as great. They are getting up rolls and organizations inside, much of which we learn, and of course more we do not. What the objections are to the *Michigan* coming here I do not know. She is in the harbor at Erie much of the time."[777] On the 19th, Colonel Hoffman wrote the Secretary of War explaining Pierson's concerns and his thoughts on the matter: "The small steamer [*Eastern*] which runs as ferry-boat to Sandusky is provided with a mountain howitzer, and by its means the escape of prisoners from the island can readily be prevented. The guards are armed with muskets and revolvers, and with ordinary vigilance should always be prepared to defeat any attempt on the part of the

---

[774] Thompson, M. Jeff, *The Civil War Reminiscences of General M. Jeff Thompson*, 215.

[775] Bingham, Robert, *Diary*, 84.

[776] *War of the Rebellion: A Compilation of the Official Records of the Union and Confederate Armies*, Series II, Vol. VI., 333.

[777] *War of the Rebellion: A Compilation of the Official Records of the Union and Confederate Armies*, Series II, Vol. 6, 385.

prisoners to make their escape. The daily guard occupy two two-story block houses, which have loop-holes for musketry in the upper stories, within each a howitzer in the lower story, and cannot be taken by unarmed men. I do not think additional guard is necessary, but if the U. S. steamer *Michigan* can be in Sandusky Bay as well as at Erie [Pennsylvania] her presence would prevent any thought of an attempt at escape."[778]

Colonel Pierson had put his guards on full alert. The *Michigan* arrived on October 24, and created the affect desired by Pierson. The prisoners believed the plan was exposed and foiled. Captain Bingham recorded in his diary: "There was a plan afloat to take possession of the Island and go to Canada—but the Yankees heard of it & the whole battalion [was] under arms all day."[779] General Thompson expressed the feelings inside the camp after the guard was alerted and the *Michigan* arrived: "The whole project 'flashed in the pan.' We now laughed at the matter as having been a good joke. We had evidently been betrayed by some man of the select 500."[780] Thompson may not have had all the information, as General Archer, the leader of the revolt, received a message from the raiders in Canada, via the personal columns in the *New York Herald*, that stated: "a few nights after the 4th of November a carriage would be at the door, when all seeming obstacles would be removed, and to be ready."[781]

Colonel Pierson's actions had effectively ended the revolt inside the prison and should have been commended for his sleuthing and strong leadership; instead, Colonel Hoffman criticized him for being an alarmist and a complainer. On November 9th, Colonel Hoffman blasted him for the request of the *Michigan* and on its effective use. Hoffman then stated: "I have no more confidence in the reports of revolt you hear this year than I have of similar reports made to you last year." He then belittled Pierson for saying the escaped prisoners could head to Canada. Hoffman stated: "I doubt if one-fourth of them could make that journey without assistance if you were to invite them to go." Hoffman criticized Pierson for complaining of the "arduous services of your command." He continued in his demeaning tone, "If you put one company with its officers on guard every day, it would only be light garrison duty, and to make this duty lighter cannot be [argued] as a good reason for increasing the guard."[782]

On the same day Pierson received the scathing reprimand, the plot in Canada to raid Johnson's Island was discovered. The Provost-Marshal of Detroit received word

---

[778] *War of the Rebellion: A Compilation of the Official Records of the Union and Confederate Armies*, Series II, Vol. 6, 385–386.

[779] Bingham, Robert, *Diary*, 84.

[780] Thompson, M. Jeff, *The Civil War Reminiscences of General M. Jeff Thompson*, 215.

[781] Bell, John, *Rebel on the Great Lakes Confederate Naval Commando Operations Launched from Canada 1863–1864*, 31.

[782] *War of the Rebellion: A Compilation of the Official Records of the Union and Confederate Armies*, Series II, Vol. 6, 490–491.

that a rebel agent had arrived in Windsor, Canada, with $100,000 in certificates of deposits. The authorities also learned that steamers were to be purchased in Montreal and the rebels had received funds to do so. A Union agent, John M. Jones, was in Toronto and had confirmed the presence of Confederate naval officers in Canada. The letter of the 9th stated: "That some project of magnitude is in contemplation I feel very certain, . . . and the information points more positively to Johnson's Island."[783] Colonel Pierson received a telegram from Brigadier-General Cox in Cincinnati, which acknowledged: "within a few days an attack will be made upon Johnson's Island to release the prisoners, and that a boat for that purpose has been purchased at Montreal."[784] General Cox sent Hoffman a telegram informing him of the situation and he "ordered a detachment of Infantry and a six-gun rifled battery to the island today." He then added, "The U. S. steamer *Michigan* is somewhere in Lake Erie. Cannot the Navy Department send her to the assistance of Colonel Pierson?"[785] Hoffman must have felt like a fool.

On November 11, 1863, the British Minister, Lord Lyons, officially notified the U. S. government of the plot to destroy the city of Buffalo, New York, and to surprise the garrison on Johnson's Island.[786] Everything along the Great Lakes became a beehive of activity. Reinforcements and General Cox arrived at Johnson's Island.[787] One prisoner, Captain Barziza, noticed the increased vigilance: "The Yankees were greatly alarmed; they ordered off the sutler, stopped the mails and express, dug rifle-pits lakeward, planted artillery, fortified Cedar Point, which commands the entrance to the bay, and received a whole regiment of reinforcements which kept increasing [with militia], until General Terry's brigade from the Army of the Potomac swelled the number to some six or seven thousand."[788] General Cox explained in his memoir the defensive situation: "A lighthouse on [Cedar Point] and range lights near it give direction to vessels approaching, which run from the northwest, head on, till they seem almost ashore at the foot of the lighthouse tower, when they turn sharply to the southwest. It did not need a second glance to determine that Cedar Point was the place to fortify, and

---

[783] *War of the Rebellion: A Compilation of the Official Records of the Union and Confederate Armies*, Series III, Vol. 3, 1008.

[784] *War of the Rebellion: A Compilation of the Official Records of the Union and Confederate Armies*, Series II, Vol. 6, 491.

[785] *War of the Rebellion: A Compilation of the Official Records of the Union and Confederate Armies*, Series III, Vol. 3, 1012–1013.

[786] *War of the Rebellion: A Compilation of the Official Records of the Union and Confederate Armies*, Series III, Vol. 3, 1013.

[787] *War of the Rebellion: A Compilation of the Official Records of the Union and Confederate Armies*, Series III, Vol. 3, 1024.

[788] Barziza, Decimus et Ultimus. *The Adventures of a Prisoner of War, 1863–1864*, 80.

that batteries there would rake any vessel approaching the harbor."[789] Edmund Dewitt Patterson, a prisoner, noted that the Yankees had been practicing with solid shot and shell to prepare for an attack from the lake. From observing the practice, Patterson realized they could put accurate fire on any ship approaching the island.[790]

Brigadier General Cox received on the 15th a telegram stating: "Rebels who left Windsor to join the raid are returning, saying that the plans are frustrated for the present, and will have to be postponed for a time." Cox added, "I regard this as ending the immediate danger, but will keep the force here as it is till the above is confirmed."[791] A few days later, General Cox told the Secretary of War that "he shall dismiss part of the militia tomorrow and the rest [the] next day, retaining here artillery and the battalion of recruits first sent up. I think a battery, part long-range guns and part Napoleons, intrenched [sic] in such earth-works as they could construct themselves, with the increase of the garrison to a full regiment, would make the island permanently safe. The long-range guns would perfectly command the channel, and the Napoleons would destroy the prisoners if they attempted escape."[792] A prisoner noted on the 21st: "The Yankees have got over their big fright."[793]

Captain Robert D. Minor was one of the conspirators who explained in a *Richmond Dispatch* article the particulars of the expedition. The group of Rebels he was with would gain passage on a steamer from Ogdensburg, New York, bound for Chicago. Once the steamer made its way to the middle of Lake Erie, they would overpower the crew and steam to Sandusky, surprise the *Michigan*, demand the surrender of the island, commandeer several ships at the Sandusky docks, and carry the prisoners to Canada. Then they would rain havoc on the Great Lakes.[794]

The fear of the raid had quite an effect on Johnson's Island. The raid had vindicated Pierson in his own mind, even though he would resign shortly afterward. Johnson's Island was now more secure with a full regiment of troops, the 128th Ohio, and two forts would be constructed with more firepower for the guards. Johnson's Island would now get reinforcements more easily than before to secure the growing number of prisoners.

---

[789] Cox, Jacob D., *Military Reminiscences of the Civil War,* 60.

[790] Patterson, Edmund Dewitt. *Yankee Rebel: The Civil War Journal of Edmund DeWitt Patterson,* 143–145.

[791] *War of the Rebellion: A Compilation of the Official Records of the Union and Confederate Armies,* Series III, Vol. 3, 1043.

[792] *War of the Rebellion: A Compilation of the Official Records of the Union and Confederate Armies,* Series III, Vol. 3, 1075.

[793] Patterson, Edmund Dewitt. *Yankee Rebel: The Civil War Journal of Edmund DeWitt Patterson,* 145.

[794] Frohman, Charles E. *Rebels on Lake Erie,* 42.

THE RAID OF JOHN YATES BEALL

In 1864, the Confederacy was losing the war. The Rebels became more desperate to turn things around and turn the tide of war. The situation on the battlefield was dire, and bold action was needed to convince Washington to abandon the prosecution of the war. A presidential election was scheduled for the fall, and if Lincoln were to be clearly rebuffed by the population of the North, the war might cease. Copperhead activity was abundant in Illinois, Indiana, and Ohio. The Confederates thought they only needed a little encouragement to break from Washington.[795] The "Northwest Conspiracy" was hatched.

The Northwest Conspiracy was a multifaceted operation with the aim of fracturing the Union. It contained, among other things, attempts to increase membership and the activities of the "Order of the Sons of Liberty," a quasi-military group distrustful of Lincoln, and to have locals release the Rebel prisoners in Chicago, Indianapolis, and Columbus. The Confederate government wanted to have covert activities and attacks emanating from Canada to demoralize the citizens and increase anti-Lincoln activities.

Jacob Thompson, former U.S. Congressman and Secretary of the Interior, was sent to Canada by Jefferson Davis in May 1864 to organize harassing activities.[796] In July, Captain Charles H. Cole, of General Nathan Bedford Forrest's Cavalry, made contact with Thompson in Canada. He represented himself as an escaped prisoner, a captain in the army and a lieutenant in the Confederate Navy. Cole was actually a prisoner of war at Memphis in April 1864, paroled not to take up arms against the United States or give any aid or comfort to the enemy. When he took an oath of allegiance to the U. S. government, he was allowed to go to Harrisburg, Pennsylvania, with the condition he reported to the provost marshal.[797] Instead, he made his way to Canada. Thompson sent "him around the lakes, with instructions to go as a lower deck passenger, to familiarize himself with all the channels, and different approaches to the several harbors, the strength of each place, the depositories of coal, and especially to learn all that he could about the war steamer *Michigan*, and devise some plan for her capture or destruction."[798]

Captain Cole sent Thompson a report that stated: "I have formed the acquaintance of Captain Carter, commanding United States steamer *Michigan*. He is an unpolished man, whose pride seems to be touched for the reason that, having been an old United

---

[795] *War of the Rebellion: A Compilation of the Official Records of the Union and Confederate Armies*, series I, Vol. XLIII, 930–931.

[796] Bell, John, *Rebel on the Great Lakes Confederate Naval Commando Operations Launched from Canada 1863–1864*, 68–69.

[797] *War of the Rebellion: A Compilation of the Official Records of the Union and Confederate Armies*, Series II, Vol. VIII, 708–709.

[798] *War of the Rebellion: A Compilation of the Official Records of the Union and Confederate Armies*, Series I, Vol. XLIII, part 2, 932.

States naval officer, he is not allowed now a more extensive field of operation. I do not think he can be bought." He then made a request: "Sir – I have the honor to ask to be placed in secret detached service, in undertaking the capture of the gun-boat *Michigan* at Johnson's Island. Combination can be made without infringing the neutrality laws of Canada." Thompson responded:

> Sir—By the authority in me vested, specially trusting in your knowledge and skill, you are assigned to the secret detached service for the purpose mentioned in your letter. To aid you in this undertaking John Y. Beall, Master in the Confederate States Navy, has been directed to report to you for duty. In all you may do in the premises, you will carefully abstain from violating any laws or regulations of Canada or British authorities in relation to neutrality. [799]

John Yates Beall was known as a daring naval officer who was recently exchanged from a prisoner of war camp. He desired to go to Canada and raid upon the Great Lakes.[800] In his diary he stated: "Immediately on my arrival in Canada I went to Col. Thompson at Toronto, and made application to start a privateer on Lake Huron. He informed me of a plan to take the *Michigan* (14 guns), and release the Confederate officers confined at Johnson's Island. I immediately volunteered, and went to Sandusky, Ohio, to meet Capt. Cole, the leader. We arranged our plans, and separated. Cole staid [sic] at Sandusky."[801]

Captain Cole spent August and September in Sandusky at the West House hotel. Sometimes he registered with his "wife." Cole represented himself as a secretary of the Mount Hope Oil Company of Harrisburg, Pennsylvania, in which he may have been acquainted. He spent a lot of money, playing the part of a well-off businessman spending heavily in saloons, wooing the officers of the *Michigan* and of the guards on Johnson's Island.[802] Cole apparently had won over quite a few as he was reported to be a guest aboard the *Michigan* several times and had visited Union officers on Johnson's Island.[803]

The plan of Beall and Cole was for a coordinated attack upon the *Michigan*, to seize the ship and to free the prisoners and Johnson's Island. Cole was to drug the wine of the officers of the *Michigan*. A messenger, sent by Cole, was to travel to Kelly's

---

[799] *The Northwest Conspiracy,* 568.

[800] Bell, John, *Rebel on the Great Lakes Confederate Naval Commando Operations Launched from Canada 1863–1864,* 71.

[801] *Diary of John Yates Beall,* 296.

[802] Frohman, Charles E. *Rebels on Lake Erie*, 73; Phillips, George M. *Glimpses of the Nation's Struggle,* 249–250.

[803] *War of the Rebellion: A Compilation of the Official Records of the Union and Confederate Armies,* Series I, Vol XLIII, part 1, 916–917.

Island in Lake Erie and rendezvous with the other party. At the same time, Beall was to board the *Philo Parsons* with his men near Detroit take over the steamer and sail to Kelly's Island near Sandusky. At the rendezvous point, they would be given the "go ahead" from Cole's man. The *Philo Parsons* would sail to Sandusky Bay where a signal from Cole would indicate the *Michigan* is ready to be taken over. A shot fired through the officer's quarters on Johnson's Island would let the prisoners know to rush the guards. This was all to coordinate on September 19, 1864.[804]

The prisoners on Johnson's Island were ready for the raid as there was coordination from the outside. R. L. McClung told of his readiness: "I have some rocks in my haversack and a club lying under one side of my blanket and a dagger which I made of an old case knife. You say, 'What do you want with these?' I say 'To burst out of here when the word of command is given.'"[805] Captain McKennon recollected in a 1906 article: "We were organized into companies and regiments and had armed ourselves with clubs, which were made of stove wood and other material at hand, with which to make a fight. I think I was a captain of the organization, for I occupied some position by which I had information of the contemplated movement.

I remember I had several conferences with the Colonel as to my duties, and we were in constant expectation of orders, which never came, to make the fight."[806] Colonel Hundley was asked to join "a secret organization which has for its object the surprise and capture of the island."[807] The prisoners were ready.

Lieutenant Colonel B. H. Hill, Commanding District of Michigan (not to be confused with Colonel Hill commandant of Johnson's Island), received information of the plot on September 17, 1864. He explained how he acquired the information and his actions, which is excerpted here:

> [A] person called upon me at my hotel and introduced himself to me as having been for some years a rebel soldier, and recently a refugee in Canada. He informed me that some of the officers and men of the U.S. Steamer *Michigan* had been tampered with, and that it was the intention of the rebel agent in Windsor, Jacob Thompson . . . to send a party to Windsor, who, with the assistance of the officers and men, would endeavor to get possession of the steamer. The statement of the man and his earnestness made some impression on me, and I telegraphed to Capt. J. C. Carter, the commanding officer of the steamer *Michigan*, that night. On Sunday evening, the 18th instant, my informant again

[804] Bell, John, *Rebel on the Great Lakes Confederate Naval Commando Operations Launched from Canada 1863–1864,* 73.

[805] McClung, R. L., *Diary,* 20.

[806] *The Johnson's Island Plot,* 10.

[807] Hundley, D. R. *Prison Echoes of the Great Rebellion,* 89–90.

crossed the river and saw me. He said, that the party was to take passage on board the *Philo Parsons* at Malden, and would take possession of her before reaching Sandusky; that certain officers and men of the steamer *Michigan* had been tampered with by a man named Cole; and that an officer of the steamer named Eddy could not be bought, and that the intention was to drug him and others. I went down to the steamer *Philo Parsons* the next morning at 6 o'clock and saw her. She was too small to be of any danger if taken by the persons, and, after mature consideration, I came to the conclusion that it would be better to let the steamer go, and place Captain Carter on his guard in a way that would make an impression on him, so that the whole party could be taken.[808]

Captain John Carter received the information on the 17th and arrested Captain Cole on the 19th. Upon arrest, Cole confessed the whole plot and said that more men were coming in on trains from various points. He also implicated six citizens of Sandusky. Colonel Hill, at about 5 o'clock, ordered half dozen officers of the Hoffman's Battalion to go across the bay on special duty.[809] According to Lieutenant Phillips of the 128th Ohio, the ship *Little Eastern*, "was then serving as a government ferry, was already receiving a detail of one hundred men, the party was rejoined by [Colonel Hill] who stated that a plot for the capture of the steamer *Michigan* on that night had just been discovered and might yet be attempted. The chief conspirator, the genial Cole, was already under arrest on the *Michigan*, and others were yet to be captured if not too late. Arriving at Sandusky, small details were sent in various directions and soon returned to the boat, bringing with them under arrest six or eight of the leading citizens, some of whom were 'copperheads' of the most pronounced type. Pickets were placed around the incoming passenger trains, and none were permitted to pass through the lines who could not identify or satisfactorily account for themselves."[810] The people of Sandusky had quite an excitement over the arrests and rumors of the raid spread quickly. Many of the citizens of Sandusky believed the raiders "were intending to come in and liberate the Rebels and burn the city; but their plot was discovered, and now we have pickets posted in the streets here night and day."[811]

The prisoners watched the drama unfold from inside the bull pen with astounding lucidity. Colonel Hundley noted in his diary when the raid became known: "And, lastly, we have tonight a grand excitement, which is not confined to the prisoners

---

[808] *War of the Rebellion: A Compilation of the Official Records of the Union and Confederate Armies,* Series I, Vol. XLIII, part 1, 233.

[809] *War of the Rebellion: A Compilation of the Official Records of the Union and Confederate Armies,* Series II, Vol. VII, 850–851.

[810] Phillips, George M. *Glimpses of the Nation's Struggle,* 249–251.

[811] Dear Sister Alida, *Stowell Letter,* Sept. 27, 1864, Copy at Follett House.

alone. Indeed the excitement outside seems to be even greater than it is inside. The Yankees report that a big fight is going on over in Sandusky, on account of the draft, but it is suspected by the knowing something else is on foot." He continued later, "Col. Hill seemed to be in a great fright, and had his forces under arms, not excepting cooks and laborers. His battery, too, was placed in position on the shore, as if expecting an attack from the water, and no rations whatever were issued to prisoners. [T]here are many vague rumors of an exploded Canada plot to relieve the prisoners confined here."[812]

John Yates Beall arrived in Windsor with a party of men, crossed over to Detroit half hour before the *Philo Parsons* was to depart for Kelly's Island. The steamer departed at 8 a.m. with 25 to 30 passengers. Beall asked the captain to stop at Sandwich and Malden to pick up more passengers, which were to be the remainder of the conspirators. Five more men boarded at Sandwich. A crewmember of the ship overheard Beall ask, "Where the rest of them were." One of them responded: "They did not come."

The ship stopped at Malden and picked up about fifteen more, including "one corded pine box, which seemed heavy."[813] The conspirators spread out on the ship to preassigned stations. The ship arrived at Kelly's Island, as scheduled, with passengers departing and boarding. When the ship left the dock for Sandusky, Beall's men sprang into action.

> Beall approached the first mate, De Witt C. Nichols, and asked: "Are you the captain of this boat?"
>   Nichols responded, "No, sir; I am mate."
>   Beall asked: "You have charge of her at present, have you not?"
>   Nichols: "Yes, sir."
>   Beall: "Will you step back here for a minute? I want to talk to you."
>   The two men then walked to the rear of the ship.
>   Beall said: "I am a Confederate officer. There are thirty of us, well armed. I seize this boat, and take you as a prisoner. You must pilot the boat as I direct you," and pulling a revolver out of his pocket, "here are the tools to make you. Run down and lie off the harbor."[814]

Michael Campbell, an engineer, recalled what happened: "I was standing in the saloon. I heard a shot, a yell, and then another shot. I then ran onto the main deck, and

---

[812] Hundley, D. R. *Prison Echoes of the Great Rebellion,* 135–136.

[813] *War of the Rebellion: A Compilation of the Official Records of the Union and Confederate Armies,* Series 1, Vol. XLIII, part 1, 240.

[814] Ibid., 240.

saw a man run after the fireman with a cocked revolver in his hand, shouting to him to go down the main hatch, or he would shoot him. The fireman escaped, and the man turned to me and made the same order. I told him to 'go to hell,' and he shot at me, the [bullet] passing between my legs as I was ascending from the main to the upper deck. On reaching the upper deck I saw five others with revolvers in their hands driving the passengers forward and detaining them. From the cabin they were driven down to the main deck and down the fire-hold."[815]

Beall's men had control of the ship, and the passengers were held below deck. The conspirators asked if the ship had enough wood to steam for seven or eight hours. When they discovered the ship did not have a sufficient supply to make the raid, they turned back for Middle Bass Island to refuel arriving at about dark. The conspirators fired several shots at the owner of the wood to pacify him and forced part of the crew to load it aboard. The captain of the ship, Sylvester Atwood, was at home on Middle Bass Island when a little boy ran up and said there was shooting down at the dock from the *Philo Parsons*. The captain walked up and asked what was happening when three or four men twirled around with their pistols. With the wood and the captain loaded aboard, the *Philo Parsons* was ready to steam on to Sandusky. But Cole's man, who was to update the conspirators of the *Michigan's* status, was not there.

The *Island Queen*, a steamer that ferried many of the prisoners from Sandusky to Johnson's Island, made her appearance in the drama. The captain of the *Philo Parsons*, Atwood, heard "the whistle of the *Island Queen*." He heard Beall order to his men, "as many as could be spared from the cabin, come this way."[816] Henry Haines, engineer of the *Queen*, gave his testimony of the event: "As we were nearing Kelly's Island we met the *Parsons*, about a mile from Kelly's Island, and seemingly bound for Sandusky. After passing us she turned to the east, went down the lake, and turned and came back again, and then steered her course for Middle Bass, where she arrived before us, and was lying at the dock. We came along side of her, and men came on the *Island Queen* from her. I was in the engine-room attending to the working of the engine. I heard some one [sic] exclaim, 'Shoot the son of a bitch,' and was immediately shot, the ball ping my nose and through my left cheek. One of the capturing party, who was called Captain Morgan, asked me where the valves were. I showed him the pony pipe in the hold, and he thereupon chopped it off. He then took a big sledge hammer and broke the big [valve] off the side of the boat and let the water in."[817] The passengers of the *Queen* were moved to the *Philo Parsons*. The woman and children and a few others under direction of Captain Atwood were sent ashore on Middle Bass. The men were then

---

[815] *War of the Rebellion: A Compilation of the Official Records of the Union and Confederate Armies,* Series I, Vol. XLIII, Part I, 237.

[816] Ibid., 239.

[817] Ibid., 244–245.

released, which included about twenty-five unarmed soldiers going home to Toledo to be mustered out.[818] All had sworn not to mention what happened for 48 hours.

The *Philo Parsons* started out on the lake with the *Island Queen* in tow. Just a few miles out, near Ballast Island, the line was cut and the *Queen* was set adrift to sink.[819] The conspirators sailed for Sandusky with most crew members locked below decks. Some of the crew from the two ships had to perform various tasks to keep the ship running and to build fireballs of hemp.[820]

When the conspirators arrived off of Sandusky, the signal from Cole to attack did not appear. Michael Campbell, wheelman of the *Philo Parsons*, explained what he witnessed off Sandusky Bay: "I told the one whom they called colonel that it was dangerous to run into Sandusky Bay by night. I told him the channel was too narrow. He then called his men forward, conversed with them a few minutes, and then came and told me to head the boat for Malden [Canada]."[821] John Yates Beall reported that "seventeen of my twenty men mutinied, and refused to go forward, and this necessitated my turning back, thus abandoning Cole." Beall continued with his consternation, "a most cowardly and dishonourable affair."[822]

The conspirators went back to Malden, plundered the *Philo Parsons*, and scuttled her on the shore of Canada.[823] Beall was arrested on December 16, 1864, in upstate New York, apparently trying to derail a train. He was tried and found guilty of "violation of the law of war" and being a spy. He was hanged on February 24, 1865.[824] Charles Cole was interrogated along with the men he had implicated. All but three were released immediately. Cole, as everyone soon found out, was a pathological liar, which embarrassed not only the Confederates and Thompson, but the Union authorities as well. With Cole lying to everyone, a case was not possible and in February 1866, he was released a free man.[825]

---

[818] Ibid., 244.

[819] Ibid., 243.

[820] Ibid., 244.

[821] Ibid., 237.

[822] *Beall Diary*, 296.

[823] *War of the Rebellion: A Compilation of the Official Records of the Union and Confederate Armies*, Series I, Vol. XLIII, Part I, 237–238.

[824] Frohman, Charles E. *Rebels on Lake Erie*, 102–104, 109.

[825] Bell, John, *Rebel on the Great Lakes Confederate Naval Commando Operations Launched from Canada 1863–1864*, 110–114.

Chapter 10

FROM HELL TO HEAVEN

"An ideal family resort, for picnics and campers"

—Post-war advertisement for Johnson's Island

THE OATH

The federals offered the prisoners at Johnson's Island, as well as the other northern camps, an option to their current situation: the Oath of Allegiance. At first, when the Confederates were considered traitors, if a prisoner signed an oath to be faithful to the United States, the prisoner was released from prison. This was an applicable option for men from the border states who could return home and live peaceful lives officially inside the federal lines. The issue became more complicated with the men who lived in states that had seceded from the Union. They would return to face the wrath of hostile neighbors. It was decided that Confederates who took the oath would be sent to the frontier to guard against Indian attack. This worked out well as the ex-Confederates did not have to take up arms against the southern states. Most prisoners still saw this as an act of treason that affected them. Colonel Murphey gave his opinion: "The oath takers are enlisted for the purpose of waging war in the far west against our true allies the Indians. Thus they are indirectly contributing to our subjugation, the act they vowed they would not commit."[826]

The prisoners were very angry over these men betraying the Rebellion. They were seen as traitors to the cause. Creative names were used to describe the Oath takers.

---

[826] Murphey, V. S., *Diary*, 103.

They were called "Galvanized Yankees" and "Razorbacks." The term "Galvanized Yankee" meant they were southerners on the inside and had a coating of Yankee on the outside. The term Razorback meant they had no spine.[827]

To take the oath, one had to apply with the authorities. This was a very dangerous prospect, for if discovered, the prisoner might receive some rough treatment. In September 1863, the prisoners found a letter written by a lieutenant from North Carolina giving his reasons to be allowed to take the oath. He said he was and "always has been a union man. He [was] born Yankee & has been south only 3 or 4 years." Captain Bingham continued with his report: "Among other amiable things he says that he wishes that not only Greek fire, but Hell fire might rain down on Charleston for 6 weeks," adding the lieutenant "might be mobbed if he does not take care of himself."[828] A prisoner in Block 5, apparently born in France, "wrote to take the oath, & his letter got out of the Yankees pocket & into rebel's hands." The Razorback was "kicked downstairs by his room mates [sic]" until a Union officer came in with about twenty to thirty men to rescue the "scoundrel." The guards formed a firing line to protect the man when the prisoners from every side started pelting the group with snowballs. The Union officer threatened to have his men open fire and the snowballing stopped.[829]

A Captain Stephens of Arkansas "wrote a petition for the oath, and started, after reveille, one morning to the 'big gate' to deposit his petition. It dropped from his pocket on the sidewalk, and was brought to [Block 8]." When Captain Stephens returned to his block, someone "kicked him out at the door." His regiment's Colonel then slashed him with his cane. His bed sack and two blankets were thrown out the door.[830] He then went around to the other blocks begging entrance, but met only insult, contempt, and rougher treatment. He openly pleaded that he had intended to take the oath to fool the authorities to release him. Since he did not intend to keep his oath, he plead "perjury as an apology for an equal crime."[831] Three months later, Stephens was discharged from the hospital where he sought refuge and began "causing trouble again."[832] None of the blocks welcomed him. Stephens was delivered by a federal officer to the chief of a Mess in Block 7, holding the chief responsible for his safety.

---

[827] Luther R. Mills, 8.

[828] Bingham, Robert, *Diary,* 59.

[829] Bingham, Robert, *Diary,* 2, 52; Dooley, John, *John Dooley, Confederate Soldier: His War Journal,* 158; Patterson, Edmund Dewitt. *Yankee Rebel: The Civil War Journal of Edmund DeWitt Patterson,* 158.

[830] McClung, R. L., *Diary,* Confederate Veteran Vol. XV, 495.

[831] Caldwell, James Parks, *A Northern Confederate at Johnson's Island Prison: The Civil War Diary of James Parks Caldwell,* 99.

[832] Caldwell, James Parks, *A Northern Confederate at Johnson's Island Prison: The Civil War Diary of James Parks Caldwell,* 120.

Major Caldwell stated repugnantly: "Notwithstanding he was turned out to sleep on the ground as was right and proper."[833]

The authorities were having difficulty protecting the men who wanted to take the oath. General Shaler, who was in command at that time, "issued an order, promising protection to all [applicants] and threatening offenders with punishment." This order was laughed at since the Rebels knew "it is necessary to catch a dog before you hang him."[834] Colonel Inzer recorded how difficult it was for the guards to fulfill the promise of safety in his diary: "We expelled Lt. Combee of the 22nd Ga. from our room for trying to take the oath. Major Fowler, yankee, said if we did not let him stay in the room, he would cut off our rations." The rations were cut, but "our friends from other blocks and messes . . . sent us the greatest plenty." The federals brought back Lieutenant Combee and "threatened [the rebels] with punishment if we mistreated him. Combee was kicked out of the room." The supply of rations was restored nevertheless.[835]

In September 1864, Lieutenant Colonel Scovill (USA) wrote in an inspection report that he "recommended the construction of a building the size of the wash-house for the occupancy of prisoners desirous of taking the amnesty oath." He was concerned about their safety. Colonel Hill acknowledged there had been "persistent effort to intimidate men in the prison who show the least disposition to yield to the United States Government" but did not like the idea of a separate barrack as it "yields the government of the prison to the prisoners."[836] Scovill once again requested that a separate building be constructed "surrounded by a line of stakes, beyond which neither class of prisoners should be allowed to pass." Colonel Hill finally relented and concurred with Scovill's idea of separate quarters. Colonel Hill realized: "Some better encouragement and more efficient protection for prisoners desirous to take the amnesty oath is undoubtedly required. If they had one of the barracks by themselves I presume it would be soon filled. At present but a very few dare let their sentiments be known."[837] Colonel Hoffman suggested a compromise: "There would seem to be no objection, however, to assigning them to rooms in one of the barracks nearest the guard-house, where protection could more readily be extended to them."[838] The order

---

[833] Ibid.

[834] Wash, W. A. *Camp, Field and Prison Life*, 206.

[835] Inzer, John Washington, *The Diary of a Confederate Soldier: John Washington Inzer 1834–1928*, 94.

[836] *War of the Rebellion: A Compilation of the Official Records of the Union and Confederate Armies*, Series II, Vol. VII, 766.

[837] *War of the Rebellion: A Compilation of the Official Records of the Union and Confederate Armies*, Series II, Vol. VII, 803–804.

[838] *War of the Rebellion: A Compilation of the Official Records of the Union and Confederate Armies*, Series II, Vol. VII, 811.

to implement this idea was issued four months later. On January 21, 1865, Colonel Hill posted inside the prison the following order:

Hdqtrs US Forces
J I and Sandusky
Jan 20, 1865

Special Orders No. 20- Extract

Par 2. – The Supt of the prison will cause so many rooms in the end of block No. 1, next to the fence, as may be necessary to provide quarters for prisoners who have applied to take the oath of amnesty, to be vacated by the present occupants, (who will be assigned to other quarters,) and will assign such rooms on both floors to the applicants for the Oath of Amnesty. Next to those applicants, he will, from time to time, assign quarters to other applicants for the oath as they shall be enrolled.

In like manner he will assign quarters in block No. 2, (beginning at the end next the fence,) to those who, though not now applicants for the Amnesty Oath, desire not to be exchanged, and thence on from Block to Block as numbers in each class may require.

He will obtain the names, in each class, from Capt Manor, Supt Pris. Rolls, etc, or act upon his own knowledge, and make changes from time to time in each class, by addition, or otherwise, as shall be consistent with the foregoing directions; and will transfer from one Company to another, so that the members of the same Company may occupy the same, or contiguous rooms.

He will, if he shall find it necessary, cause the prescribed rations to be issued and delivered with reference to the classification of prisoners herein ordered.

By command of Col Chas H Hill
(Capt) J F Huntington[839]

This order angered the prisoners. V. S. Murphey recorded in his diary the reasons of the order: "They are placed in these quarters for two reasons. 1st: The rooms are sealed and more comfortable and pleasant than the others. 2nd: They are in close proximity to the barracks of the Yankee troops who could afford them protection from the vengeance the officers would visit upon their traitorous heads. They are to receive additional rations as an award for their treachery and as alluring prize to the hungry of like treatment on taking the precious amnesty oath."[840] Colonel Inzer, who was lodged in one of the rooms in question, penned: "It is hard to be thus imposed on by traitors

---

[839] Murphey, V. S., *Diary,* 137–138.

[840] Murphey, V. S., *Diary,* 140.

and scoundrels. A man must be very corrupt, indeed, to be a member of this villainous crowd. I fear we will have to move."[841]

On January 30, the transfer to the near quarters of the men applying for the oath took place. Murphey continued his tirade upon oath takers: "Our sluggish blood has been aroused from its usual tranquil status, and our minds excited by a sad humiliating spectacle. The oath takers were mustered (numbering twenty-three) paraded and under the protectiveness of Yankee bayonets were marched to be installed in the most comfortable commodious and convenient quarters in the 'pen,' the rebels being compelled to vacate to those galvanized gentry. Crowds gathered upon the boulevard of the prison to scrutinize their faces learn who they were and what state they represented. They marched by amid horrid groans and billing sarcasms with penitent heads abjectly bowed, eyes fastened intently upon the earth."[842] The first half of Block 1, nearest the gate, became, as McHenry Howard put it, a "plague spot to the rest of the prisoners, being occupied by the 'galvanized' men." Howard continued, "These were contemptuously ignored by their former comrades and herded together, looking very uncomfortable in their isolation and degradation."[843] As the number of oath takers grew to 42[844] by February 1, V. S. Murphey warned: "I shall get their names and record them in this book of Yankee infamies. They will learn some day that 'there is a child among them taking notes, and faith he will print them too."[845]

EXCHANGE COMMENCES

By January 1865, special exchanges became more common, and prisoners started to exit Johnson's Island for the first time in about eighteen months. The Rebels received notice that Trans-Mississippi prisoners should "be prepared to leave at a moment's notice." Three days later, John Dooley, recorded: "One hundred and seventy prisoners of the trans-Mississippi department (captured at Port Hudson and Vicksburg) left today for exchange. This is cheering indeed; for although they are returning where the Confederacy has long been asleep and a dead weight, it gives us some hope that they will not be the only ones who may be exchanged and once having set the ball in motion we may all be rolled to our homes."[846] In January, two small groups of seventeen men

---

[841] Inzer, John Washington, *The Diary of a Confederate Soldier: John Washington Inzer 1834–1928*, 121.

[842] Murphey, V. S., *Diary,* 168.

[843] Howard, McHenry, *Recollections of a Maryland Confederate Soldier and Staff Officer under Johnston, Jackson, and Lee,* 398–399.

[844] Caldwell, James Parks, *A Northern Confederate at Johnson's Island Prison: The Civil War Diary of James Parks Caldwell,* 180.

[845] Murphey, V. S., *Diary,* 141–142.

[846] Dooley, John, *John Dooley, Confederate Soldier: His War Journal,* 158; Patterson, Edmund Dewitt. *Yankee Rebel: The Civil War Journal of Edmund DeWitt Patterson,* 165.

each and a few individuals departed on special exchange.[847] They most likely were sent home to areas occupied by the Union army and would not be a threat to the federals.

By February, a general exchange was being finalized between the North and the South. Colonel Hoffman issued an order to prepare "parole-rolls for exchange, of all prisoners of war, who wish to be exchanged, in parties of 100. Those who have been longest in confinement will be first exchanged."[848] John Dooley's spirits were high when he penned on February 16, 1865: "The excitement is growing intense. 120 prisoners leave today. They will leave according to States. Those from 'free' States have preference of being freed before the others."[849] The first to leave were men from Missouri, Kentucky, Arkansas, and Louisiana. These areas were under Union occupation.[850] Colonel Hill went into the pen on the 18th and gave a speech to the prisoners that exchange was commencing.[851] February and March became a beehive of activity. On February 20th prisoners captured up to July 1, 1863, are exchanged in alphabetical order. Three hundred officers, most captured at Gettysburg, departed for exchange on the 23rd. [852] On March 12th a reported 1,000 prisoners departed the island in one group. By March 31st the official number of prisoners stood at 1,817. The exchange system was in full swing emptying the prison of old inmates. New captures from the battlefield were also arriving, keeping the overall number fairly stable. The exchange system ended in April, stabilizing the number at 2,778.[853]

THE END OF THE WAR

Robert E. Lee surrendered to Ulysses S. Grant at Appomattox Courthouse on April 9, 1865. The Army of Northern Virginia, the deciding battle force of the Confederacy, was no more. The news reached Sandusky and Johnson's Island the next day. A prisoner noted: "When the news came of Lee's surrender, we were sad and glad at the same time: sad to know that it had to be, and glad to know that we would soon see our loved ones at home."[854] The Loyal League was organized by the prisoners after

---

[847] Inzer, John Washington, *The Diary of a Confederate Soldier: John Washington Inzer 1834–1928,* 122.

[848] *War of the Rebellion: A Compilation of the Official Records of the Union and Confederate Armies,* Series II, Vol. VIII, 237.

[849] Dooley, John, *John Dooley, Confederate Soldier: His War Journal,* 158; Patterson, *Yankee Rebel,* 166.

[850] Wash, W. A. *Camp, Field and Prison Life,* 299.

[851] Inzer, John Washington, *The Diary of a Confederate Soldier: John Washington Inzer 1834–1928,* 125.

[852] Caldwell, James Parks, *A Northern Confederate at Johnson's Island Prison,* 184; Dooley, John, *John Dooley, Confederate Soldier: His War Journal,* 158; Patterson, Edmund Dewitt. *Yankee Rebel: The Civil War Journal of Edmund DeWitt Patterson,* 165.

[853] *War of the Rebellion: A Compilation of the Official Records of the Union and Confederate Armies,* Series II, Vol. VIII, 988–1004.

[854] *Confederate Veteran,* Vol. II, 243.

the surrender. It was formed because "men began to ask for paroles that they might go home." This was seen as defeatist and traitorous to the cause to promise not to fight. In response, a "Loyal League was formed and all asked to join it with the pledge that no officer would accept a parole not to serve in the Confederate Army as long as there was an organization of Confederate forces in the field. Col. Boles of Louisville was the head of this Loyal League."[855]

The federals started celebrating the surrender of Lee and the now-guaranteed defeat of the Confederacy. Two hundred guns were fired as a salute to the victory.[856] Colonel Inzer inked in his diary: "The Yanks had a big day of it, fired a national salute, fireworks at night. Decorated buildings with color and flags."[857] A guard wrote to his daughter describing the scene on the island: "There is a candle burning in every house of each window on the island and the city is very highly illuminated. The salutes were fired as perported [sic] . . . [and the] fire works would fairly frighten you. The boys have just returned . . . with likeness of Jef[ferson Davis] on a pole. Jef [sic] looked a little as I used to think the Devil looked. The firecrackers are bursting everywhere and sound not a little unlike the musketry of the battlefield when one is a little distance from the scene of action."[858] Then on the 14th, news of Lincoln's assassination reached the area. The month of April became a mix of joyous celebrations, much like the end of a victorious sporting match and reverence and mourning the fact President Lincoln had been martyred. The guards wanted to have a bonfire and set fire to the guard's pest house. Thompson, a Union soldier, wrote "a very bright light was seen suddenly to spring up on the hill near the fort and nearly on the highest point on the Island. It was no doubt set by some of the boys for a bonfire . . . its light extended all over the Island and was as bright perhape [sic] as any island ever stood under the Sun."[859] On the 26th, the Yankees fired thirteen guns at sunrise, one every half hour until sun set when a national salute of thirty-six guns was fired.[860]

The war was now all but over. The months of April and May saw one Confederate command after another surrender. Westwood Todd noticed the changed attitude of the entire prison: "After the surrender of our armies, the prison rules and discipline were very much relaxed. The guards sometimes talked to the prisoners from their posts. In order to "make a raise" the prisoners frequently sold their blankets to the guards for a trifle, the weather being then warm enough to dispense with them."[861]

---

[855] Hayden, S. A., *Letters*, 7.

[856] Inzer, John Washington, *The Diary of a Confederate Soldier: John Washington Inzer 1834–1928*, 134.

[857] Ibid.

[858] M. Jeff Thompson, *The Civil War Reminiscences of General M. Jeff Thompson*, April 14, Follett House.

[859] Ibid, April 16, 1865.

[860] Inzer, John Washington, *The Diary of a Confederate Soldier: John Washington Inzer 1834–1928*, 134.

[861] Todd, Westwood, *Reminiscences of Westwood Todd*, 329.

With the Confederate forces surrendering, the exchange system was put on hold. Now the only way out of prison was to take the Oath of Allegiance or have a special release procured by powerful friends. On April 25th, Colonel Hill posted an order from the Secretary of War, which stated that to be released, prisoners would have to take the Oath of Allegiance.[862] Throughout the month of May, prisoners started to trickle out. Colonel Inzer tried to keep a record of this departure and counted 200 prisoners left who had previously taken the oath.[863]

Taking the Oath was a wrenching experience for the Rebels, who called it "Swallowing the Eagle." Luther Mills recalled the phrase came from a prisoner who had a dream: "I saw something like a dark cloud rise up out of Lake Erie far off in the East. As it rose higher and higher, it appeared to be an enormous eagle stretching its wings from the North toward the South. When it came vertically over the stockade, it burst with a loud noise, and thousands upon thousands of little eagles fell into the prison pen. And then every prisoner began to catch the eaglets and to swallow them."[864] R. L. McClung made an eloquent argument: "If I break one oath, I'll break another. If I break mine oath, what is my word? If I am false in one thing, I would be in another and how can I be false to the loved ones I left in the distant land? How can I be false to . . . my gray haired parents who are now trembling on the very verge of the grave and most of all, how can I be false to myself?"[865] Prisoners who were hesitant to take the oath started to receive letters from friends and loved ones to "take the oath and come home."[866]

Captain Blackman wrote in a letter dated May 30: "All here except about fifty have applied for the amnesty and anxiously await the action of the war department."[867] The prisoners eagerly awaited release, but nothing seemed to be happening, causing confusion inside the pen. On either June 9 or 10 Colonel Hill entered the bullpen to give a statement. Westwood Todd remembered the event: "Colonel Hill, the Commandant, came 'into the pen,' one morning, and mounting the steps to one of the blocks, drew a large audience. As it was to be his last chance of airing his oratory 'he spread himself.' After indulging in much 'buncombe' and glorification of the American Eagle, he announced to the prisoners that all under the rank of [major] would be released on taking the oath."[868] Almost daily men were leaving to the point that 119 prisoners remained at the end of June. W. A.

---

[862] Inzer, John Washington, *The Diary of a Confederate Soldier: John Washington Inzer 1834–1928*, 136.

[863] Inzer, John Washington, *The Diary of a Confederate Soldier: John Washington Inzer 1834–1928*, 138.

[864] Luther R. Mills, 8.

[865] McClung, R. L., *Diary*, 15.

[866] Todd, Westwood, *Reminiscences of Westwood Todd*, 329.

[867] Blackman Letter, May 30, 1865.

[868] Todd, Westwood, *Reminiscences of Westwood Todd*, 329.

Wash described the feeling of departure: "The scene reminded me of the parting of students at the close of a collegiate year. Friends were saying goodbye, never to meet again, and many pleasant, happy associations and ties were being severed forever. I felt attached to my room, my books, my bunk and our rustic furniture, and I experienced a like feeling for the very prison and even some of the Federal garrison."[869] Westwood Todd volunteered to be a clerk to facilitate a quick departure of his comrades. He recollects: "As many as could be conveniently transported were released every day. About fifty men at a time were drawn up, before Colonel Hill, who administered the oath, the prisoners being required to lift up their right hands. Every fellow looked like he was taking the oath 'on compulsion.' Each man was handed his discharge order for transportation home, and whatever money was due him."[870]

The war ended and the prisoners were once more citizens of a United States of America. They left the island with varying emotions regarding their time in prison. They felt disappointment, regret, and sometimes hate. Most went home and picked up the pieces of their disrupted lives, never forgetting the memories of what they experienced in battle or in prison. One prisoner left behind a handwritten poem inscribed on a wall of Block 4, about his feelings:

> Farewell! Farewell! thou giant inland sea:
> Thou, too, subservest the moods of tyranny—
> Girding this Isle, washing its lonely shore
> With moaning echoes of thy melancholy roar.
> Thou hast the curses of this patriot band,—
> All, save the spot, the holy sacred bed,
> Where rest in peace our southern warriors dead.[871]

THE END OF AN ERA

By June 30, there were only 119 prisoners on the island. Most had refused to take the oath and were considered diehard secessionists. At one point, Colonel Hill left the island and was replaced by Major S. P. Lee. The last communique from Colonel Hoffman to Johnson's Island was on September 1, 1865. Hoffman ordered all the prisoners (302 in number) to be transferred to Fort Lafayette in New York, with the exception of Henry P. Esteph, who was ordered to Fort Delaware.[872]

---

[869] Wash, W. A. *Camp, Field and Prison Life*, 300–301.

[870] Todd, Westwood, *Reminiscences of Westwood Todd*, 329–330.

[871] Thomas Usher Tidmarsh, "Farewell to Johnson's Island," *Confederate Veteran*, Vol. III (1894), 252.

[872] *War of the Rebellion: A Compilation of the Official Records of the Union and Confederate Armies*, Series II, Vol. VIII, 739.

On November 7, 1865 an announcement was printed in the *Register*:

Quartermaster's Property   At Auction
   Will be sold at public sale on Wednesday, November 15, at Johnson's
Island near Sandusky, Ohio
   69 Buildings
Of various dimensions, all of seasoned pine lumber and in good order, mostly
of rough boards and battened roofs, some with shingle roofs and plastered
inside, with doors and windows.
Also, a quantity of unserviceable quartermaster stores, comprising stoves,
pipes, carts, harness, tools, &c &c.
Terms cash, in United States currency. Bidders will be required to make deposit
of ten per cent when bids are accepted. Thirty days will be allowed to remove
the buildings; all other property to be taken away immediately after the sale.[873]

Another auction was held on the 21st consisting of butcher knives, saws, scales,
and other such items. The sales were well attended and brought in a reported
$7,000. The federal officers' buildings were not part of the option. The officers
of the post offered for auction their personal furniture, horses, buggies, and miscellaneous items two days before Christmas. Assumedly, they were about to be
discharged as an African American regiment had arrived on the island December
1, 1865. The last government auction was April 2, 1866, and consisted of the rest
of the buildings and equipment not sold in the previous auctions. Like before,
bidders had thirty days to remove the buildings. Mr. Johnson reportedly bought
the officers' buildings. On June 8, the federal government relinquished control of
Johnson's Island.[874]

THE CEMETERY

Mr. Johnson built a fence around the cemetery "at his own expense" and repaired
it from time to time. An unknown officer from the Columbus Barracks put up iron
posts with flat steel wire sometime in the mid 1880s. McMeen's Post of the G.A.R.
of Sandusky maintained the cemetery and held Memorial Day services at the site.
In 1889, a group of prominent editors, farmers, and fruit growers from Georgia visited the cemetery. They saw the decayed state of the original wooden markers, raised
funds, and replaced the markers with Georgia marble.[875] The wood was rotted, and
many mistakes were made in transcribing what was thought to be the information

---

[873] *Register,* November 7, 1865.

[874] Frohman, Charles E. *Rebels on Lake Erie,* 69–71.

[875] *Descriptive Booklet of Johnson's Island,* 2

onto the marble. Many simply have carved "Unknown." The cemetery grounds were purchased in 1905 by the Robert Patton Chapter, United Daughters of the Confederacy of Cincinnati. The group also purchased a strip of ground from the cemetery all the way to the bay. This extra land would be useful for a park area and allow boats to land to visit the cemetery. An iron fence surrounded the cemetery.[876] On June 8, 1910, the U. D. C. erected a monument at the bay side of the cemetery. The monument is of a Confederate sentry standing with a watchful eye. The lower pedestal on which the monument stands was placed by the Grand Lodge of Mississippi "in remembrance of the Masons who sleep here." An iron gate to welcome visitors from the shore stands in front with the inscription "Confederate Soldiers 1861–1912."

JOHNSON'S ISLAND IN TRANSITION

An 1889 article described the island. Of the 300 acres of the island, "seventy-five of which are covered by magnificent young groves of black walnut, hickory and other trees native to this section, grown up almost wholly since the dark and unhappy days of civil war." About 50 acres were peach orchards and 25 acres was a quarry of "inexhaustible lime stone." The rest of the island, about 150 acres, was tilled farmland. The article then made an accurate prediction: "The time is coming when Johnson's Island will be converted by the landscape gardener into one of the most beautiful resorts in all this summer resort region, and when cottages and summer homes by the dozen dot its charming shores."[877]

The Johnson's Island Pleasure Resort Company was established on Johnson's Island. In 1894, L. S. Johnson, son of L. B. Johnson who leased the island to the federal government, leased twenty acres of land on the eastern end of the island for the construction of a pleasure resort. It is interesting to note that the lease also allowed a walkway to the old fort on the east side of the island. The company leased the land for three years, with an option to extend to ten years. The handwritten map enclosed with the contract showed the quarry and two families living on the northwestern side of the island, nearest to the peninsula. It also showed that the western tip had been dedicated as the Villa Site, an apparent attempt to start a village.[878] The pleasure resort advertised: "An ideal family resort, for picnics and campers. Cottages for rent. Fine bathing beach and good fishing. Baseball grounds. Roller skating rink. Dancing pavilion and vaudeville shows. Restaurant and hotel accommodations."[879] The resort burned down

---

[876] *Sandusky Register,* March 1905. Article copy at Follett House.

[877] *Descriptive Booklet of Johnson's Island,* 4.

[878] Lease Contract, Follett House.

[879] Johnson's Island Pleasure Resort Co. Flyer, Follett House.

in 1897. A second attempt was made in 1904 with a new pavilion. It lasted a couple of years until it was purchased and moved across the bay to Cedar Point.[880]

Lieutenant E. O. Mitchell of the 128th Ohio visited the island in 1896. He went back to reminisce about his time as a guard. He found: "Where the prisoners' quarters were located is now a wheat field. A few of the old officers' quarters are standing, now occupied by families who live there. The old fort is distinguishable, although covered with long grass and underbrush. Today about two hundred and fifty graves remain, the others having been removed by relatives and friends. A marble slab is located at the head of each grave, with the name, rank and regiment carved thereon, the whole inclosed [sic] by a wire fence."[881]

In 1897, Mr. Johnson sold the island to Charles Dick and Minnie Emerich of the Breakwater Company.[882] At about that time, a quarry was in operation upon the area where the federal buildings were located. The quarry had a promising future for a few years as the work force increased around 150 to 200. A small village, a school, and a post office were in operation until about 1905 with the quarry closing in 1908.[883]

In 1907 or 1908, Robert Crouch, a former prisoner, made a visit back to the island. He described this visit in the *Confederate Veteran* magazine. He related: "This long period had wrought many changes on the island, and it was with difficulty that I could locate any part of the old prison." The federal officers' quarters must have been removed or destroyed because Crouch did not mention them like Mitchell had in his 1896 visit. The blockhouse and the main gate fortification were still there as was one part of the western ditch that ran beside the fence. A rock quarry was in operation to the western side of the island where the union building once stood. A pleasure resort was located on the eastern side of the island butting right up to the edge of the cemetery. When he visited the cemetery he noticed it was in "so much better condition than [he] expected . . . and shows more care than the ordinary country cemetery."[884]

Johnson's Island almost became another military establishment when the Navy had an interest in establishing the Naval Training Station Great Lakes on the island. In 1902 and 1904 the location was scouted, but it was decided to build the station near Chicago where it still exists today.[885] The idea was to have a training center in the Midwest to ease training recruits and reserves from the area.

---

[880] Frohman, Charles E. *Rebels on Lake Erie*, 122–123.

[881] Mitchell, E. O., *Sketches of War History,* 129.

[882] Lawsuit document, Case Number 6106, copy at Follett House.

[883] Frohman Collection, Rutherford B. Hayes Library, 123.

[884] Crouch, Robert, "A Visit to Johnson's Island", *Confederate Veteran,* Vol. XVI, 76.

[885] Frohman Collection, Rutherford B. Hayes Library, 123.

In 1959, the military decided to conduct a training exercise on Johnson's Island. The plan was called "Operation Ready Reserve." It was conducted September 19th to 20th, in "the spirit of 'unification,' [of] Air, Land and Sea Units of the Marine Corps Reserve, Naval Reserve and the Ohio Air National Guard." The exercise was to rescue prisoners of war from a work camp at the quarry. The 8th Infantry Battalion, USMCR, made an amphibious attack on the north side of the island from the *USS Turkey*, a WWII minesweeper stationed in Toledo. The island was defended by the 11th Infantry Battalion, USMCR, from Cleveland, Ohio. Air support was provided by 112th Jet Fighter-Interceptor Squadron ONG and Marine Air Reserve Squadron VHA-231. Over 500 men participated in the mock invasion and camped on the island in combat conditions with meals of C rations.[886]

Johnson's Island today is connected via causeway to the peninsula to the north. This bridge improved access to the island and as a result, beautiful summer homes now dot the island. The old quarry is now a marina with sailboats and yachts. Across the bay at Cedar Point is an amusement park with some record-holding rollercoasters. Almost all traces of the prison complex have been erased by time, save for the cemetery, which will be a permanent reminder to the pleasure seekers that this island was once home to thousands of Rebels suffering for a "lost cause."

---

[886] U.S. Marine Corps Release No. 10–60, Rutherford B. Hayes Presidential Library.

APPENDIX

THE OATH OF ALLEGIANCE

United States of America

I, McHenry Howard, of the county of Baltimore, State of Maryland, do solemnly swear that I will support, protect, and defend, the Constitution and Government of the United States against all enemies, whether domestic or foreign; that I will bear true faith, allegiance and loyalty to the same, any ordinance, resolution or laws of any State, Convention, or Legislature, to the contrary notwithstanding; and further, that I will faithfully perform all the duties which may be required of me by the laws of the United States; and I take this oath freely and voluntarily, without any mental reservation or evasion whatever.

McHenry Howard.

Subscribed and sworn to before me at Johnson's Island, O., this Twenty-sixth day of May, A. D. 1865.

Chas. W. Hill, Colonel Comd'g[887]

---

[887] Howard, 404.

BIBLIOGRAPHY

Primary Sources

Published Materials:

[Allen, Captain L. W.] "A Plan to Escape" in *Southern Historical Society Papers, Volume XIX*. Richmond, VA: Southern Historical Society, 1891:239–289.

Archer, J. J. "The James J. Archer Letters." *Maryland Historical Magazine*. Vol. LVI. Baltimore: Maryland Historical Society, 1961.

Barber, Flavel C. *Holding the Line: The Third Tennessee Infantry, 1861–1864*. Edited by Robert H. Ferrell. Kent State University Press, 1994.

Barbiere, Joe. *Scraps from the Prison Table, At Camp Chase and Johnson's Island*. Dolestown, PA: W. W. H. Davis, Printer, 1868.

Barziza, Decimus et Ultimus. *The Adventures of a Prisoner of War, 1863–1864*. Edited by R. Henderson Shuftler. Austin: University of Texas Press, 1964, originally pub. 1865.

Caldwell, James Parks. *A Northern Confederate at Johnson's Island Prison: The Civil War Diary of James Parks Caldwell*. Edited by George H. Jones. Jefferson, NC: McFarland & Company, 2010.

Carpenter, H. "Plain Living at Johnson's Island." *Century Magazine* (March 1891): 705–718.

Chamberlayne, Ham. *Virginian – Letters and Papers of an Artillery Officer in the War for Southern Independence*. Richmond, VA.: Press of the Dietz Printing Co., 1932.

Confederate Veteran. Nashville, Tennessee. 40 vols., 1893–1932. Reprint, Wilmington, N C: Broadfoot Publishing, 1987.

Cox, Jacob D. *Military Reminiscences of the Civil War*. New York: C. Scribner's Sons, 1900.

Dooley, John. *John Dooley, Confederate Soldier: His War Journal*. Edited by Joseph Durkin. South Bend, IN: University of Notre Dame Press, 1963.

Douglas, Henry Kyd. *I Rode with Stonewall*. Chapel Hill: The University of North Carolina Press, 1940.

Drummond, Edward W. *Confederate Yankee: The Journal of Edward William Drummond: A Confederate Soldier from Maine*. Edited by Roger S. Durham. Knoxville: The University of Tennessee Press, 2004.

Dunaway, Wayland Fuller. *Reminiscences of a Rebel*. New York: The Neale Publishing Co., 1913.

Fell, T. E. "Escape of Prisoners from Johnson's Island." *Southern Historical Society Papers*, Vol. XVIII. Richmond, VA: Southern Historical Society, 1891.

Green, Wharton Jackson. *Recollections and Reflections: An Auto of Half a Century and More*. [no place]: Presses of Edwards and Broughton Printing Company, 1906. Electronic Edition, University of North Carolina at Chapel Hill, NC, 1998.

Hicks, Irl. *The Prisoner's Farewell to Johnson's Island*. St. Louis: Southwestern Book Publishing Co., 1872.

Hines, Captain Thomas H. [and John B. Castleman] "The Northwestern Conspiracy," *Southern Bivouac II* (June 1886–May 1887), 437–445, 500–510, 567–574, 699–704.

Houston, Thomas D. *Prisoner of War Letters: 1863–1865. From Johnson's Island*. Edited by Charles W. Turner. Verona, VA: McClure Printing Company, Inc., 1980.

Howard, McHenry. *Recollections of a Maryland Confederate Soldier and Staff Officer under Johnston, Jackson, and Lee*. [no place]:Williams and Wilkins Co., 1914.

Hundley, D. R. *Prison Echoes of the Great Rebellion*. New York: Green Printer, 1874.

Inzer, John Washington. *The Diary of a Confederate Soldier: John Washington Inzer 1834–1928*. Edited by Mattie Lou Teague Crow. Privately Printed, 1977.

Kenan, Thomas S. "Johnson's Island." *Histories of the Several Regiments And Battalions from North Carolina in the Great War 1861–65*. Edited by Walter Clark. Vol. 4. Goldsboro, NC: Nash Brothers, 1901.

Lewis, John H. *Recollections from 1860 to 1865*. Washington, DC: Peake & Company, 1895.

Lucas, Daniel Bedinger. *Memoir of John Yates Beall: His Life; Trial; Correspondence; Diary; and Private Manuscript Found Among His Papers, Including His Own Account of the Raid on Lake Erie*. Montreal: John Lovell, 1865.

Mason, F. H. *The Twelfth Ohio Cavalry: A Record of Its Organization and Services in the War of the Rebellion, Together with a Complete Roster of the Regiment*. Cleveland, OH: Nevins Steam Printing House, 1871. Published on the web by Larry Stevens, 2006.

McNamara, M. "Lieutenant Pierce's Daring Attempts to Escape from Johnson's Island." *Southern Historical Society Papers*, Vol. VIII. Richmond, VA: Southern Historical Society, 1880.

Mitchell, E. O. "Johnson's Island: Military Prison for Confederate Prisoners." *Sketches of War History, 1861–1865*. Vol. V. Cincinnati, OH: The Robert Clark Company, 1903, 118–119.

Norman, James. *Southern Letters and Life in the Mid 1800s*. Edited by Susan Lott Clark. Waycross, GA: S. Clark, 1993.

Norman, William M. *A Portion of My Life*. Winston-Salem, NC: John F. Blair Publishing, 1959.

Nisbet, James Cooper. *Four Years on the Firing Line*. Jackson, TN: McCowat-Mercer Press, 1963.

Olivier, P. D. *What the Confederates Endured on Johnson's Island*. Publisher Unknown. Copy at Western Reserve Historical Society Library.

Olmstead, Charles H. "The Memoirs of Charles H. Olmstead." *The Georgia Historical Quarterly*. Edited by Lilla Mills Hawes. Vol. XLIV. Savannah: Georgia Historical Society, 1960.

Patterson, Edmund Dewitt. *Yankee Rebel: The Civil War Journal of Edmund DeWitt Patterson*. Edited by John G. Barrett. Chapel Hill: The University of North Carolina Press, 1966.

Phillips, George M. "Johnson's Island and the Lake Erie Raid of 1864." *Glimpses of the Nation's Struggle*. Third Series. New York: D. D. Merrill Company, 1893. Poe, James T. *The Raving Foe: The Civil War Diary of Major James T. Poe, CSA*. Edited by J. C. Poe. Unknown Binding, 1967.

Shepherd, Henry. *Narrative of Prison Life at Baltimore and Johnson's Island*. Baltimore: Commercial Ptg & Sts. Co., 1917.

Speer, W. H. A. "A Confederate Soldier's View of Johnson's Island Prison." *Ohio History*. Edited by James B. Murphy. Vol. 79. Kent, OH: Kent State University Press, 1970.

Stakes, Edward T. "The Heightes Exercis of Masonic Virtures," *The Scottish Rite Journal*. Hall, Alvin L. Ed. Washington, D. C.: Supreme Council, 1994.

Stiles, Robert. *Four Years Under Marse Robert*. Third ed. New York: The Neale Publishing Company, 1904. Electronic Edition, University of North Carolina at Chapel Hill, NC, 1999.

Thompson, M. Jeff. *The Civil War Reminiscences of General M. Jeff Thompson*. Edited by Donal J. Stanton, Goodwin F. Berquist, and Paul C. Bowers. Dayton, OH: Morningside House, Inc., 1988.

Thrasher, Robert Mullins. "Prisoner of War." *The Register*, Sandusky, OH (May 8, 1938).

Trimble, Isaac Ridgeway. "The Civil War Diary of Isaac Ridgeway Trimble." *Maryland Historical Magazine*. Vol. XVII. Baltimore: Maryland Historical Society, 1922.

Unknown, "Determined to Escape." Rutherford B. Hayes Presidential Library.

U. S. Department of the Navy. *Official Records of the Union and Confederate Navies in the War of the Rebellion*. 30 vols. Washington: GPO, 1894–1927.

U. S. War Department. *War of the Rebellion: A Compilation of the Official Records of the Union and Confederate Armies*. 128 vols. Washington: GPO, 1880–1901.

Wash, W. A. *Camp, Field and Prison Life*. St. Louis: Southwestern Book and Publishing Co., 1870.

Webb, R. F. "Prison Life at Johnson's Island." *Histories of the Several Regiments and Battalions from North Carolina in the Great War 1861–65*. Edited by Walter Clark. Vol. 4. Goldsboro, NC: Nash Brothers, 1901.

Newspapers:

Sandusky *Register* (OH)

Unpublished Materials:

Bingham, Robert, *Diary,* Rutherford B. Hayes Presidential Library.

Blackman, Felix Hays, *Letters to Maggie Sexton* (1863–1865), Author's Collection.

Brochure, Frohman Collection, Rutherford B. Hayes Presidential Library.

Bullitt, Henry, *Letters to Helen Bullitt*. Ohio Historical Society. Photocopy at Rutherford B. Hayes Presidential Library.

Douglas, Henry Kyd. *Letters*. Rutherford B. Hayes Presidential Library.

Ellis, E. J. to "My Dear Sister." Rutherford B. Hayes Presidential Library.

Hayden, S. A., *Letters*. Ohio Historical Society.

Johnson's Island Pleasure Resort Brochure, Follett House.

Lawsuit Document No. 5964, 6106. 1897. Follett House.

Lease Document, Johnson's Island Pleasure Resort, Follett House.

McClung, R. L., *Diary,* Follett House.

Mills, Luther Rice, Papers, Ohio Historical Society.

Murphey, V. S., *Diary,* Rutherford B. Hayes Presidential Library.

Official U. S. Marine Corps Release No. 10–60. Rutherford B. Hayes Presidential Library.

Rives Letter to Mr. H. A. Rives, Rutherford B. Hayes Presidential Library.

Sells, Hiram. Prisoner's Letter of 1863. Preserved, Edited by Fern Sharp. Sandusky Library.

Scates, James M., *Diary*, Follett House.

Scovill Papers, Western Reserve Historical Society.

Stem Family Collection (Letters etc.). Rutherford B. Hayes Presidential Library.

Stowell Letter to Dear Sister Alida, Follettt House.

Swift Letters, Rutherford B. Hayes Presidential Library.

Thompson, Mortimer C., *Letter,* Ohio Historical Society.

Thompson, P. E., *Letter,* April 14, 1865, Follett House.

Todd, Westwood. *Reminiscences of Westwood Todd.* Copy at Rutherford B. Hayes Presidential Library. Original at Southern Historical Society Collection at University of North Carolina.

Wescott, G. G. Letter to Dr. Sereno Watson, Rutherford B. Hayes Presidential Library.

Woodson, William D. *War Recollections of Lieut. Wm. D. Woodson.* Lynchburg, VA: Liggan & Holt.

Secondary Sources

Published Materials

Bell, John. *Rebel on the Great Lakes Confederate Naval Commando Operations Launched from Canada 1863–1864.* Toronto: Dundurn, 2011.

Fetzer, Dale, and Bruce Mowday. *Unlikely Allies, Fort Delaware's Prison Community in the Civil War.* Mechanicsburg, PA: Stackpole Books, 2000.

Frohman, Charles E. *Rebels on Lake Erie.* Columbus, OH: The Ohio Historical Society, 1965.

Hesseltine, William. *Civil War Prisons.* Kent, OH: Kent State University Press, 1972.

Knauss, William H. *The Story of Camp Chase.* Nashville, TN: Publishing House of the Methodist Episcopal Church, 1906.

Levy, George. *To Die in Chicago, Confederate Prisoners at Camp Douglas 1862–65.* Gretna, LA: Pelican Publishing Company, 1999.

Long, Roger. "Johnson's Island Prison." *Blue and Gray Magazine,* Vol. 4, Issue 22. March 1987.

Shepard, Frederick J. "The Johnson's Island Plot." In Frank H. Severance, ed., *Publications of the Buffalo Historical Society, Volume IX.* Buffalo, NY: Buffalo Historical Society, 1909:1–51.

Speer, Lonnie R. *Portals to Hell: Military Prisons of the Civil War.* Mechanicsburg, PA: Stackpole Books, 1997.

Unknown Author, *Descriptive booklet of Johnson's Island and Confederate Cemetery.* Sandusky, OH: Register Star News, 1945.

Unpublished Materials:

Schultz, Charles R. "The Conditions at Johnson's Island Prison during the Civil War." M.A. Thesis, Bowling Green State University, 1960.

www.aandc.org/research/rush-bagot_agreement.html